CW01369010

Heinrich Böll and Ireland

Heinrich Böll and Ireland

By

Gisela Holfter

With a Foreword by Hugo Hamilton

CAMBRIDGE SCHOLARS
PUBLISHING

Heinrich Böll and Ireland,
by Gisela Holfter

This book first published 2011

Cambridge Scholars Publishing

12 Back Chapman Street, Newcastle upon Tyne, NE6 2XX, UK

British Library Cataloguing in Publication Data
A catalogue record for this book is available from the British Library

Copyright © 2011 by Gisela Holfter

All rights for this book reserved. No part of this book may be reproduced, stored in a retrieval system, or transmitted, in any form or by any means, electronic, mechanical, photocopying, recording or otherwise, without the prior permission of the copyright owner.

ISBN (10): 1-4438-3195-6, ISBN (13): 978-1-4438-3195-6

Table of Contents

Introduction and Acknowledgements vii

Foreword ix
Hugo Hamilton

Part I: Background

Chapter One 2
Writers and Places—An Introduction to Irish-German Relations

Chapter Two 8
Heinrich Böll—A Biographical Sketch

Part II: Early Irish Influences and Heinrich Böll's Visits to Ireland

Chapter Three 18
An Early Preference—Links to Ireland before the First Visit

Chapter Four 27
The First Trip: A Homecoming? Heinrich Böll's Visit in 1954

Chapter Five 38
Discovering Achill Island

Part III: The *Irish Journal*

Chapter Six 54
Background, Structure and Formation

Chapter Seven 64
The Usage of Time—Past, Present, Future

Chapter Eight 73
Germany: 'A Cursed Country'—but 'I am still a German'

Chapter Nine 80
Irish People, Traditions and Landscape

Chapter Ten 86
A Multimedia Experience through Different Art Forms

Chapter Eleven 95
Poverty and Emigration

Chapter Twelve 104
Religion

Chapter Thirteen 115
Reception in Germany

Chapter Fourteen 123
Reception in Ireland

Chapter Fifteen 133
The *Irish Journal* in Context

Part IV: Later Works on Ireland

Chapter Sixteen 144
Translations and Reviews

Chapter Seventeen 158
The Emerald Isle in Black and White—The Film *Children of Eire*

Part V: Legacy

Chapter Eighteen 172
Reverberation

Select Bibliography 183

INTRODUCTION AND ACKNOWLEDGEMENTS

For most of my academic career I have been interested in Heinrich Böll and Ireland. This interest is shared worldwide: invitations for lectures or requests for publications have come from academics and journals in countries ranging from China, South Korea, Italy and Sweden not to mention Germany and Ireland. Specifically in Ireland a number of people have asked about a comprehensive publication on Heinrich Böll and Ireland and his influential *Irish Journal*. This volume will hopefully at least provide an introduction. Given that in 2007 it was fifty years since *Irisches Tagebuch* and forty years since the English translation *Irish Journal* were published, it seems somewhat overdue.

The basis of this study is informed by a number of my own earlier writings, specifically parts of a study of German travel descriptions of Ireland in the 20th century, and numerous articles and lectures. Of great importance for any research on Böll is the new complete edition of Böll's works, the *Kölner Ausgabe* ('Cologne edition') that has been published since 2002 in 27 volumes. It has brought to light many new aspects of Böll's work and it is of immense value to have the well written and informative commentaries. Of interest here is particularly volume 10 which contains *Irisches Tagebuch* and to which the Centre for Irish-German Studies in Limerick was able to contribute some aspects. Also, the 2007 publication of *Irisches Tagebuch*, edited by René Böll and Jochen Schubert, contains a lot of background material.

As always, the co-operation from the Heinrich Böll Archive in Cologne and the Heinrich Böll Foundation has been excellent, especially the support and interest of Markus Schäfer and Jochen Schubert. Heinrich Böll's son René Böll has patiently encouraged me with this undertaking and supported me throughout its development, I am especially indebted to him and his daughter Samay regarding the tracing of and permission to use photographic material. Hugo Hamilton immediately agreed to write a foreword when I approached him.

Of great inspiration was a stay in the Heinrich Böll Cottage on Achill Island as writer in residence in the late summer of 2006 which enabled me to write a good part of this book in a truly magical place. No one could ask for a more congenial work environment! The people in Achill contributed greatly to this endeavour, especially the Heinrich Böll Committee and everyone connected with it. I want to thank especially Elizabeth & John Barrett, Sean and Margaret Cannon, John F. Deane, Edward King, John McHugh, Sheila McHugh, also Elisabeth Sweeney, the late Vi McDowell, Michael O'Malley and Mary Colohan. I am grateful to Jean Tansey for her permission to use interviews she conducted on Achill Island in the early 1990s and I want to thank Aidan O'Beirne, Dublin, Peter Williams, Limerick, and everyone else who helped with information and support. This means, as always and foremost, Glenn, but also everyone else who read parts of this book at different draft stages and contributed with suggestions and constructive criticism, especially Sophia Kingshill, Hermann Rasche, Amelie Dohna, Horst Dickel, Bill O'Keeffe, Rose Little, Susan Woods, John McHugh, René Böll, Eda Sagarra, Ian Wallace and especially to Alison McConnell, who kept at me to keep going. Any errors are my own.

Thanks also to the University of Limerick College of Humanities Research Committee who provided seedfunding for this project.

Foreword

Hugo Hamilton

There has never been a better time to examine what the Germans think of the Irish and what the Irish think of the Germans. At times it seems like the people at the centre of Europe and the people on the periphery of Europe gazing at each other with a mixture of astonishment and admiration. The attraction is mutual, full of love and misunderstanding.

At times Germany and Ireland seem more like continents apart, glancing over the shoulder at each other with envy and baffled interest. Different in the way that we are shaped by history, different in the character of the landscape and the expression of the imagination, different in our optimism and our melancholia, different in many of the essential ways in which we deal with reality, with truth, with money. Profound differences which have inspired such ongoing fascination between these two places. Perhaps it is this continued attempt to understand each other which makes us so close.

In this timely book, Dr. Gisela Holfter investigates one of the most important literary events to engage both Ireland and Germany directly over the past half century. Since the publication of Heinrich Böll's collection of personal sketches in the fifties, *Irisches Tagebuch* (Irish Journal) has claimed an extraordinary place for itself in Irish-German relations. It has acted like one of those clustered signposts on the Irish landscape, pointing the way for many Germans to an idyllic place of rescue on the edge of Europe. At the same time it also points back to Germany and to the historical reasons for this great swell of enthusiasm for Ireland. In describing the waves of German visitors who came here on the strength of reading Böll's book, Holfter refers to the fact that former president Mary Robinson once suggested that Ireland should claim Böll as a national saint.

The details which have been stacked up in this new book allow us to form great insight into the perception of this country from the outside over the years. Holfter compares Böll's impressions of Ireland with the pre-existing view and asks if England had acted as a screen hiding Ireland away from Germans until Böll's book appeared to such widespread acclaim. She examines the contents of *Irisches Tagebuch*, what interested the outsider and what, for example, had been ignored by the German writer. Why did Heinrich Böll not speak about Irish music? Why did he ignore his own early fascination with Irish folk tales and turn to the description of realities in front of his eyes on arrival. Why did he avoid Northern Ireland and why did he not touch on the troubled historical anxieties between Britain and Ireland?

By focussing on Böll's literary impressions of Ireland, we learn so much about this country through German eyes. There is a kind of outsider politeness which may have prevented the German writer from being more critical. Heinrich Böll was well aware of the grip of the Catholic church on Ireland. His entire work became a lifetime engagement with Catholic morality and the emergence of a new social and political awareness in Germany. But his writing on Ireland seems to have avoided any substantial commentary on these matters apart from describing the Irish people as being 'closer to heaven' because of their extraordinary spiritual life.

It becomes clear now from this incisive study of his work how Böll's legendary critical faculties became inhibited in his encounter with Ireland. Perhaps, as Holfter points out, he was here as a guest and could only allow himself to see Ireland with great affection. His intellectual preoccupations were more concerned with the creation of a 'piece of art' rather than with social reform, something for which he needed all his energies to deal with back home in Germany.

Böll's controversial views on Irish poverty are examined here with forensic precision in a chapter which seems to have a long echo. One of the first meetings in Dublin is with a beggar outside St Patrick's Cathedral. He discusses Limerick poverty long before it was acknowledged even in Ireland. Emigration is a recurring theme in *Irisches Tagebuch*, but the description of the desperate economic conditions in the 1950s is something the Irish were not particularly keen to hear about from the point of view of the outside.

There is also a kind of 'dignity' in poverty which the German writer comes to admire and which, in Holfter's perceptive assessment of the text and its critical response, may have emerged from Böll's own Catholic influences such as Chesterton and Bloy. Holfter draws attention to the fact that Böll was strongly marked by the destitution he saw unfolding across Europe during the war, by his own experiences of poverty in post-war Germany and also by the rush of material adjustment which followed during the German economic miracle.

Böll's observation of the absence of any obvious obsession with money in Ireland in the 1950s is something which will continue to intrigue us in present times. It seemed rude and un-catholic to talk about money here up to a particular point. As Böll puts it in his own words, Ireland seemed to be 'outside the European social order.' The slow emergence of material aspirations makes this such an interesting investigation both from a literary and social, as well as intercultural aspect.

It is the lack of money that seemed to characterize Ireland. The episode in which Böll describes the woman in a fish and chip shop in Limerick chiding a young customer for freely using too much vinegar and potentially causing her financial ruin, seems to demonstrate perfectly the predicament in which the country existed. A man present in the chip shop at the same moment then pays over the odds for the extra drops of squandered vinegar. The man is quite probably the German visitor, Böll himself, though these frequent acts of generosity throughout his life remained mostly hidden.

The economic stagnation of the country is connected by Holfter to another piece of writing by Böll in which he explores the prevailing attitudes towards employment at the time. Work was something that was switched on and off like a tap, whenever it was needed. Something which the German writer perceives, in contrast to his own country, as the Irish way of keeping a perfect balance with the enjoyment of life.

With her background expertise in German-Irish studies, Holfter has placed Heinrich Böll's writing on Ireland in the context of its time, showing us the diverging reception and also its ongoing impact. It is sometimes hard to believe that Böll was so fashionable at one time that he was mentioned twice by Woody Allen in his film *Manhattan*. In the intervening years, his literary reputation has become eclipsed a little, perhaps on account his gentle but unflinching political engagement. But Holfter is among many others who increasingly see his enormous relevance to the contemporary world and point to his importance as an international writer returning to a prominent place.

Heinrich Böll's writings about Ireland have never been out of the public eye. Compiled here are the most telling reactions to the *Irisches Tagebuch* and also to the film *Children of Eire* which followed the book and which caused great controversy at a time of high sensitivity in Ireland's self-image in the 1960s. It caused great offence and opened a heated debate, demonstrating how far apart we were from Europe. The film was not screened again until recently and shows us, as Holfter explains, how we deal with the views of the outsider.

To all German visitors, of course, Ireland is green, an emblematic attachment which has formed in the imagination over the years, not for any ecological reasons but from the reputation of the landscape and the sheer abundance of green growth. Holfter, above all, gives us the expanding legacy of this German writer's literary interest in this green island and locates some of the most enduring reasons why the Germans and the Irish are so well matched in their differences.

As Heinrich Böll saw it, in spite of all our troubles, the Irish people were always happier than they knew it themselves. Perhaps this is a natural faculty which the Germans wanted to learn and which we may need to relearn ourselves at some point. Böll repeatedly found an easy fluency of poetry here, a natural spring of creativity which Holfter refers back to Ireland's historical inheritance, a kind of 'poetry of unhappiness' in the words of Böll, which inspired him and which continues to fuel the fascination between the Germans and the Irish.

© Hugo Hamilton

PART I:

BACKGROUND

CHAPTER ONE

WRITERS AND PLACES—
AN INTRODUCTION TO IRISH-GERMAN RELATIONS

A relationship with a specific country can play a significant role in a writer's work and its reception. The writer's view may, in turn, influence the perception of that country among the reading public. Writers can become champions of their own land, their names becoming synonymous with that land. Their portrayal of a nation other than their own becomes a basis for discussion both in the place described and in their homeland. Madame de Stäel's *De l'Allemagne* was a case in point in the nineteenth century. More recently Peter Mayle's account of his new life in France, *A Year in Provence*, inspired millions of English-speaking readers to dream about a similar move – and influenced tens of thousands to buy their own place in France. Bruce Chatwin wrote notably about Patagonia and Australia; Elias Canetti's *The Voices of Marrakesh* created a vivid image of a seemingly timeless encounter with Morocco, while several decades earlier Somerset Maugham's *On a Chinese Screen* brought the country which many had imagined to be a fiction perpetrated by Marco Polo, closer to European readers. That travel literature could be viewed as fiction, whether commended as such or condemned, underlines its hybrid nature.

James Joyce portrayed his own country, especially its capital, from a distance. That such distance – in some extreme cases, exile – can be necessary to capture the essence of a place has been widely acknowledged. Robert Lloyd Praeger's *The Way that I Went*, Dervla Murphy's *A Place Apart* and Pete McCarthy's *McCarthy's Bar* capture important aspects of (Northern) Irish twentieth century life, and though very different in tone and style, all bring both familiarity and distance to the task.

What about the perspective of complete outsiders such as Heinrich Böll? Is a portrayal of another place merely a clandestine sketch of their own home? It has always annoyed me to read comments such as that of the influential critic Marcel Reich-Ranicki, that the *Irisches Tagebuch* (*Irish Journal*) is really only 'a hidden book on Germany'.[1] Was that not a somewhat trite comment? Which traveller is able to observe another, foreign place completely outside the framework of his or her own experience, his or her own background? Is not the real question whether he or she achieved something more, brought another place closer, contributed to that often postulated but equally elusive idea of intercultural understanding? Could a literary portrayal of a distant place give the readers a better understanding of their own home country? Problems arise from that as well, of course, if a book creates a utopian place for the readers (possibly not intended or even described) – a place to dream about and to escape to, but one that meets their own needs rather than giving an appreciation of the actual destination. Arguably Ireland has become such a place for many German readers and tourists thanks to Heinrich Böll. How was it possible – intentionally or unintentionally – to create this phenomenon? What was it about the readers' minds or needs that contributed to it? What explains its tremendous immediate and ongoing success? And what was the personal background as well as the literary development of the man behind it?

Böll always championed a concept of 'Fortschreibung', continuous and constantly developing writing in which the sequence is of great importance. Where, then, is the place of the *Irish Journal* in his literary oeuvre? In what way are his own experiences or his own imaginings described – and does it really matter, given that this is a literary travel description? And what about the third element in this triangular relationship of author, home country and country visited? Is not the portrayal of one's own place by an outsider always viewed with slight suspicion unless infused with delight and praise? What if a description meant entirely positively conflicts with one's own ideas about what is positive and what might be derogatory and hurtful? What kind of power relationship is behind this? In what way can the passage of time come into the equation? After all, more than fifty years have passed since the *Irisches Tagebuch* appeared for the first time, and both Ireland and Germany have changed almost beyond recognition.

---

[1] Marcel Reich-Ranicki, Der Poet der unbewältigten Gegenwart, in: *Deutsche Literatur in West und Ost*, Munich: Piper 1963, pp. 120-142; see also Rolf Becker's earlier (though less influential) review of the *Irisches Tagebuch*: Irland hat, was uns abhanden kam, *Sonntagsblatt*, 5 May 1957.

In the case of Heinrich Böll and Ireland, these questions must concern more than one book, regardless of how influential that book might have been. There is far more to Heinrich Böll and Ireland than the *Irish Journal*. The relationship between man and country is more controversial and more complex than most people suspect. In Böll's case we have not only the *Irish Journal*, but also the many German translations of Irish literature published by him and his wife Annemarie, including works by Brendan Behan, Flann O'Brien, Tomás O'Crohan, Eilis Dillon and George Bernard Shaw.

Then there is his film, *Irland und seine Kinder* (*Children of Eire*), which was received very favourably in the Federal Republic of Germany, but caused great controversy in Ireland in 1965, resulting in one critic demanding an apology from the German government. Despite the controversy, the film had been long forgotten, both in Germany and in Ireland, until it was re-broadcast some forty years later on Christmas Day 2006 on Irish national television. This time the reception was entirely different, raising again the question of how perceptions change over time, and what factors contribute to the change. Finally, how can one creatively use a legacy of so many facets, one which has had such a unique impact, as Böll's relationship with Ireland?

To begin answering these questions this book will start with some background on Heinrich Böll, particularly for readers who might not be familiar with his life and impact in Germany. This is the backdrop to his encounter with Ireland, and helps to explain how and why it could function as a second home or at least a refuge for Böll. The background would be incomplete without some information on Böll's wife Annemarie, neé Cech. Böll's relationship with Ireland was both shared and enhanced by her.

This is followed by an analysis of Heinrich and Annemarie Böll's existing links with Ireland and Irish literature before they set foot on Irish soil. The question of Böll's preconceptions about Ireland and specific Irish characteristics, his first encounters with Irish literature and authors and their significance for him as a young writer are at the core of this section. Böll's visits to Ireland are examined next, concentrating especially on his first trips in 1954 and 1955 and his time on Achill Island where he stayed regularly throughout the sixties and seventies and where he bought a holiday cottage.

The literary creation of Böll's *Irish Journal*, a distillation of comings and goings to Ireland over a period of years, needs to be examined as much for what it leaves out as for what it says and contains. Chapter three therefore attempts to plot overlapping charts of the real and fictional peregrinations. Prior to the book's publication most of the eighteen chapters had already appeared in newspapers or been broadcast on the radio, contributing significantly to the book's immediate popularity. The unusual structure, the title and the main themes are explored. This chapter also includes an examination of the differences between the German *Irisches Tagebuch* and the English language version *Irish Journal*, particularly the addition of the chapter 'Thirteen years later'. The different responses to *Irisches Tagebuch* and *Irish Journal* are analysed next, contrasting the overwhelmingly positive reception in Germany with the relative lack of interest for a long time in Ireland.

A short overview of Irish-German (literary) relations

The uniqueness of Böll's portrayal of Ireland can best be understood by considering it alongside other contemporary publications about Ireland by authors from Germany and from other foreign countries. Also, we need to bear in mind that the *Irish Journal* was not created out of a vacuum – Ireland had been attracting varying degrees of interest over the ages. The following is a very short summary of the German literary view and an overview of the different approaches and agendas.[2]

Following encounters with Irish monks on the continent, medieval Europe began to imagine Ireland as 'the island of the saints', the home of St. Brendan and later of Isolde, fatefully in love with Tristan. Yet up to the nineteenth century, very little attention was paid to Ireland in Germany. While early travel descriptions about Ireland by German travellers can be traced from the sixteenth century onwards, it was only at the end of the eighteenth century that a number of English travel accounts were translated into German and the first relatively comprehensive German view of Ireland based on personal experience was published. Ireland was mostly seen as a colonial appendix to Great Britain, a very minor and insignificant player. Images and concepts which were based on the English

---

[2] For more details see John Hennig, Irish-German Literary Relations, in: *German Life and Letters*, No. 3, 1950, pp. 102-110; Patrick O'Neill, *Ireland and Germany — A Study in Literary Relations*, New York: Peter Lang 1985; Doris Dohmen, *Das deutsche Irlandbild*, Amsterdam/Atlanta: Rodopi 1994 and Gisela Holfter, *Erlebnis Irland*, Trier: WVT 1996.

perspective in turn determined the German perception, in some instances well into the nineteenth century.

The English view itself was based in part on classical texts, often denouncing Ireland's wildness and lack of civilisation, which had been taken up by writers such as Giraldus Cambrensis in the twelfth century who had a colonial mission at hand.[3] A clear shift in the German perception took place in the nineteenth century when three more or less distinct phases, especially as far as German-speaking travellers are concerned, can be discerned:

Firstly, the orientation towards England up to about 1830. Secondly, the period between 1830–1850, marking a pronounced increase in the attention paid to Ireland, influenced by ideas of Romanticism, a fascination with Irish fairy tales, and political circumstances, personified in the charismatic figure of Daniel O'Connell. Besides numerous travel descriptions (more in these twenty years than during the rest of the century added together, the most influential being Hermann von Pückler-Muskau's *Briefe eines Verstorbenen*, published in English translation only a year later in 1831/1832 as *Tour of a German Prince*), the translations of Irish fairy tales by the Grimm Brothers, first published in 1825, generated much enthusiasm. However, in the third phase, from the 1850s, following the famine and O'Connell's death, until the end of the century, there was a noticeable waning of German interest in Ireland as a travel destination, with Julius Rodenberg and Friedrich Engels providing exceptions from the rule.

At the same time, in the context of a growing fascination with other languages, Irish received much scholarly attention. Indeed a great deal of the groundwork of Irish language studies was laid by German-speaking academics such as Johann Caspar Zeuss, Rudolf Thurneysen and Kuno Meyer. The awareness of Ireland in the first decades of the twentieth century was often politically motivated: Ireland was noticed again thanks to its close connection with England, particularly in the periods leading up to each of the two World Wars. Still, despite all interest in Ireland, the era when 'everyone always mistakes Ireland for Iceland', as Richard Bermann wrote in 1914, lasted for a long time: Joachim Gerstenberg repeated the phrase in 1940. Similarly Karl Surenhöfener called Ireland 'the country we

---

[3] For more details see Joep Leerssen, *Mere Irish & Fíor Gael: studies in the idea of Irish nationality, its development and literary expression prior to the nineteenth century*, Amsterdam/Philadelphia: Benjamins 1986.

hardly know' in 1948. Not least thanks to Böll's *Irish Journal* Ireland has since become a familiar concept, a seeming proof that a different life-style, values and mindframe exist. This became a decisive part of the ongoing attraction of Ireland as a tourist destination, one which includes the traditional image of the 'Emerald Isle', the forty shades of green as well as Irish literature and music. Of these traditional attractions some proved more stimulating for Böll than others as we will see when analysing the *Irish Journal* and also his other works on and references to Ireland, including his own and his wife's translations. Of particular importance here is the examination of his film *Children of Eire* and its widely differing reception in Germany and Ireland. But maybe of even greater significance today is the question of the ongoing impact of the *Irish Journal* as well as Böll's personal legacy in Ireland. This will form the last part of this book.

CHAPTER TWO

HEINRICH BÖLL— A BIOGRAPHICAL SKETCH

It is my firm belief that the period in which an author lived is of crucial importance [1]

Heinrich Böll was born in Cologne on 21 December 1917, the youngest of six children. The German Kaiser was still in power, the First World War was raging and Konrad Adenauer, later to become German Chancellor, was mayor of Cologne. The Bölls were a lower middle-class family. According to family tradition their ancestors had emigrated from England several centuries previously, preferring emigration to Henry VIII's state religion.[2] Heinrich's father, Viktor Böll, was born in 1870 in Essen as one of nine children. After the early death of his first wife Katharina, he married Maria Hermanns in 1906. Among Viktor's brothers were a successful architect and a priest; Viktor himself followed in the footsteps of his father Heinrich Böll, who was a master-joiner, and specialised in wood-carvings for churches. He had a great appreciation of art history and shared this with his children, while teaching them 'to honour God and not to fear earthly rulers'.[3]

Maria Böll was by all accounts a very generous and intelligent person. Her son would write about her that she was a great and wonderful woman,

---

[1] [Ich glaube folgendes: daß man sehr genau unterscheiden muß, aus welcher Zeitbiographie ein Autor stammt.] 'Ich habe nichts über den Krieg aufgeschrieben' – Ein Gespräch mit Heinrich Böll und Hermann Lenz, in: Nicolas Born, Jürgen Manthey (eds), *Literaturmagazin 7 – Nachkriegsliteratur*, Reinbek: Rowohlt, 1977, pp. 30-74, 31. All translations by the writer unless otherwise stated. At least in the case of texts by Heinrich Böll, the original German might be of interest especially for students of literature. It will therefore be provided in the footnotes in square brackets.

[2] Heinrich Böll, Über mich selbst. (Autobiographische Notiz) I, in: *Der Mann mit den Messern*, Stuttgart: Philipp Reclam jun. 1959, pp. 76-78.

[3] Alfred Böll, *Die Bölls. Bilder einer deutschen Familie*, Bergisch Gladbach: Lübbe 1981, p. 239.

always helping others, even if her own family was struggling. The family was a close-knit unit, which helped when the economic situation took a turn for the worse. Viktor Böll had invested in a small bank for craftsmen that collapsed during the Great Depression in 1929. The family had to sell their house in Cologne-Raderthal and move; it was the first of many changes of address at short intervals. Unemployment, visits to pawnbrokers and scarcity of food were the common lot. The young Heinrich Böll was clearly affected by these experiences: together with the trauma of the Nazi rise to power they formed the source of a lifelong anxiety.[4] Böll's own assessment of the family's situation following their reduced circumstances was that they were 'neither proper petit bourgeois nor conscious proletarians, but with a strong Bohemian streak.'[5]

After attending the elementary school in Cologne-Raderthal Böll went to the prestigious Kaiser Wilhelm Gymnasium, a grammar school where the curriculum included Latin and Greek, subjects he found interesting. He obtained his Abitur (Leaving Certificate) in 1937.

Any discussion of Heinrich Böll's family background must include the specific form of Catholicism in which he was reared, which influenced his later life and had a surprising amount in common with the faith he was to encounter in Ireland. The Böll family was Catholic, in an almost puritan fashion, which led to a contempt for 'bourgeois' society displayed in many of Böll's early texts, and a sceptical outlook regarding Church institutions.[6] While the latter aspect would not have been a strong feature of religion in Ireland, where the Church authorities were revered, temporal authorities were viewed with much greater mistrust, doubtless engendered by Ireland's colonial past. Scepticism towards Church authorities is strongly reflected in Böll's early writing, which contains a strong religious element, a love for the marginalised such as the poor and prostitutes, and passionate outbursts against hypocrisy.

---

[4] Heinrich Böll, Christian Linder, *Drei Tage im März*, Cologne: Kiepenheuer und Witsch 1975, p. 39.
[5] [Wir waren weder rechte Kleinbürger noch bewußte Proleten, hatten einen starken Einschlag von Bohème] Heinrich Böll, *Was soll aus dem Jungen bloß werden*, in: *Werke 1979-1981*, Kölner Ausgabe volume 21, edited by Jochen Schubert, Cologne: Kiepenheuer & Witsch 2006, p. 398. In the following abbreviated as *KA 21*.
[6] See Böll, *Werke 1936-1945*, Kölner Ausgabe volume 1, edited by J.H. Reid, Cologne: Kiepenheuer & Witsch 2004, pp. 470f. In the following abbreviated as *KA 1*.

Böll's religious thinking was influenced by his reading of the French writer Léon Bloy, whose essay *Le Sang du Pauvre* (*Blood of the Poor*) was published in German in 1936. Indeed, Böll describes Dostoyevsky and Bloy as being for him literary 'bombs', and Chesterton a 'firecracker'.[7] Bloy was a part of the 'Renouveau catholique', a movement for religious renewal which advocated spiritual revival through poverty and suffering; his writings led to animated discussions among Heinrich Böll, his siblings and their friends, a group of young people trying to escape the growing pressure from Nazi ideology. These early experiences and his family background were instrumental in forming what J.H. Reid calls the 'strong existentialist or anarchist element in Böll's outlook which made him suspicious of all rigidities in social life, whether structures of authority in Church or State'.[8] The more mature post-war Böll was later able to turn all this youthful passion into bitingly humorous satire with a strong visual element, as in his description of the pompously pious, bishop-led church procession in Cologne,[9] the centre of powerful Rhenish Catholicism, where State and Church authorities were strongly interlinked.

Following his 'Abitur', the German Leaving Certificate which showed that Böll was by no means an 'A' student, he had a brief stint as an apprentice with the bookseller M. Lempertz in Bonn. Heinrich Böll was then enlisted for labour service in 1938, compulsory work experience introduced by the National Socialists which included everyone who wanted to study at university. He enrolled at the University of Cologne before being called up for military service in the autumn of 1939. During the war he was first at a training camp in Osnabrück, then after two months in Poland in May and June 1940 he was transferred to France for four months and then back to Germany until May 1942. During this time he got married to Annemarie Cech.

Annemarie Cech was the daughter of Eduard Cech, who worked for the Austrian Railway Company, and his wife, Stefanie Cech, neé Hagen. She was born in 1910 in Pilsen, Bohemia, now in the Czech Republic, and for

---

[7] Böll, *Was soll aus dem Jungen bloß werden*, Munich: dtv 1983, p. 90.
[8] J.H. Reid, *Heinrich Böll: A German for His Time*, Oxford: Berg 1988, p. 6.
[9] Böll, *Und sagte kein einziges Wort*, Cologne: Kiepenheuer & Witsch 1953, chapter 5. First translated as *Acquainted with the Night* in 1954 by Richard Graves, using the title of a Robert Frost poem. Nearly 25 years later, Leila Vennewitz, who also translated the *Irisches Tagebuch* and had by then become the main translator of Böll's work into English, reinstated the original title in her new translation *And Never Said a Word,* New York: McGraw-Hill, 1978.

Heinrich and Annemarie Böll on their wedding day, 6 March 1942. © Samay Böll.

the first few years of her life she spoke German and Czech bilingually. After the early death of both her parents Annemarie moved to Cologne, where she lived with her grandparents and later attended the St Ursula School, run by nuns. In 1933 she met Heinrich Böll's elder sister Mechthild at the University of Cologne, where, like Mechthild (called 'Tilla' or 'Tilde'), she studied German and English literature, and trained to become a teacher. The house of the Böll family became a second home for Annemarie.[10]

Due to the high rate of unemployment she had great difficulty in finding a job. She worked for a while as an administrator in a business firm and then tried to get an au pair position (for which no work permit was required) in an English school, with the help of contacts provided by her old school.

---

[10] See Dieter Kühn, *Auf dem Weg zu Annemarie Böll*, Berlin: Heinrich-Böll-Stiftung 2000, p. 23.

Eventually she was offered a place in Upton Hall in the Wirral, near Liverpool, a private Catholic boarding school run by the Society of the Sisters Faithful Companions of Jesus (SFJ). Annemarie went there in 1935 and taught mathematics and Latin and prepared students for the entry examinations to tertiary level. Sometimes she accompanied students when they had to go to medical or dental appointments in Liverpool – something she preferred to teaching, as she found it difficult to keep strict discipline.

At Upton Hall she met and became friends with an Irish woman, one of many at the school. This contact with Mary Kelleher, later Daly after her marriage to Robin Daly, was to have a profound impact regarding the connection with Ireland; Annemarie argued that her own and Heinrich's relationship with the country was rooted in this friendship.[11] Annemarie greatly enjoyed her time in Upton Hall and would have liked to stay, but felt she had to return to Cologne after one year in order to be with her grandmother, who had supported her in England with a monthly grant. The employment situation in Germany was still very difficult but as the war started and an ever growing number of men were needed to serve in the army, women were suddenly in demand to fill the ensuing gaps. Annemarie obtained a position at the Mittelschule Rothgerberbach, a secondary school in Cologne. Here she taught German, English and gymnastics, having gained experience of the latter at Upton Hall, where she had assisted her friend Mary Kelleher, who was sports teacher there.

Not long after his wedding in 1942, Böll returned to France as part of the occupation force and remained there until October 1943 before being posted to Russia, to the Crimea and to Odessa. Despite the possibility of being promoted to officer, Böll decided against it. While tempted by the advantages he felt it would be a betrayal, he did not want to join the 'caste' of the officers.[12] From March 1944 he was at various places on German territory until he was taken prisoner of war in April 1945. Following his release from an American prisoner-of-war camp in September 1945, he worked in his brother's carpentry shop, on building sites and in administrative jobs. From 1948 onwards he tried to make ends meet through his writing and giving private tuition: the family was, however, dependent on the steadier income of Annemarie, who went back to

---

[11] Ibid., p. 24: 'That's where our relationships with Ireland have their roots.' [Da haben auch unsere Beziehungen zu Irland ihre Wurzeln.]
[12] Cf. his letter of 19 July 1942 to his mother from France, in: Heinrich Böll, *Briefe aus dem Krieg 1939-1945*, edited by Jochen Schubert, Cologne: Kiepenheuer & Witsch 2001, vol 1, pp. 398-399.

teaching at a secondary school. She was also to be the first reader of all her husband's works, helping with editing and doing most of the translations.

Heinrich Böll's writing career started with the publication of *Der Zug war pünktlich* (*The train was on time*) in 1949, followed in 1950 by a collection of short stories about war experiences, *Wanderer, kommst Du nach Spa ...* (*Stranger, Bear Word to the Spartans we ...*). In 1951 *Wo warst Du, Adam?* (*Where Art Thou, Adam?*) appeared, and Böll received the Gruppe (Group) 47 Prize for his story 'Black Sheep'. In the immediate post-war era Gruppe 47 was an influential association of writers and critics of contemporary German literature who met regularly at the invitation of Hans Werner Richter. The prize was designed to promote new writing and was very prestigious – later prize-winners were Ilse Aichinger (1952), Ingeborg Bachmann (1953) and Günter Grass (1958). For Heinrich Böll it was the long-hoped-for break that allowed him to concentrate on writing full time. Two years later, with his new publisher Kiepenheuer & Witsch, he achieved his first commercial success with *Und sagte kein einziges Wort* (*And never said a word*). This was followed in 1954 by *Haus ohne Hüter* (*Tomorrow and Yesterday*), in 1955 *Das Brot der frühen Jahre* (*The Bread of Those Early Years*), in 1959 *Billard um halbzehn* (*Billiards at Half-past Nine*), in 1963 *Ansichten eines Clowns* (*The Clown*), in 1971 *Gruppenbild mit Dame* (*Group Portrait with Lady*), and in 1974 *Die verlorene Ehre der Katharina Blum* (*The Lost Honour of Katharina Blum*) – to name only his most important works. Shortly after his death in 1985, *Frauen vor Flusslandschaft* (*Women in a River Landscape*) was published. His books are generally set around the time of writing, and deal with current social, political, and (in the earlier novels) religious issues: J.H. Reid points out that Böll's 'point of departure was always the particular, the today, even if this meant that his work did not take on the appearance of having been written for eternity – later readers may well be puzzled by allusions to events or people long since forgotten'.[13] The exception is the *Irish Journal*, published in 1957 – the only one of his works not set in Germany.

Böll also wrote many essays and satires and was increasingly viewed as a moral authority. He was known as 'the good man from Cologne' or 'the moral conscience' of the Federal Republic of Germany. He did not appreciate such labels, maintaining that expressions such as 'the conscience of the nation' were fatal: the real conscience of a nation was to

---

[13] Reid, *Heinrich Böll*, p. 8.

be found in its parliament, code of law and judicial system, roles that neither could nor should be replaced by authors.[14]

His relationship with Germany became fraught, particularly in the aftermath of an article he published in the context of the debate on terrorism and the general unease in Germany in the early 1970s. While Böll never approved or supported the violent means adopted by the Red Army Faction in their fight against the system and the institutions of the Federal Republic of Germany, he was outspoken against the prejudices of the gutter press. His attempts to break down frontiers and reduce tensions were ignored by the terrorists but led to a smear campaign by the conservative media and political commentators in which Böll was denounced as one of the spiritual fathers of terrorism. Böll's public standing became controversial, his increasingly political engagement, as well as his criticism of the Catholic Church making him the target of numerous conservative critics. However, his fame as a writer continued to grow, both in Germany and abroad, especially after 1972 when he was awarded the Nobel Prize for Literature. By 1977 over 17 million copies of his books had been printed worldwide; by 1987 this had more than doubled,[15] and today one could estimate at least 36 million.[16] When Heinrich Böll died on 16 July 1985 in Langenbroich (about 55km southwest from Cologne) he had become one of the most important German writers of the 20th century, as demonstrated not only by his Nobel Prize but also by his pre-eminent position among his colleagues in Germany in the decades after the war.

For many people outside his home country he embodied 'the other Germany', one that people could trust again after Fascism. He was seen as someone for whom morality and aesthetics were congruent. This, however, had also its downside in that his writing was often regarded – and dismissed – as political literature. In this respect an examination of the *Irisches Tagebuch* can be particularly enlightening: it can be categorised in a number of ways – as travel literature, personal reflections, a collection of

---

[14] [Das halte ich für lebensgefährlichen Wahnsinn, das G.d.N ist eigentlich ihr Parlament, ihr Gesetzbuch, ihre Gesetzgebung und ihre Rechtsprechung, das können wir nicht ersetzen und das maßen wir uns auch gar nicht an.] Interview with Hans-Peter Riese, Schriftsteller in dieser Republik. Gespräch über Selbstverständlichkeiten, in: *L'76*, 1977, No. 6. pp. 5-37, 7.
[15] Bernd Balzer, *Heinrich Bölls Werke,* Cologne: Kiepenheuer & Witsch 1977, p. 16.
[16] Thanks for this information to Markus Schäfer, Böll Foundation, and Iris Brandt, Kiepenheuer & Witsch, Cologne, 20 January 2011.

poetic impressions, – but most people would agree that it scores low on political content, both in the German and in the Irish context. Given this example it might become easier to assess his abilities in his other novels, especially today when the immediate political and socio-historical context has changed so greatly. Thus Böll's literary qualities may be rediscovered. The new critical edition of his complete works will help furnish fresh insights into his thought. There is hope that a new generation of literary scholars will be able to work towards a new appreciation of Heinrich Böll and his legacy: this book, dealing with a very specific area of his life and work, hopes to contribute to that understanding.

PART II:

EARLY IRISH INFLUENCES AND HEINRICH BÖLL'S VISITS TO IRELAND

CHAPTER THREE

AN EARLY PREFERENCE—
LINKS TO IRELAND BEFORE THE FIRST VISIT

> *Anyone who writes is firstly a reader, and everything that he has read influences him. It started, I remember, when as a boy of eight or nine years, I was given Irish fairy tales as a present*[1]

Heinrich Böll's interest in Ireland was awoken early, perhaps by his reading of Irish fairy tales as a child to which he refers in interviews as one of his first literary memories or indeed the very first fictional influence he received. This partiality is also reflected in his early writing before the war. In one of Böll's first literary efforts, 'Das Mädchen mit den gediegenen Ansichten' (The girl with sound views), written in 1939,[2] the

---

[1] [Jeder, der schreibt, ist zuerst einmal der Leser, und alles, was er gelesen hat, beeinflußt ihn. Das fing damit an, ich erinnere mich, daß ich als Junge, so mit acht, neun Jahren irische Märchen geschenkt bekam.] Böll, *Eine deutsche Erinnerung, Interview mit René Wintzen*, Cologne: Kiepenheuer & Witsch 1979, p. 36 and Böll, *Werke Interviews II 1976-1979*, Kölner Ausgabe volume 25, edited by Robert C. Conard und Werner Jung, Cologne: Kiepenheuer & Witsch 2010, p. 319 (in the following abbreviated as *KA 25*). As early as 1959, when he was asked about books that were important for him, Böll named a volume of Irish fairy tales that he read when he was nine or ten years old as one of three influential books [Ich kann Ihnen drei Bücher nennen, von denen ich sicher bin, daß sie für mich von entscheidender Bedeutung geworden sind: Johann Peter Hebels Schatzkästlein, das ich als Sieben- oder Achtjähriger geschenkt bekam, das erste Buch, das ich wirklich gelesen habe, immer wieder las, bis es im Krieg verlorenging. Ein oder zwei Jahre später ein Band irischer Volksmärchen, und Weihnachten 1936 Léon Bloys: Blut der Armen, das in der Übersetzung von Clemens ten Holder erschien]. See Böll, Kein Selbstbetrug, *Ruhr Nachrichten* (Essen), 24 December 1959, in Böll, *Werke 1959-1963*, Kölner Ausgabe volume 12, edited by Robert C. Conrad. Cologne: Kiepenheuer & Witsch 2008, p. 20. In the following abbreviated as *KA 12*.
[2] It remained unpublished until 2004 when it appeared in *KA 1*. Interestingly, it is the only piece of Böll's early writing (which runs to an impressive 455 pages in the *KA*) that was handed in for publication. He offered it for a short story competition,

main character, a boy called Peter, is reading the collection of Irish fairy tales given to him by his sister. Together with the setting, a park in June, it creates a marvellous atmosphere: 'Peter had a wonderful book, from which the great and colourful truths of the fairy tales grew like flowers, whose scent and colours brought out all the splendour of their indescribable beauty.'[3] He is fascinated by the adventures of Finn Mac Cool and Cu Chulainn and the tale of the poor son of the fisherman, in the web of the Gruagach. The stories develop magic qualities in their own right:

> [...] he floated into a cloud of incredible dreams; time stood still; the book was never-ending; Peter was reading and the book would never end; it was bewitched like that pot of sweet mush, and Peter became entangled in a web of stories as if he were in a mist, a sweet mist prepared from a thousand herbs by a witch sitting at the other end of the world. Peter had forgotten everything; it was as if he was lying by a spring, deep in a dark forest, a spring whose waters would never run dry, whose rippling noise was gentle and soothing.[4]

This enchanted world is then contrasted with that of two amoral young students, early versions of Böll's often-described symbols of the establishment – coldly and hatefully denouncing the poor and the dejected of society, in this case the unmarried mother of Peter's friend, who has just had a second child out of wedlock.

---

but was not successful. 'Just imagine if I had got the prize,' he commented many years later, apparently somewhat relieved at his failure (supposedly fearing he would not have been able to cope with the early success, or feeling he needed his war experiences to mature as a writer) – although the 1000 Marks offered to the winner was a lot of money at the time. See Fritz Raddatz, *Lieber Fritz. Briefe an Fritz J. Raddatz 1959-1990,* Reinbek: Rowohlt 1991, pp. 126f. or *KA 1*, p. 628.

[3] [Peter hatte ein wunderbares Buch, aus dem die großen und bunten Wahrheiten der Märchen wuchsen wie Blumen, deren Geruch und deren Farbe alle Pracht ihrer unsagbaren Schönheit offenbart.] *KA 1*, p. 318. Translation of this quote and the next by Susan Tebbutt, London.

[4] [[...] er versank in einer Wolke wunderbarer Träume; die Zeit blieb stehen; das Buch nahm kein Ende; Peter las und das Buch würde nie ein Ende nehmen, es war verzaubert wie jener Topf mit dem süßen Brei, und Peter wurde von Geschichten eingesponnen wie von einem Nebel, von einem süßen Nebel, der aus tausend Kräutern bereitet wurde von einer Hexe, die am anderen Ende der Welt saß. Peter hatte alles vergessen; es war, wie wenn er an einer Quelle läge, an einer unerschöpflichen, tief in einem dunklen Wald, dessen Rauschen mild und besänftigend ist ...] Ibid.

In another story written in 1939, 'Am Rande der Kirche' (On the edge of the Church) the first-person narrator has a 'wonderful' present for his girlfriend: 'a beautiful old volume that contained Gulliver's Travels by Swift with old and delightful illustrations'.[5] An *Irish Times* article by Desmond Fennell (who met Böll in Cologne in 1956) indicates that not only Irish fairy tales but also more contemporary Irish literature might have influenced the young Böll: 'He had always felt attracted to Ireland. As a boy before the war, he had got to know some of the writings of Sean O'Faoláin and Frank O'Connor, Liam O'Flaherty and Yeats.'[6] This statement is also borne out by the selected exhibition of his library, now on view as part of his study in the Heinrich Böll Archive in the Central Library of the City of Cologne at Neumarkt, where one can find extensive holdings of the named Irish writers as well as, for example, Sean O'Casey, Flann O'Brien and George Bernard Shaw. A 1916 German edition of Yeats' stories and essays is inscribed 'Heinrich Böll 1938', with a picture of Yeats glued on the first page. Other indications of his ongoing interest during the war in Irish writing include inscriptions such as 'Heinrich Böll Im Kriege [during the war] 1939' in Swift's *Lemuel Gullivers Reisen* (a bargain as it was reduced from 5RM to 1.85RM) or Shaw's *Kleine Dramen*, published in Berlin in 1921, inscribed with 'Heinrich Böll 1940 Osnabrück Wahlkommando Winkelhausenkaserne'.

The early fascination with Ireland was to provide solace even in extreme circumstances, as can be seen in *Briefe aus dem Krieg* (Letters from the War), published in 2001.[7] One letter written in spring 1942 is particularly poignant. Böll writes to his fiancée Annemarie Cech, whom he was to marry a few months later. Rather than addressing her immediately, he quotes a sonnet which, he explains to Annemarie, has cheered him up tremendously. He describes how he came back very sad and tired to his bunk bed after being on watch, when he happened to open a book containing the poem and upon reading it immediately felt consoled, nearly healed. The poem that had such impact on him was 'Irland' by Reinhold

---

[5] Böll, Am Rande der Kirche, *KA 1*, p. 405.
[6] Desmond Fennell, Report from Cologne – Heinrich Böll in Ireland, *Irish Times*, 23 June 1956, p. 7.
[7] Despite a number of reviews there has not so far been a detailed analysis of the letters. An initial appraisal can be found in Philipp Alten's contribution 'Heinrich Böll: Der lesende Soldat – eine Teilrekonstruktion auf Grundlage der veröffentlichten Feldpostbriefe' in: W. Jung, J. Schubert (eds), *'Ich sammle Augenblicke' - Heinrich Böll 1917-1985*, Bielefeld: Aisthesis 2008, pp. 49-80.

Schneider.[8] It employs the image of a holy island, with monks singing, surrounded by the sea, and dreams of greatness overwhelmed by a

---

[8] Irland
Aus grauem Meere tönt dein Mönchsgesang;
Wie von der Welle, die sich ruhlos bäumt,
So ist Dein Strand vom Heiligen umsäumt,
Und Heiligstes ward Dir zum Untergang.

Dir war dein Erbteil wie ein Harfenklang
Und herrlich nur, was ohne Spur zerschäumt;

Das Größte deines Seins hast du erträumt,
Bis überm Traum dein Feind sein Zepter schwang.

Doch als sie deinen Königsthron zerschlagen
Und in das Meer dein Kreuz geworfen hatten,
Da hast du dir das Heiligste errungen,

Denn Völker sind, um Gottes Last zu tragen.
Dich hat der Herr verstoßen zu den Schatten,
Und nun erst wardst du ganz vom Kreuz durchdrungen.

Ireland
Out of the grey sea your monks' singing sounds
As though from a restlessly mounting wave
Your beach is surrounded by holiness
And holiness became your downfall.

For your heritage was like a harp's sound
And only that was magnificent, which foamlike disappeared;

You dreamt of the greatness of your being
Until above the dream the enemy showed his sceptre.

But when they destroyed your king's throne
And threw your cross into the sea
Then you achieved holiness

Because people exist to shoulder God's Burden.
The Almighty threw you to the shadows
And only now were you fully penetrated by the cross.

Böll, *Briefe aus dem Krieg 1939-1945*, vol. 1, p. 245. Thanks to Deirdre Kelliher for her improvement of my translation.
    Reinhold Schneider (1903-1958) was a German writer who had chosen 'inner emigration' during the Hitler regime. Publication of his work during that time was illegal but many copies were in private circulation. Like Böll years later, Schneider was referred to with the problematic title of the 'conscience of the nation'. Schneider spoke out against rearmament after the war as he was convinced that the 'Gnade des Unglücks' (mercy in misfortune), as he called the German experience, incorporated the duty for peace. According to Jochen Schubert, Böll Archive, Cologne, Böll knew all Schneider's early works.

conquering enemy. It is a place which has to suffer, but through its suffering it is infused with the spirit of the cross, or, in other words, becomes one with the suffering Christ, an idea that would have appealed very much to Böll's religious understanding.

While the images used to describe Ireland are very traditional, it is likely that what struck a chord with Böll was the idea of suffering, of 'carrying God's burden', and through that acquiring a true elevation. Böll speaks of his 'eternally torturing impatience and desire to live and to be free' that was quietened by reading the poem and absorbing its idea of finding real freedom in suffering. One can find parallels to these themes in Böll's early writing that was published only posthumously, for example 'Die Brennenden'[9] (The Burning Ones), written in 1936/7 and 'Eine kleine Geschichte'[10] (A Little Story), written in 1939 – where Heaven is described as split into two parts: one for God and the Holy Spirit, with all the good Catholics, full of popes, bankers, diplomats; the other for the suffering Christ who came to live with the poor. Here would be all the saints, all children, prostitutes and beggars, as well as the writers Chesterton and – interestingly for this study – Swift.[11] In 1956 Böll stated that he had read all of Jonathan Swift's works several times in the 1930s. A fragment titled 'Sonderbare Erlebnisse des jungen Pankratius Sundagsplaat' (Strange Experiences of the Young Pankratius Sundagsplaat) written by Böll in 1939 was explicitly conceived as a 'Gulliver II'.[12]

Böll's early affinity with Ireland was shared by Annemarie, who had had her own experience of a form of Ireland in exile in her time at Upton Hall in 1935/36. Her lifelong friendship with Mary Daly, neé Kelleher, started there and was to have a strong and positive impact on the whole Böll family after the war when Mary Daly helped them with care parcels which contributed to the well-being and perhaps even survival of the children. When the Bölls' second son Raimund, born on 19 February 1947, fell ill, these parcels provided the desperately needed extra rations of egg powder, chocolate and flour.[13] It must have been a particularly anxious time for the young parents as their first son Christoph, born on 19 July 1945, had died

---

[9] *KA 1*, pp. 48-67.
[10] *KA 1*, pp. 446-457.
[11] *KA 1*, pp. 450f.
[12] *KA 1*, p. 652.
[13] Herbert Hoven (ed.), *Die Hoffnung ist ein wildes Tier - Der Briefwechsel zwischen Heinrich Böll und Ernst-Adolf Kunz 1945-1953*, Munich: Deutscher Taschenbuch Verlag 1997, p. 67 (letter 54, 21 April 1948).

from severe diarrhoea on 14 October 1945, less than three months old.[14] The parcels could not be sent direct from England, where Mary Daly and her husband Robin lived, but were packed and posted by a Swiss organisation to whom the Dalys sent instructions and payment in US dollars.[15] Some years later in 1954 the Dalys' daughter Mary, then a student at Trinity College Dublin,[16] showed Heinrich some of the sights in Dublin during his first visit.

The link to Ireland and Irish writing remained strong after the war and as one of Böll's early reference points at times led him to adopt an over-positive view of anything or anyone Irish. Jonathan Swift's *Gulliver's Travels* appeared in Böll's first long publication, *Der Zug war pünktlich* (*The train was on time*), published in 1949 by his first publisher Friedrich Middelhauve.[17]

Shortly afterwards Böll discovered the Irish writer Francis Stuart and in 1952 he wrote a radio play *Das Lächeln* (The Smile) based on Stuart's novel *Redemption*, which had been published in 1949 (and appeared in translation as *Das Lächeln* in 1957, the same year that Böll's radio play was finally broadcast).[18] In 1953 Böll wrote a review of the German translation of Stuart's autobiographical novel *Pillar of Cloud* which appeared in German as *Die Wolkensäule*.[19] In it Stuart uses his experiences in a refugee camp in Germany to create a convincing picture of the pervading sense of disorientation and poverty. Böll refers especially to Stuart's critical portrayal of Germans, and states: 'These lines are written not by someone who indulges in cheap hatred of Germans, but by one who

---

[14] Ibid., p. 431 (commentary letter 4).
[15] Ibid., p. 445 (commentary letter 37, 4 January 1948).
[16] Mary was a student of History in TCD 1952-56: information thanks to Professor David Simms of Trinity College, who was a good friend of hers and remembers having tea with Mary and Böll in 1954.
[17] Böll, *Werke 1949-1950*, Kölner Ausgabe volume 4, edited by Hans Joachim Bernhard, Cologne: Kiepenheuer & Witsch 2003, p. 383. In the following abbreviated as *KA 4*.
[18] The Böll radio play was broadcast on 19 January 1957, see Hoven, *Die Hoffnung ist ein wildes Tier*, p. 538. According to the commentary in Böll, *Werke 1956-1959*, Kölner Ausgabe volume 10, edited by Viktor Böll, Cologne: Kiepenheuer & Witsch 2005, p. 623 (in the following abbreviated as *KA 10*), there are no references to the writing of the play among Böll's papers.
[19] Böll, *Werke 1953-1954*, Kölner Ausgabe volume 7, edited by Ralf Schnell in cooperation with Klaus-Peter Bernhard, Cologne: Kiepenheuer & Witsch 2006, pp. 196f. and commentary pp. 586f. In the following abbreviated as *KA 7*.

voluntarily shared the German time of need in the years 1945-1948 and gave up the security of a life in Ireland.'[20] The reader is not told – and perhaps Böll himself was not aware – that Stuart also spent the war years in Germany and that his stay in Germany afterwards was not entirely voluntary since he spent nearly ten months in prison. He had been involved in German radio propaganda, first writing speeches for William Joyce, better known as 'Lord Haw-Haw', and later broadcasting his own texts. Furthermore, Stuart's acquaintance with Hermann Goertz, a German spy in Ireland, would not have helped to endear him to the British and French authorities. He had given Goertz the address near Dublin of his estranged wife Iseult (daughter of Maud Gonne) who was consequently to face trial on charges of harbouring and helping a spy.[21] We do not know whether Böll was aware of these connections and Stuart's activities. However, there is no doubt that Stuart's writing appealed to Böll, due both to the writing style and the chosen themes.[22]

Ireland figures prominently in Böll's novel *Haus ohne Hüter*, published in 1954, which appeared in translation in 1957 as *Tomorrow and Yesterday*.[23] Albert, one of the main characters, has been married to Leen, an Irish woman he met in London. Leen (who incidentally is described as a young sports teacher in a convent school – just like Annemarie's Irish friend Mary Daly, neé Kelleher[24]) appears as one of the wild but pious Irish colleens, loving 'kitschy' Franciscan churches, movies and betting games with a passion. Her strong dislike of order and especially of providing for the future make her a perfect contrast to traditional German sentiments. Before her sudden death she tells Albert to go to Ireland. Many years later at the time of the novel he still regrets not having followed her suggestion

---

[20] ['Diese Sätze sind geschrieben nicht von jemand, der billigem Deutschenhaß frönt, sondern der die deutsche Not der Jahre 1945 und 1948 freiwillig teilte, auf die Sicherheit eines Lebens in Irland verzichtete.']
[21] See Geoffrey Elborn, *Francis Stuart: A Life*, Dublin: Raven Arts 1990, pp. 185-194; Francis Stuart, *Black List, Section H*, London: Penguin 1996; Brendan Barrington (ed.), *The wartime broadcasts of Francis Stuart 1942-44*, Dublin: Lilliput 2000 (especially the introduction pp. 1-65).
[22] See also Richard Heinen, 'Geh nach Irland – Das Irlandbild in *Haus ohne Hüter*', in: Gisela Holfter, Joachim Lerchenmueller (eds), *Yearbook of the Centre for Irish-German Studies 1998/99*, Trier: WVT 1999, pp. 66-76.
[23] Heinrich Böll, *Tomorrow and Yesterday*, New York: Criterion Books 1957, trans. Mervyn Savill.
[24] Another parallel between the Dalys and Leen's family exists regarding support after the war. Leen's parents send food parcels to Albert, containing ham, tea and tabacco, cf. *KA* 8, p. 144.

and wonders how it would have changed things. Ireland becomes an unfulfilled dream.

Another interesting feature in the novel is the description of Irish tea. Before ever setting foot in Ireland, Heinrich Böll had very precise ideas about it: Leen always makes it 'very dark, deeply golden glimmering up from deep down'.[25] In the *Irish Journal* the description is similar: the tea has 'the dark, glimmering tones of Russian icons'.[26] Tea was sometimes included in the care parcels that were sent by the Bölls' Irish friends in the late 1940s and was described by Böll at the time as giving great joy and acting as a perfect way to soothe anxiety and provide inspiration.[27]

To summarise: Heinrich Böll was intrigued by Ireland and its literature from an early age long before he experienced it by travelling there. The above examples show that Ireland had a lasting impact on and importance for him as a writer. Given the spectrum of different images already displayed, one could argue that Böll did not really need to go to Ireland, that before he ever went there Ireland appeared to be a kind of spiritual home for him. He had found 'his' Ireland even before actually experiencing it.[28] 'Actual' encounters with Ireland, both in literary form through Irish writers and fairy tales and through acquaintance with Mary Daly, the close friend of his wife, were, however, the foundation of this vision.

---

[25] Heinrich Böll, *Haus ohne Hüter*, Cologne: Kiepenheuer & Witsch 1954, p. 346.
[26] Heinrich Böll, *Irish Journal*, translated by Leila Vennewitz, New York/Toronto/London/Sydney: McGraw-Hill 1967, p. 9 (quoted from now on in the text with page numbers).
[27] Hoven, *Die Hoffnung ist ein wildes Tier*, p. 67 (letter 54, 21 April 1948).
[28] Böll felt strongly that literature was the best way to get to know a country. See Böll, *Eine deutsche Erinnerung - Interview mit René Wintzen*, in *KA 25*, p. 393: '[...] literature provides better information than politics, the economy or whatever. How do I know America? From its literature. How do I know Spain, where I was only once briefly? I know it because I know Cervantes, and only him but also other Spanish writers and books about Spain [...] and out of all of this my image develops' (Natürlich, ich hab ja schon in einem anderen Zusammenhang, ich glaube, im Zusammenhang mit Südamerika, gesagt, daß die Literatur die besseren Auskünfte gibt als die Politik, die Wirtschaft und was immer. Woher kenne ich Amerika? Aus der Literatur. Woher kenne ich Spanien, wo ich erst einmal im Leben kurz gewesen bin? Ich kenne es, weil ich Cervantes kenne; und nicht nur ihn, auch andere spanische Erzähler und Bücher über Spanien, von Andersen-Nexö zum Beispiel, aus dem allen setzt sich doch für mich ein Bild zusammen).

What should be kept in mind is that except for Reinhold Schneider's sonnet no reference to the traditional German view of Ireland appears. To the reader it would appear that the wealth of German literature on Ireland, particularly from the nineteenth century had not left a mark on Böll or even been known to him.[29] His context of reference remains firmly rooted in Irish prose literature, mainly from the twentieth century.

---

[29] This is not to say that Böll entirely forgets German writers, see for example his reference to Johann Peter Hebel's 'Kannitverstan' (p. 8) – though he does not name Hebel, one of his favourite writers, he only refers to 'the old tale'. However, none of the literature about Ireland by German writers is mentioned.

CHAPTER FOUR

THE FIRST TRIP:
A HOMECOMING?
HEINRICH BÖLL'S VISIT IN 1954

Heinrich Böll's first actual visit to Ireland seems to have been instigated by Moira Fleischmann, neé Moore, an Irish woman who lived in Cologne. According to Aidan O'Beirne, who was in diplomatic service in Germany from 1951 to 1956 and knew her, she was in a bookshop one day and met a man who wanted to find a book on Ireland. She mentioned where she came from, they had a conversation and the man (none other than Heinrich Böll, of course) expressed his wish to go to Ireland. The way she told the story later to Aidan O'Beirne, this encounter ended with her putting her hand in her pocket, getting out the key to her holiday home in Wicklow and giving it to Böll with the words "stay as long as you like".[1] In any case, shortly afterwards Böll went to see O'Beirne regarding a visa for Ireland and this in turn led to an ongoing acquaintance between the two.[2] Moira Fleischmann continued to help Böll with getting travel documents and arranged accommodation for him with her husband Georg Fleischmann in Dublin while she was away.[3] Böll's trip seems to have been motivated not only by a desire to get to know Ireland but also by his wish to escape from the exhausting experience of building a house and

---

[1] Conversation with Aidan O'Beirne, Dublin, 31 July 2008.
[2] Aidan O'Beirne went to visit the Böll family a number of times, was impressed by Böll's father's "charming way of complaining" and especially the "wonderful sense of family life the Bölls had at home, much more than in other German homes" (ibid). O'Beirne also remembered with a smile that Böll and the official church didn't mix well, that, for example, at St Patrick's Day receptions at the Irish embassy, Böll would make sure that he and the archbishop were at opposite ends of the room. The contact continued after O'Beirne's time in Germany, and when Böll was made President of the International PEN in 1971 he spent an evening with O'Beirne in his house in Dublin.
[3] See *KA 10*, p. 637.

incurring substantial debt,[4] and to avoid the reviews and press attention following the publication of his novel *Haus ohne Hüter* in the week of his departure.[5]

Heinrich Böll set off for Ireland on 23 September 1954 and travelled via Ostend, Dover, London, Holyhead and Dun Laoghaire to Dublin, where he was based until 21 October, although his four weeks in Ireland included more than Dublin. He went on several trips around the country, often with Georg Fleischmann, and explored Bray, Limerick, Killarney, Drumcliff and Hare Island in Lough Ree.

Georg (later George) Fleischmann (1912-1995) is himself a fascinating figure who had significant influence in the development of the Irish film industry. Born in Graz in Austria, he had moved to Berlin and assisted Leni Riefenstahl with her film on the 1936 German Olympic Games.[6] In 1939 he won a Gold Medal at the Venice Film Festival for his documentary *Styria*. During the war he served in the Luftwaffe as a photographer until 1941 when his plane had to make an emergency landing in Ireland. He then spent several years interned in the Curragh, where the situation was quite different from that in most other camps in Europe: the internees were allowed out during the day, bound only by their word of honour to return, and attended dances, played golf, even took courses at university. After the war several of the internees stayed on in Ireland, having found a new home.

---

[4] Deutsch ungenügend, *ZEIT-Magazin*, 3 November 1978, p. 10: 'Ja, es war eine Flucht, weil ich mich in Köln durch einen Hausbau hoch verschuldet hatte und Ruhe vor meiner Familie brauchte' [Yes, it was an escape, because I had a huge mortgage due to building a house and needed peace from my family]. See also Dorothee Pribil, Heinrich Bölls Irisches Tagebuch, Gießen 1989 (unpublished academic essay), p. 17; Dieter Kühn, *Annemarie Böll*, p. 119: 'Als das Haus soweit fertig war, da waren auch Annemarie und Heinrich Böll fertig, und zwar 'völlig' wie sie im Gespräch betont.' [Once the house was finished, Annemarie and Heinrich Böll were through, too – 'totally exhausted', as she [Annemarie] emphasised in the conversation.]
[5] See Böll's letter to Ernst-Adolf Kunz, 22 September 1954: 'Tomorrow I will depart and you will hear from me from Ireland [...] My trip is halfway a flight. The novel arrives this week [...]' *KA 10*, p. 637.
[6] Brian McIlroy, Interview with George Fleischmann, in: Brian McIlroy, *Irish Cinema: an Illustrated History*, Dublin: Anna Livia Press 1988, pp. 109-113.

George Fleischmann (left). © Irish Film Archive of the Irish Film Institute.

George Fleischmann (right) filming the Royal Dublin Society (RDS) Horse Show. This was the first live TV transmission in Ireland. The transmission from the RDS to the Gresham Hotel demonstrated 'Live TV' to the government at the time and predated RTE. Information and © Irish Film Archive of the Irish Film Institute.

Fleischmann, who had insisted on retrieving his camera every six months during his period of internment in order to clean it thoroughly, managed to re-establish himself as a cameraman, and when Böll visited him he had already been involved in the filming of important Irish occasions such as the hurling championships and had acted as director of photography on a number of films sponsored by the Departments of Foreign Affairs, Health, Post and Telegraphs and Local Government. In 1950 he shot *Ireland – Rome*, a film about the state visit of President Sean T. O'Kelly to the Vatican, and made a film on William Butler Yeats, *W.B. Yeats – A Tribute*, which was well received, its opening night being attended by the Taoiseach and numerous members of the Government. The production had brought together a number of Ireland's best artistic talents – the script was written by John Desmond Sheridan, Éamonn Ó Gallchobhair composed the music for it, Cyril Cusack gave the commentary, Micheál MacLiammóir and Siobhan McKenna read the poetry, while the introduction was given by Lennox Robinson. Fleischmann's direction and editing attracted a number of newspaper articles, for example, 'German ex-pilot directs Yeats film'.[7] Fleischmann is possibly best remembered as photographic director

---

[7] *Sunday Empire News* (Manchester), 28 May 1950.

of the film *Return to Glennascaul* (1951), starring Orson Welles and directed by Hilton Edwards, based on a ghost story that Micheál MacLiammóir was told by a police sergeant in County Kerry.[8] It received an Oscar nomination.

Böll was able to accompany Fleischmann on several of his assignments: to Limerick (basis for the *Irish Journal* chapter 'Portrait of an Irish Town – Limerick in the Morning and Limerick in the Evening'), to Killarney and to a 'little island in the Shannon' (p. 101), the setting for the chapter 'A Small Contribution to Occidental Mythology'. Böll's descriptions are so precise that one can often follow his route through Dublin and Limerick and on to the island (actually in Lough Ree near Athlone), but while using authentic details he is creating his very personal imaginative portrayal, a method he used to a far greater extent in his novels but which is also apparent in his Irish impressions.

Upon his arrival in Ireland, Böll ventured from Dun Laoghaire to Dublin City, arriving in Westland Row, now Pearse Station, a six mile train trip that was Ireland's first railway connection, dating from 1834. Close by is St. Andrew's Church from where on his first morning in Ireland he heard the 'sudden roar, a sound almost like thunder' (p. 9) that turned out to be the powerful opening bars of the *Tantum ergo*, leaving Böll with a lasting impression of Irish piety. St. Patrick's Cathedral and St. Nicholas of Myrna in Francis Street were further ports of call as were Nelson's Pillar, later also the Georgian houses in slum areas and St. Teresa's near Grafton Street. On his first morning Böll had his first cup of tea in an unnamed B&B (not wanting to disturb his host[9] too early on a Sunday morning) and thoroughly enjoyed it: 'a heavenly brew [...] worthy of renown' and 'thrown in for free was the smile of the young Irish girl who served it' (p. 9). Böll must have been quite taken with her friendliness as he later repeats that he 'enjoy[s] the free smiles of the tousled tea goddess' (ibid). Another powerful impression is conveyed here in his personal experience of a place with a different attitude towards time and a different appreciation of the past. The lasting impact of past generations on the present ones was something that he found in a quote and came to regard as a key to the Irish

---

[8] McIlroy, Interview with George Fleischmann, p. 112. This ghost story makes an appearance on Böll's long list of ninety Irish themes of which only some were developed, dating from 1954, 1955 and 1956. See photo in Jochen Schubert's Nachwort, in: Heinrich Böll, *Irisches Tagebuch*, edited by René Böll, Cologne: Kiepenheuer & Witsch 2007, pp. 149-195, 186.

[9] Georg Fleischmann lived in 53 Pembroke Road, Ballsbridge.

temperament: 'The cemeteries are full of people the world could not do without.' (p. 10)

In Limerick, Böll gives a succinct overview of its historical settlement and the relationship between the old city, English Town on King's Island, and the newer part. Fleischmann and Böll 'parked the car near the cathedral' (p. 43); from St. Mary's Cathedral they crossed Ireland's foremost river, the Shannon ('this river was too big, too wide, too wild for this gloomy little town,' ibid.), to the Treaty Stone on the other side of Thomond Bridge. ('At this stone the Irish were promised freedom of religious expression and a treaty was concluded that was later revoked by the English parliament, so Limerick is also sometimes called 'the town of the broken treaty' p. 44.) Böll describes the butcher shops, symbolic of Limerick, which has traditionally been called 'Pigtown' and is still famous for its ham and bacon. His description is not a tourist guide's: no routes are mapped out, nor is much background given. King John's Castle, a medieval stronghold between St. Mary's and the Treaty Stone, he mentions only as something that 'reared grimly out of the darkness' (p. 50), the background to a scene of extreme poverty, where a child is scolded for using a few extra drops of vinegar on his chips and where an unlikely hero, a 'dark, blood-stained drunk' (p. 50), overcomes pettiness with courtesy and by paying 'ten thousand per cent interest' (ibid.). Similarly, a church is woven into the story with a 'great Sacred Heart' that 'shone crimson' and from which the faithful 'cannot bear to part' (p. 51). This is very likely Limerick's Redemptorist St. Alphonsus Church where the Chapel of the Sacred Heart dating from 1903 is located at the head of the left-hand aisle.[10] The devotion of 'the faithful' in the story has much to do with a desperate belief that, through prayer, a wager on 'Crimson Cloud' may be successful. During Böll's short stay in Limerick there was indeed a horse race on 7 October 1954, and another horse mentioned in the chapter 'Limerick in the Evening', 'Isle of Innisfree', was indeed among the runners,[11] but 'Crimson Cloud' owes its name more to the transference of symbolic meaning from the 'crimson Sacred Heart', several times repeated in the German text though lost in the English translation.[12]

---

[10] In 1904 the church became notorious as the origin of the 'Limerick pogrom', initiated by Fr John Creagh's sermon against the Jews and leading to a boycott of Jewish traders: Böll would not have been aware of this at the time.

[11] Thanks to William O'Keeffe for this information.

[12] Another reason for the name 'Crimson Cloud' could have been a book with the same title (*Purpurwolke*) by Willy Kramp published in the same year. According to Jochen Schubert of the Böll Archive, Böll knew Kramp's work.

The small island in the Shannon with a church built by St. Ciaran of Clonmacnoise where Fleischmann wanted to try out a new colour film was Hare Island or Inis Ainghin in old annals. It had attracted visitors for centuries. The 'vacant manor house' (p. 99) where they had tea was most likely Hare Lodge, a hunting and fishing retreat designed by the architect Richard Morrison for the then owner Lord Castlemaine in the early 19th century.[13] The family who lived there when Böll visited, the Duffys, had already been there since the 17th century and the old man with 'white, fluffy, and thick' hair (p. 97) whom Böll portrays ('a contemporary of Sun Yat-sen and Busoni, he was born before Rumania became what it has for years no longer been: a kingdom; he was four years old when Dickens died – and he is a year older than dynamite', p. 98) was Thomas Duffy, who died in 1961 aged 94.[14]

The 'retired English Colonel who had brought us over in his boat – with his long red hair, pointed red beard, he looked like a mixture between Robinson Crusoe and Mephistopheles' (p. 99) was a retired doctor named Harry Rice who had served as a colonel with the British army in India and who lived with his wife and daughter at Cusack Point. Rice was one of the founders of the Inland Waterways Association in 1953, Seán MacBride called him the prime mover.[15] He would have been an excellent guide for Fleischmann and Böll, his interest in and knowledge of the Shannon and Lough Ree had led to a publication two years before Böll's visit, *Thanks for the Memory – Being Personal Reminiscences, Traditions, History and Navigational Details about the River Shannon*.[16] Böll's observation that 'Rommel's "fairness" during the "war" was one of the colonel's favourite topics' is backed up by Rice's grandson, Peter Williams, who recalls that

---

[13] Detailed information on Hare Island has been published by Westmeath County Library on www.askaboutireland.ie, see http://www.askaboutireland.ie/readingroom/environment-geography/physical-landscape/lakelands-of-westmeath/loughree/islands-of-lough-ree/hare-island-the-annals/hare-lodge-and-lord-castl/
(accessed 8 March 2011). This very informative website on the history of Hare Island from early times also refers to other visitors, among them Leonard Alfred George Strong, who was inspired to write *The light above the lake* following his visit. The book was published posthumously by Methuen in 1958.
[14] Information from Noel Duffy, owner of Hare Island and grandson of Thomas Duffy, 8 November 2005.
[15] Cf. Seán MacBride, *That Day's Struggle – A Memoir 1904-1951*, edited by Caitriona Lawlor, Dublin: Currach 2005, p. 227.
[16] Harry Rice, *Thanks for the Memory*, Athlone: Athlone Printing Works 1952, reissued 1974 by the Athlone Branch of the Inland Waterways Association of Ireland and reprinted 1975, second edition 2002.

Rommel was respected as 'the gallant foe' and 'straight'. (An interest in the German war general seems to have been a family trait: Harry Rice's sister-in-law had a dog that was named 'Rommel'.)[17] Rice's involvement in photography might have been the connection that led to the acquaintance with George Fleischmann: he also knew the photographer and cameraman Tom Stobart.

LANDING PLACE AT HARE ISLAND.

Sir Cusack P. Roney, *How to Spend a Month in Ireland*, London: John Camden Hotten 1872, p. 115; thanks to Brendan Bolger for pointing me to the publication.

---

[17] Conversation with Peter Williams, Limerick, 8 October 2007.

Harry Rice in his boat on the Shannon, picture courtesy of Peter Williams.

The episode on Hare Island is interesting for another reason, as the reader gains an insight into the question of Heinrich Böll's command of the English language. He describes how hard it was for him to understand the English colonel 'although he was kind enough to try and speak "very, very slowly"' (p. 99). Böll had learned English at school, and in fact his 'Abitur' (Leaving Certificate/ A-level) grades indicate 'good' (B) for English and only 'sufficient' (ausreichend – C-) for German.[18] In 1948 he had started working along with his wife on translations from English into German[19] (and persisted for decades, as he enjoyed collaborating in the search for the *mot juste*, although he acknowledged later that Annemarie did the lion's share of the work).[20]

---

[18] See copy of his grade sheet in Gabriele Hoffmann, *Heinrich Böll*, Bornheim-Merten: Lamuv 1986, p. 49.

[19] In the summer of 1948 Heinrich and Annemarie translated Stephen Spender's essay 'W.H. Auden and the Poets of the Thirties' for *Literarische Revue*, see Böll, *Werke 1947-1948*, Kölner Ausgabe volume 3, edited by Frank Finlay and Jochen Schubert, Cologne: Kiepenheuer & Witsch 2003, p. 552 (in the following abbreviated as *KA 3*). Böll hoped that such translations would provide for the financial needs of the family.

[20] See a letter from Böll to J.C. Witsch, 30 June 1956: 'in fact 90% of the work is actually done by my wife.' *Heinrich Böll - Life and Work*, ed. Stadt Köln/Heinrich Böll Stiftung, Cologne: Steidl, 1995, p. 29, for more details see chapter on translation

However, he would have lacked practice in spoken English, especially compared with Annemarie who had had the advantage of a year in an English-speaking environment at Upton Hall. Clodagh King, who met the couple in 1955 in Keel, remembers that Annemarie spoke very good English and hence the language difficulty was overcome 'as you could speak to him through her because he didn't know English at the time'.[21] This may have been an exaggeration, or may indicate that Böll preferred to leave conversations to Annemarie and to concentrate on observation.

Böll himself acknowledges in several chapters that he had difficulties with conversation. Apart from the difficulty of comprehending the slowly speaking English colonel he mentions his 'meager (sic) knowledge of the language' (p. 8) in 'Arrival II' in the context of relying more on his eyes than his tongue or the ears of other people. Shortly afterwards, at the first attempt of a local to engage him in conversation on Irish soil, he is 'engulfed in words of which I only understood one: Germany', and decides 'to strike back, in friendly but determined fashion, with the weapon of the country, "Sorry"' (p. 9).

While in Ireland for the first time he took the opportunity of improving his English by going to the cinema.[22] However, it is a considerable tribute to his (improving) language skills that during his extended stays in Ireland he was the one – at his wife's urging – to pull 'the tooth of Hitler admiration' in some of the locals' minds during pub visits (see chapter six of the *Irish Journal* entitled 'Itinerant Political Dentist').

---

in this volume.

[21] Interview with Clodagh King by Jean Tansey in the early 1990s.

[22] Böll, *Rom auf den ersten Blick*, Munich: dtv 1987, p. 59. Years later, on a trip in the Soviet Union, Böll referred to his having learned English in Ireland and seems to have confused a New Zealander travelling in the same train compartment through Russia with his statement that he learned English in Ireland, as it was unclear to the New Zealander whether Böll was a Russian who managed to go to Ireland, or an Irishman travelling in the Soviet Union – Cf. Böll, Entweder – Oder (1963), *KA 14*, pp. 98-101, 100f. [Sogar Johann Peter Hebel wäre mit einer Geschichte nach Hause gekommen: der von dem jovialen älteren Mann aus Wellington, Neuseeland, der sich unverhofft im D-Zug nach Leningrad einem Englisch sprechenden Zeitgenossen gegenüberfindet, ihn fragt, wo er Englisch gelernt habe, die Antwort: ‚In Irland' notwendigerweise mißversteht: ein Ire in Rußland, ein Russe, der in Irland Englisch lernte – Kopfschütteln über einen Deutschen, der in Rußland das in Irland gelernte Englisch mit dem jovialen älteren Herrn aus Neuseeland spricht.]

Overall, he enjoyed his first time in Ireland tremendously and wrote home: 'It is so beautiful here that I am very sad that you are not here with me. Lakes, mountains, clouds and these indescribable ever-changing lights that I have never seen before. I am very happy that I went to Ireland,'[23] and later: 'I think if we get some money we should really come here with the children.'[24]

At this stage he might already have been aware that his Irish experiences could have literary potential and bring benefits beyond a successful escape and holiday. While he was still in Ireland he had an offer from a Sunday paper, the *Sonntagsblatt*, wanting to publish his impressions of the country and expressing particular interest in comparisons between the two countries or views on Irish cultural life,[25] and a little later he received another enquiry from Karl Korn, in charge of the Arts Section of the prestigious *Frankfurter Allgemeine Zeitung* (*FAZ*), about anything suitable for the Christmas edition. Böll finished his first story inspired by his Irish experiences on 7 December, and on Christmas Eve 1954 'Der erste Tag' ('The first day', which became later, after some changes, 'Arrival II', the second chapter of the *Irish Journal*) was published in the *FAZ*, under the additional heading 'Tagebuch aus Irland' (Diary from Ireland) and accompanied by three photos.[26]

The reaction to this publication was so positive that only ten days later Korn requested more and a tug of war ensued between different possible outlets.[27] Four other stories from his stay in 1954 that were later revised to become part of the *Irish Journal* appeared in the following months – 'Pray for the Soul of Michael O'Neill' in February 1955,[28] 'Portrait of an Irish Town' in March (broadcast on radio as a reading by Böll a day before the article appeared in the *FAZ*),[29] 'A Small Contribution to Occidental Mythology' in May[30] and 'The Dead Redskin of Duke Street' in September

---

[23] Böll, *Rom auf den ersten Blick*, p. 57.
[24] Ibid., p. 58.
[25] Cf. *KA 10*, p. 638. For more details see ibid., chapter on 'Entstehung', pp. 637-662.
[26] Der erste Tag – Tagebuch aus Irland, *FAZ*, 24 December 1954, p. 39, see also *KA 10*, p. 639.
[27] Letter from Karl Korn to Heinrich Böll, 4 January 1955, cf. *KA 10*, p. 639; regarding the other interested parties see *KA 10*, pp. 638-643.
[28] Bete für die Seele des Michael O'Neill – Aus dem Irland-Tagebuch von Heinrich Böll, *FAZ*, 26 February 1955, p. 32.
[29] 'Porträt einer irischen Stadt' [only 'Limerick Am Morgen' ('Limerick in the Morning')], *NDR* (Northern German Radio), 25 March 1955 / *FAZ*, 26 March 1955.
[30] 'Auf einer kleinen Insel', *FAZ*, 14 May 1955, p. 42.

in a yearbook called *Jahresring 55/56*,[31] published by the national culture association of German industry. All four stories were also broadcast under different titles as radio programmes during the summer of 1955 by RIAS Berlin,[32] indicating again the immediate interest in and success of Böll's Irish impressions.

---

[31] 'Der tote Indianer in der Duke Street', *Jahresring 55/56*, edited by Kulturkreis im Bundesverband der Deutschen Industrie, Stuttgart, September 1955, pp. 206-209; it later also appeared in the *FAZ*, 31 March 1956, p. 46.
[32] *KA 10*, pp. 641f.

CHAPTER FIVE

DISCOVERING ACHILL ISLAND

As planned in 1954, the following year the whole family and a family friend, Christine Assenmacher, did come to Ireland, this time with a base not in Dublin but in the north-west of the country, on Achill Island in County Mayo. This time Böll stayed not four weeks but four months and it proved to be the beginning of a lifelong contact with Achill for the whole family.

The origin of tourism in Achill can probably be attributed to the Achill Mission in 1834 and the subsequent opening in 1839 of the Achill Mission Hotel which provided accommodation for travellers.[1] Memories of the Mission (aimed at converting local Catholics) are still alive today in Dugort, especially of Reverend Edward Nangle, a colourful missionary, under whose instruction cottages, a school, an orphanage, a hospital, a hotel and a church were erected. He even installed printing presses that regularly produced a newspaper called the *Achill Missionary Herald*.

Achill Island, one of the most western points in Ireland, has been connected with the mainland by a bridge since 1887. In many respects its development followed a quiet pace. Electricity was introduced in 1952, but as Kenneth McNally writes in his book on Achill, many islanders declined to have their homes connected to the supply at the outset and several years elapsed before the Electricity Supply Board offered a post-development scheme.[2] In 1969 there were still only 145 telephone connections and these mainly in hotels, guest houses and administrative premises.[3]

Achill has provided a temporary home for a number of artists and writers – one of the best known being Paul Henry, who was born in Belfast in 1876,

---

[1] Theresa McDonagh, *Achill Island – Archaelogy – History – Folklore*, Tullamore: I.A.S. Publications 1997, p. 43.
[2] Kenneth McNally, *Achill*, Newton Abbot: David & Charles 1973, p. 157.
[3] Ibid., p. 136.

studied art in Paris and then came to Achill for a two week holiday in 1910, and stayed for nine years in Keel and Pollagh. Henry and his wife Grace first visited Dugort, but found it too busy, and went to the – then – much quieter village of Keel,[4] where Henry decided he simply had to stay and would go no further.[5] He described it as 'the most gregarious of villages, perhaps fifty houses in all, huddled close together as if for warmth and companionship, devoid of any plan.'[6]

Among the first people the Henrys met were John and Eliza Barrett, who ran the post office and 'after some coaxing, gave them lodgings'[7] in a house that later became the Amethyst Hotel – just across the street from the house in which the Böll family spent their first years in Ireland. The Barretts later sold this house and bought a former coastguard station. Owned previously by Alexander Hector, the founder of the Achill Fishery, the building was called 'the Bervie' after his birthplace in Scotland;[8] the Barretts ran it as a hotel, which was later taken over by their niece and nephew Tony and Lilly Gallagher (who in turn became the hosts of the Böll family).[9] Paul Henry's portrait of the Barretts (*My Host and Hostess*, 1910-1913) now hangs in the Ulster Museum in Belfast.

Other well-known residents and visitors to Achill included Sean Keating, Derek Hill, Charles Lamb, Robert Henri and the novelist Graham Greene (who was brought to Achill by Lady Catherine Walston, who frequently spent time in Dooagh in the late 1940s; their relationship is captured to some extent in his book *The End of the Affair*).

For Heinrich Böll, the link to Achill was provided through George Fleischmann, who wrote to Böll in February 1955:

> I immediately inquired about a cottage for you and have found something suitable through a friend of mine at RTE, Mr. O'Reilly. Mr. O'Reilly has lived there himself and thinks it will be very comfortable for you. The

---

[4] See McDonagh, *Achill Island*, p. 42: 'The contrast between Keel and Dugort at that particular time was enormous, the former a village of thatched cottages and the latter a replica of a rural English village.'
[5] S.B. Kennedy, *Paul Henry*, New Haven and London: Yale University 2000, p. 42, quoting Paul Henry, *An Irish Portrait*, London: Batsford 1951, p. 3.
[6] Ibid., p. 42.
[7] Ibid.
[8] McDonagh, *Achill Island*, p. 261.
[9] Kennedy, *Paul Henry*, p. 160. See also Mary Cosgrave, Paul Henry and Achill Island, in: Ullrich Kockel (ed.), *Landscape, Heritage and Identity*, Liverpool: Liverpool University Press 1995, pp. 93-116.

house is in Keel, Achill, on the Atlantic coast, Co. Mayo. There are 4 bedrooms on the first floor, one living room and one dining room, kitchen, utility and a maid's room. Running water and electricity. It is next to the post office and directly off the sea. Achill is a well known peninsula off the Irish west coast, where they have shark fishing in May and June and where you will gain a vast amount of material and impressions. But do not worry, it is a great place for swimming and you won't be eaten by sharks! The rent for the furnished house is L15 (May and June) and L20 in July. You get all appliances from the owner of the house who also runs a cafe there and you can buy all food. Please write immediately to the owner: Mr. Toni (sic) Gallagher, The Bervie, Keel, Achill, Co Mayo, Ireland, and reserve the house for the time you want to spend there, as demand for such opportunities is always high.[10]

Böll did write immediately and shortly afterwards received a positive answer. On 24 February, Tony Gallagher wrote that he would be pleased to reserve the cottage for him and that there would be no need to pay a deposit on the rent. He only asked that Böll would let him know if anything 'went wrong' with his plans.[11] Further questions regarding electricity, laundry and cooking facilities as well as travel arrangements were sorted out in the followings months (see letter from 5 May 1955)[12]. Everything seemed well organised and the long anticipated sojourn started on 30 May 1955 from Cologne train station. The family spent a night in London and one on the ship. Heinrich Böll wrote later to his sister that both nights they slept well.

After the long trip, including a brief reunion with Mary Daly who collected them from the ferry in Dun Laoghaire, the Böll family arrived in Keel on 3 June 1955, having travelled from Dublin on credit as changing money proved to be far more difficult than anticipated. Böll immortalised the eventful trip in the story 'Mayo – God help us', later chapter four of the *Irish Journal*. The one thing that went wrong, according to Böll in his letter to his father and sister the next day, was that his typewriter did not work any more after a porter had dropped it. Everything else was to their satisfaction: 'The landscape is wonderful, the house quite beautiful, roomy, and comfortable [...] our chimney fire burns wonderfully [...] We

---

[10] Letter George Fleischmann to Heinrich Böll, 4 February 1955, in *KA 10*, p. 642 (Böll Archive HA 1326-4026, Bl. 75). Padraig O'Reilly knew Tony Gallagher from earlier visits to Achill, where O'Reilly's father had been a teacher.
[11] Archive Böll Erbengemeinschaft. Thanks to René Böll for sending me an image of this letter.
[12] Ibid.

The Böll family in front of the house in Keel. @ Samay Böll

are all very happy here: The children have a great appetite and enjoy everything very much, especially the donkeys, the ocean and the chimney fire.'[13] In the chapter 'Mayo – God help us' the initial impressions are presented like a painting:

> The house was painted snow white, the window frames dark blue; there was a fire burning in the grate. The welcoming feast consisted of fresh salmon. The sea was pale green, up front where it rolled onto the beach, dark blue out toward the center of the bay, and a narrow, sparkling white frill was visible where the sea broke on the island. (p. 29).

In another letter home two days later, with the typewriter mended, and having spent a long time at the beach, he described the surroundings further though more prosaically than in the *Irish Journal*: 'For the time being we are the only strangers in the village [...] there are enough shops and every week a big truck with groceries comes. And everything is very cheap: a huge loaf of bread costs 65 pfennig, butter 2,20 DM. A half

---

[13] Letter Heinrich & Raimund Böll to Viktor & Tilde Böll, Keel, 4 June 1955. In *Rom auf den ersten Blick*, p. 60. English version on the wall of the small study in the Böll Cottage, Dugort.

pound of tea 1,80 DM etc.'[14] Thanks to the electric stove not yet being installed they had their first larger meal with the Gallaghers 'who are very very nice (eight children and one hotel!)'.

Overall Böll had reason to find all the people in the village 'nice' and writes that he was able to test their benevolence due to the family's cashflow problems. He borrowed the money to call George Fleischmann in Dublin asking him to send a postal order: this was promptly done, but it could not be paid out as there was no money available at the post office. Böll did not receive Fleischmann's ten pounds until two days later – and exclaims, probably half exasperated and half fascinated: 'O lovely Ireland'.[15]

A final piece of advice for his sister Tilde, who was to join them later, is not to worry 'if the mail is a little bit slow: nothing works here very fast: even the prayer in church yesterday was slow and pure'. The only things missing and therefore desired in this slow-paced paradise seem to be coffee and newspapers.[16] In a later letter, Böll states 'it is a totally different world',[17] one in which electricity may not always work – but a world which is not in any way inferior. Böll tells his father that on one occasion when the electricity fails again 'we have to boil the water for the tea and fry the eggs on the peat fire – it is faster than with electricity.'[18]

The long second trip to Ireland in 1955 lasted the whole summer. The Bölls stayed in Keel until the end of September 1955. Annemarie and Heinrich Böll took over school duties and taught their sons personally. This time interest in Böll's 'Irish diary pages' was expressed not only by print publications but also by radio. Alfred Andersch, another influential writer in postwar Germany, who was trying to build up the features programmes and late night listening at the *Süddeutsche Rundfunk* (South German Radio), asked for pieces like the ones that had appeared in the *FAZ*.[19] Andersch expressed his delight with the quality of Böll's work and praised his 'sovereign prose'.[20]

---

[14] Letter 6 June 1955, in *Rom auf den ersten Blick*, p. 69, translation also in the Böll Cottage.
[15] Ibid., p. 70.
[16] Ibid.
[17] Ibid., p. 69.
[18] Ibid., p. 70.
[19] Letter from Alfred Andersch to Böll, 7 June 1955, *KA 10*, p. 643.
[20] Ibid.

Clodagh and Edward King, photo thanks to René Böll. © Edward King.

Four more articles appeared based on the time in Keel in 1955, two of them written in Ireland – 'Skelett einer menschlichen Siedlung' ('Skeleton of a Human Habitation') in which Böll describes the first encounter with the deserted village on Achill, and 'Torfklumpen im Kamin', later called 'Blick ins Feuer' ('Gazing into the fire'), a meditation on peat fires, cigarettes and time. The other two were written after the return to Cologne[21] and published early in 1956 – 'Betrachtungen über den irischen Regen' ('Thoughts on Irish Rain') and 'Ambulanter politischer Zahnarzt' ('Itinerant Political Dentist').

The Böll family seem to have made immediate friends – the village doctor Dr Edward (Ned) King and his wife Clodagh, who was to have a starring role as the young doctor's wife in the tenth chapter 'Die schönsten Füße der Welt' ('The Most Beautiful Feet in the World') and their children who played with Raimund, René and Vincent. Clodagh King came to Achill when she was just married, and is remembered as being different from the locals, always beautifully dressed and made up. Her husband Ned was a dedicated doctor, who took devoted care of young mothers, poked the fire and made tea for himself, and whose door was always open.[22]

---

[21] See *KA 10*, p. 643.
[22] Conversation with Elisabeth Sweeney, Achill, 28 August 2002.

Other close contacts included the Gallagher family. Tony Gallagher and Heinrich Böll spent many hours discussing all kinds of issues in Molloy's Pub.[23] Lily Gallagher and her ninth child James Pius Martin (called James Patrick Pius in the *Irisches Tagebuch* and James Patrick Pedar in the English translation) feature in the chapter 'Mrs. D.'s Ninth Child';[24] Lily's daughter Mary appears as Siobhan[25] who will take over the post office, and who 'has eyes like Vivien Leigh' (pp. 92, 95).[26] Also in the Bölls' circle of acquaintances were Thea and Captain Robert Boyd, who ran the Amethyst Hotel and a small shop in the annex, just a stone's throw from the house where the Bölls stayed.

Though his main base from 1955 onwards was Achill Island, Böll ventured further afield and travelled around Ireland. In 1956, in the middle of his next stay in Keel (again lasting almost four months), he went south on a round trip in order to explore areas he had not yet seen, a conscious effort to base his impressions not solely on Mayo: 'and to do Ireland justice: in the south it is really southern, fertile and fairytale-like colourful and beautiful'.[27] Furthermore, as he wrote to his friend Ernst-Adolf Kunz, he planned to look for work in Dublin, any kind of job, to spend one or two years in order write a novel there.[28] After his return he enthused that he had had a wonderful trip to Dublin and the south,[29] but neither the longer stay in Dublin, a novel written there nor the more geographically balanced overall description materialised. Instead, Böll continued to return to Achill for many years, and in both the *Irish Journal* and his film *Children of Eire* one can observe a predominance of Achill experiences. Soon, the status of occasional visitor, albeit for long periods, and paying

---

[23] Lily Gallagher recalled in an interview with Jean Tansey that Böll and her husband were the best of friends, always chatting with each other 'too long sometimes I used to think.' Molloy's Pub later became the Village Inn.
[24] Böll seems to have misunderstood the name rather than changing it for publication. See Böll's letter to Annemarie Böll, 18 June 1956 (*KA 10*, p. 733): 'Mrs. Gallagher had her ninth child last winter, it is called Seamus Patrick Pius.' Correct information from Elizabeth Barrett, neé Gallagher.
[25] Information from Elizabeth Barrett, 29 August 2002.
[26] Böll's prediction that '[o]ne thing is certain, and that is that of Mrs. D's nine children five or six will have to emigrate' (p. 94) fortunately was not fulfilled as Elizabeth Barrett (Mrs Gallagher's seventh child) thankfully notes – they were all able to stay. Elizabeth herself along with her husband John Barrett took over the running of the Bervie from her parents.
[27] Letter from Böll to Witsch, 27 July 1956, *KA 10*, p. 648.
[28] Letter from Böll to Kunz, 31 July 1956, ibid.
[29] Postcard from Böll to Kunz, 13 August 1956, ibid.

The Boyd family, photo thanks to René Böll. © Samay Böll.

guest was not enough and in 1958 the Bölls bought a cottage in Dugort on the north side of Achill, close to the former mission. A few years later Böll purchased a second house close by, where his eldest son, Raimund, spent a long time with his first wife, Lila Mookerjee, whose father came from India and whose mother was German.

A large part of *Ansichten eines Clowns* (*The Clown*) was written on Achill between mid-June and mid-July 1962, the draft version being known in the definitive edition of his works as the 'Dugort Version', while the final, published version is referred to as the 'Kölner (Cologne) Version'.[30] It became one of his best known and most controversial novels, highly praised by many but also seen as a biting criticism of the Catholic Church. After the long and intense work on the novel he felt 'tired, exhausted, also

---

[30] Böll, *Ansichten eines Clowns*, Kölner Ausgabe *Werke* volume 13, edited by Árpád Bernáth, Cologne: Kiepenheuer & Witsch 2004, pp. 241ff. In the following abbreviated as *KA 13*. The 'Dugort version' provided in the section giving the background to the novel, intriguingly provides a happy ending in comparison to the open ended 'Cologne version'.

ill' and fled back to Ireland for 'standstill, complete quiet'. He felt best protected there from seeing or hearing any criticism of his new book.[31]

In Achill people liked and respected Böll – but not because he was a well-known writer, a fact that did not become generally obvious until he received the Nobel Prize. As the late Violet McDowell, proprietor of Gray's Guesthouse, just a few hundred metres away from Böll's cottage in Dugort, said: 'People loved him here, the Nobel Prize made no difference.'[32] She knew the Bölls well in their later years in Achill. They came often for meals and sometimes also had friends staying in her guesthouse. McDowell's impressions were echoed by most people I talked to in Achill. It is well remembered how every Sunday the Böll family went punctually to Pollagh Church – 'You wouldn't need an alarm clock, you'd know the time if you saw the Bölls.'[33] Michael O'Malley, who was the local tailor before he took over the post office (and who made tweed suits for Böll and his sons as well as cutting their hair which grew long over the three months they were often there) remembers that Böll did not stand out, was well liked and really quite ordinary: 'We were all surprised when we heard he was an important writer after he got the Nobel Prize,'[34] and Tom McNamara says similarly: 'Böll was a very gentle man [...] He was part of the community, mixed easily, people didn't really know who he was and how important he was until he got the Nobel Prize.'[35]

Even today, although Böll's memory and his links to Achill are cherished, not many of his books, with the possible exception of the *Irish Journal*, would be known and read in Achill. But his descriptions of his surroundings are still appreciated – especially, according to Theresa McDonald, his writings on the deserted village (she also included parts of the chapter in her monograph on the history of Achill[36]):

> His description of Deserted Village is most important, it's very evocative; it captures the essence of the place. That's most important also for people here as there is strong attachment to it from local people, probably as it is

---

[31] *KA 13*, p. 267, quoting letter to Jenny Aloni (Böll Archive, HA 1326 Erg. 2, Bll. 34-35.)
[32] Conversation with Violet McDowell, 29 August 2002.
[33] Conversation with Mary Colohan, 28 August 2002.
[34] Conversation with Michael O'Malley, 28 August 2002.
[35] Conversation with Tom McNamara, 28 August 2002.
[36] McDonagh, *Achill Island*, pp. 267f.

'Sons in the deserted village' – Vincent, Raimund and René Böll. © Samay Böll.

connected with happy memories. People still go walking there, all folklore related to it as the booley village. Booleying ended in the 1940s.[37]

All in all, Heinrich Böll spent nearly three years in Ireland. In addition to the four weeks in 1954, there were the four months in 1955 and again in 1956. In 1958 Böll spent nearly two months in Gera, in Switzerland, from late April to 20 June, and after just two days at home in Cologne the family took off again to Ireland for two months, from 30 June to 31 August. In 1960 it was a long stay again, for three months from 31 May to 31 August. In 1961 he was guest of honour at the German Academy Villa Massimo in Rome from mid June to late October, but the following year he returned to Ireland for two months (July and August), and again a year on for four months (late April to early September) in 1963. In 1964 he arrived in mid-July and stayed until October; in 1965 he came for one month from early April to early May; in 1966 for July and August; in 1967 again for a longer period, from July to September; in 1971 from August to September. During this time Böll was elected president of the International PEN at a meeting which took place in Dun Laoghaire.

Following the Nobel Prize in 1972, recognition in Ireland came swiftly. In 1973 he stayed in Ireland from 26 November to 14 December and received

---

[37] Conversation with Theresa McDonald, 27 August 2002.

an Honorary Doctorate from Trinity College Dublin. This had been initiated by a Senior Fellow in Trinity College, George Dawson, who was a Professor of Genetics but also a generous patron of the arts.[38]

Gilbert Carr, a former Senior Lecturer in TCD's German Department, remembered the following anecdote from this occasion: when Böll was in Trinity to receive his honorary doctorate that year, Hugh Sacker, the then Professor of German, invited Böll and his wife to a cup of tea in the German Department, then in House 35 in New Square. Böll liked this low-key encounter, in contrast with the College's ceremonial tribute. Carr recalls that it was not immediately before or after the ceremony, as Böll was in normal gear and not in academic robes. Carr then proceeded to ask Böll a few – and as he now thinks naive – questions, including: why he had come to the defence of Ulrike Meinhof (which Böll explained by referring to the Springer press's hate campaign); and whether Ireland in 1972 was not altogether a different place from the subject of the *Irisches Tagebuch*. Böll's answer to this included the phrase: 'Das war alles Fiktion' ('That was all fiction'). Carr knew that this was not to be taken literally, as he had already met a member of the 'Co. Mayo doctor's' family, and himself had memories of the atmosphere of early fifties Ireland, and concluded that it was both Böll's self-commentary on the style and conception of his book, and a laconic comment on the 'reality' of the modernized Ireland of 1972, against which memory of the 1950s (or the utopian aspect of the book) was being measured.[39] As in Achill, Böll left in Trinity a strong impression of someone modest, unassuming and nice.[40]

Between 1974 and 1982 there were no more visits; in the 1970s and 1980s the principal visitors in Achill were the eldest of Böll's three sons, Raimund, and his wife Lila. Use of the cottage was also given to the extended family and friends of the family, among them Petra Kelly, the German Green party activist.

---

[38] Gilbert Carr to whom I owe this information, pointed out that Dawson was also responsible for the acquisition of works by Henry Moore and for the organization of major exhibitions, such as the Picasso exhibition in the late 60s, before there was a Douglas Hyde Gallery. It is unclear but possible that he knew the Bölls personally already.
[39] Email from Gilbert Carr, 3 January 2008.
[40] Email from Tim Jackson, former Associate Professor in Trinity College Dublin, 3 January 2008.

Heinrich Böll's last visit took place between 12 and 23 May 1983, two years before his death.[41] Looking at the dates of Böll's visits, the last longer period of time in Ireland was in 1967; after that he only spent about three months altogether in the country. A number of reasons are likely to have played a role in this diminished contact. In 1967 the English translation of the *Irisches Tagebuch* appeared, which had the effect of 'blowing his cover' to a certain extent in Achill, where his descriptions of Ireland and indeed some of the people in Achill were now freely available and accessible in English. Also, in the epilogue to the *Irish Journal*, Böll indicated that his literary preoccupation with Ireland was coming to an end ('it is high time for me to close my file on Ireland, postponing my visions of writing another book about that country until some distant date in the future').[42] His Nobel Prize in 1972 only added to the increased exposure, furthermore bringing a swell of publicity about the author and his life, including his Irish hideaway, to an interested German audience (some of whom seem to have believed that Böll would be overjoyed by unannounced visits – an ongoing problem even today for writers in the Böll cottage).[43] And while Ireland had been his first experience of a foreign country (except for his war experiences) and then became according to himself a kind of second home, Böll had over the years and with increasing success become a dedicated globetrotter who had made several, at times longlasting trips to France, Belgium, Czechoslovakia, Italy, the Netherlands, Denmark, Sweden, the USSR, Austria, Greece, Israel, the USA and Ecuador. On average one can calculate that after 1956 he visited two to three different countries per year. For health reasons he went for several annual visits to Switzerland from 1976 onwards. Health concerns would also have sometimes impacted on visits to Ireland given the long and exhausting travel that was necessary to get to Achill from Cologne. In addition, the long trip to Ireland made short visits impractical and longer visits to Ireland would have conflicted with the increasing demands upon Böll's time as an internationally famous writer. But even if

---

[41] *KA 10*, p. 651.
[42] Böll, Epilogue – Thirteen years later, in: *Irish Journal*, p. 121. He charts with mixed feelings the enormous differences he perceives to have taken place in the thirteen years since his first visit.
[43] See letter from Böll to Lew Kopelew 28 August 1973: '[...] aber auch Irland ist "hinüber": jeder deutsche, der dorthin fährt, glaubt, ich freue mich wahnsinnig, wenn er mich dort besucht – und es gibt ja einige siebzig millionen deutsche (sic)!'. Thanks to Elsbeth Zylla, editor, for this excerpt from her forthcoming publication *Briefwechsel Heinrich Böll – Lew Kopelew*, Cologne: Kiepenheuer & Witsch 2012.

Böll did not come very often to Ireland in the last fifteen years before his death, nor write much about it anymore, the country was arguably always close to his heart.[44] A biographer who came to his house in Cologne in 1976 noted a model of his Achill cottage on his study desk,[45] and in the replica version of his last study in the Central Library of Cologne an enlarged photo of himself in Ireland has pride of place on the wall. In a poignant letter to an Irish schoolgirl shortly before his death, Böll emphasises that it was mainly health reasons that prevented him for a long period from visiting Ireland, but when he returned (in 1983) he found it was as beautiful and lovely as always, especially the way in which people engaged with children, adding that he was accompanied by some of his family, including his granddaughter. He reiterates that he never wanted to settle in Ireland permanently and therefore never did "leave Ireland". The following sentence expresses his lifelong emotional attachment to Ireland: 'In meinem Innern verlassen kann ich es nie', which could be translated as 'In my heart I can never leave it'.[46]

In Ireland Heinrich Böll found peace and a refuge from the constant need to give interviews on controversial topics; it helped him to withstand the pressure he suffered in Germany from the conservative media, for example following the publication of *The Clown*. Achill's remoteness helped him to retain a distance from everyday concerns – something also found refreshing by another writer, by coincidence one Böll admired, Graham Greene ('I long for somewhere like Achill or Capri where there are no telephones').[47] Greene though had other reasons, too, for his own personal affinity for Achill as the place where his extramarital relationship with Catherine Walston blossomed.[48] But Greene also appreciated the simple life on Achill and found it inspirational; he finished his novel *The Heart of the Matter* (1948) there. Especially welcome, though, was the relative anonymity for him and Walston, herself also married and recently converted

---

[44] In fact he argues in the epilogue that the main reason that keeps him from writing, is his emotional attachment: 'The thing that really prevents me from "correcting" or "adding to" what I have written about Ireland is this: I am too attached to it, and it is not good for an author to write about a subject to which he is too attached' (Böll, Epilogue – Thirteen years later, in: *Irish Journal*, p. 126).
[45] Hoffmann, *Heinrich Böll*, p. 227.
[46] Letter from Heinrich Böll to Maeve Collins, 29 May 1985, copy thanks to Joachim Fischer. Thanks to René Böll for permission to quote from it.
[47] William Cash, *The Third Woman*, London: Little, Brown & Company 2000, p. 119.
[48] Cash, *The Third Woman*, p. 117.

Heinrich Böll on Achill © Samay Böll.

to Catholicism. However, while Böll also enjoyed the privilege most people in the public eye no longer have – a location where he was private – it went much deeper for him, as it was not merely a place where he was unknown but rather one where he was known and liked as a member of a community which accepted him as one of themselves. Achill was very much a place where the whole family felt at home, where the sons as teenagers and adults accompanied their parents and later visited themselves, and where Annemarie went to visit after Heinrich's death.

Another aspect of what Ireland meant for Böll was expressed by him when literary critic Marcel Reich-Ranicki was dismissive of Böll's portrayal of Ireland. Reich-Ranicki had been shocked by the poverty in Dublin and was not in favour of how fashionable Ireland had become in Germany, a popularity possibly due to a dubious fascination with slums and squalor. Böll argued that Dublin was not Ireland and disagreed strongly with the notion that Ireland was first and foremost a poor country. Instead for him it was a place where people had an amazing sense of freedom and held a record in strike actions, an entirely positive notion for Böll. In his opinion the Irish were privileged with a simple but rich life (however, he readily agreed his description could be and was misunderstood, especially in Ireland).[49]

Ireland proved to be not only an inspiration for the *Irish Journal* – which will be the focus of the next chapter – but was also important for many of his other works. Böll not only spent his holidays in Ireland, not only found a kind of second home there, he also worked and wrote there. According to his notes in his diary on 4 September 1973, in which he lists the number of works done in different workplaces, Ireland features quite strongly with 68 pieces done in Keel and Dugort between 1954 and 1968. The house in Germany where he lived mainly at that time, in Müngersdorf, Cologne, provided in the years 1954 to 1969 the surroundings for only less than twice that number, 115 (though a further 83 were written in the garden house in Müngersdorf between 1963 and 1967).[50]

---

[49] *Im literarischen Kaffeehaus*, WDR/NDR/Freies Berlin, 21 December 1967, conversation between Heinrich Böll, Hans Mayer and Marcel Reich-Ranicki on the occasion of Böll's 50th birthday.
[50] Cf. Stadt Köln & Heinrich-Böll-Stiftung (ed.): *Heinrich Böll Life and Work*, edited by R. Böll, V. Böll, K.H. Busse, M. Schäfer, Göttingen: Steidl 1995, pp. 48f.

PART III:

THE *IRISH JOURNAL*

CHAPTER SIX

BACKGROUND, STRUCTURE AND FORMATION

In 1967 a book published some ten years previously in German as *Irisches Tagebuch* appeared for the first time in an English translation. Its title was *Irish Journal* and its author a certain Heinrich Böll. A disclaimer and a dedication appeared after the table of contents, the dedication rather unspectacular ('I dedicate this little book to the man who encouraged me to write it: Karl Korn'), but the disclaimer has since become a staple quotation for German tourists: 'This Ireland exists: but whoever goes there and fails to find it has no claim on the author.' Nevertheless, for some tourists Böll's Ireland still exists and can be found.

When the book appeared in Germany in 1957 it had been an immediate success. Nearly all reviews were euphoric and the reading public has loved it from the beginning. It is even now almost compulsory reading for any German visiting Ireland. Given the obvious changes that have occurred not only in Ireland but also to the interests and perspective of the readership, why is that the case? Also surprising are the vastly differing assessments the book has received from Böll specialists, ranging from 'unique' in the context of Böll's oeuvre[1] to 'from the first line to the last there is little new in the *Irish Journal*: the same style, the same qualities, the same themes, the same characters, the same commitment, and the same criticism of Germany.'[2] There is no such variety of opinion when it comes to rating the influence of the book on German perceptions of Ireland – everyone agrees that it has become a 'cult book'[3] and that its influence could hardly be overestimated.[4]

---

[1] Bernd Balzer, *Das literarische Werk Heinrich Bölls – Einführung und Kommentare*, Munich: dtv 1997, p. 213.
[2] Robert C. Conard, *Heinrich Böll*, Boston: Twayne 1981, p. 79.
[3] See for example Doris Dohmen, *Das deutsche Irlandbild*, Amsterdam/Atlanta: Rodopi 1994, p. 158.
[4] For an overview see Gisela Holfter, *Erlebnis Irland*, Trier: WVT 1996, pp. 140f.

The reception of the English version ten years later was somewhat different to that of the German one, both in terms of enthusiasm and in the sheer volume of commentary. There were some changes from the German version: the translation of 1967 featured two additions to the original eighteen chapters, a foreword and an epilogue. The foreword indicates fear of causing offence: 'The Ireland described in this book is that of the mid-1950s. My comments on the great changes that have taken place in that country since are contained in the Epilogue.' The epilogue accordingly concentrates on economic and social developments that had taken place in the meantime. This was clearly a reaction to the criticism and debate that had been unleashed two years earlier by the broadcasting of Böll's film *Children of Eire*, which will be discussed in a later chapter.

In the following analysis of the *Irish Journal* the focus will be on what contributed to making the book so special that it is still worth looking at it today, more than fifty years later. What does it contribute to our knowledge of Böll, to Irish-German relations, to travel writing and the understanding of another place? Why was it so successful? To evaluate the limitations of the book as well as its triumphs and to place it both in the context of Böll's work and within the large corpus of travel writing about Ireland and its influence on the German view of that country, one needs to go back to its genesis. One also needs to look at its unusual form and content, including the surprising choice of title given the structure, style and themes in comparison with other works about Ireland. Time – past, present and future – plays an important role which may be hardly noticed on first reading but has far-reaching consequences to the way Ireland has since been perceived in Germany.

It should be remembered that Böll's point of view is that of an outsider, bringing into play other perspectives and another framework, first and most obviously his position as a German writer and his relationship with Germany, but entailing also the triangle of Germany, Ireland and Great Britain, since for centuries Germany had viewed Ireland solely through English eyes. Böll's portrayal of the Irish people and of Ireland's three most powerful magnets for visitors – scenery, music and literature – is especially interesting, and his use of colour is particularly significant.

All these aspects help us to understand the main themes of the book (poverty, emigration and religion), the continuous narrative thread and Böll's experience of Ireland. The main themes are already introduced as he is on his way to Ireland, in the very first conversation presented. Indeed, already here the portrayal of the interlinked themes of poverty and emigration on one hand and religion on the other allow a glimpse into the later controversies.

The Making of the Book

As described in previous chapters, individual articles which had been published from 1954 onwards form most of the basis for the *Irish Journal*. The articles appeared in the two and a half years prior to the appearance of the book, mainly in the *Frankfurter Allgemeine Zeitung* or as hugely popular radio broadcasts. The most important of the radio features, which included the stories from 1954 and 1955 was *Der tote Indianer in der Duke Street und andere Berichte aus Irland von Heinrich Böll* (The Dead Redskin of Duke Street and Other Reports from Ireland), arranged for radio by Alfred Andersch, broadcast on the *Süddeutsche Rundfunk* on 15 May 1956. The idea of publishing the articles in book form had already been discussed as early as 1955 and was originally planned for the end of May 1956.[5] In a letter to his publisher, 'Jupp' (Joseph Casper Witsch), in January 1956, Böll encloses his latest 'Irish Impressions' and explains that added to the existing ones would be 'one chapter with all the "facts" on Ireland', concentrated in the form of a conversation, and possibly one or two shorter chapters in the same format as earlier ones.

Furthermore, everything would now be told in the first person and possibly shortened.[6] The reworking and change to a predominantly first person narrative, plus the addition of some further chapters, were indeed to happen, but Böll must have decided to leave out the factual chapter, unless one assumes that 'Ankunft I' ('Arrival 1'), the first chapter, is intended to fill that gap. A large part of that chapter is in the form of a conversation between a priest and a returning emigrant who is visiting her family and is disillusioned especially with the Church and religion but also with Kathleen Ni Houlihan, the mystical personification of Ireland, who exports her most precious possession, her children.[7] The priest gently but unsuccessfully tries to stem her bitterness.

---

[5] Böll Archive, HA 1326 – EK Witsch. Also at *KA 10*, p. 644.
[6] Letter from Böll to Witsch, 29 January 1956 (Böll Archive HA 1326 – EK Witsch, 2nd sheet, also at *KA 10*, p. 644).
[7] The use of 'Kathleen Ni Houlihan' as a symbol for Ireland was quite common also in other German accounts of Ireland in the 1950s, see for example Enno Stephan, who refers to her and continues: 'Anyone who ever saw the women of Ireland, the slender, blue-eyed, dark-haired, understands where the name comes

There is no doubt that Böll would have carefully crafted this chapter, written specifically for the book, which sets the tone and context for what follows. The key to understanding Ireland here, however, is not as originally planned through objective facts (though a number of Irish world records as announced at the time are given: tea drinking, ordination of new priests, cinema-going and the lowest official suicide rate) but through listening to the conversations of the Irish people and becoming aware that merely by boarding the ferry the traveller crosses a border to a different world, one that he can experience with all his senses ('I could see, hear and smell that I had crossed a frontier'). Böll describes the traveller experiencing a complete change from what he saw before: hearing throaty Celtic, smelling the peat, tasting the tea and whiskey – and the feeling of being in a society where Europe's social order is utterly changed and wealth and poverty are no longer indicators of honour and disgrace.[8] But the conversation between the young woman and the priest is also a form of warning that not all is as innocent and intriguing as it would have appeared to Böll on his first trips to Ireland and as appears in most of the following (but earlier written) stories.[9] In order to understand this warning it is necessary to look more closely at the structure, the title and the main topics of the *Irish Journal*.

It quickly becomes clear that this is not the normal travelogue with a set structure and a chronological and geographical order, nor, as suggested by the title, a day by day account of what happened to Böll while in Ireland. The book consists instead of 18 chapters which offer impressions of the

---

from. It is a noble visage that belongs to "Kathleen Ni Houlihan". Proud and deeply religious, it is marked by the experience of suffering and true knowledge of the ultimate things. Hospitality, openness and cheerfulness of the heart radiate from it. Anyone who has seen it once and understood it can only love it.' [Wer einmal die Frauen Irlands sah, die schlankgewachsenen, blauäugigen, dunkelhaarigen, begreift, woher der Name kommt. Es ist ein edles Antlitz, das 'Kathleen Ni Houlihan' trägt. Stolz und tiefe Frömmigkeit, erfahrenes bitteres Leid und letztes Wissen um die Dinge zeichnen seine Züge. Gastfreundschaft, Offenheit und Heiterkeit des Herzens strahlen aus ihm. Wer es einmal sah und begriff, wird es nur noch lieben können].
Eins Dritter Dublin – Reise ins Land der Rebellen (6), in *Fortschritt*, No. 33, 16 September 1953, p. 5.
[8] See *Irish Journal*, p. 1. The truth of this is obviously debatable and the topic will be explored further in the chapter on poverty and emigration below.
[9] The conversation is of special significance for the topic of religion and will be examined more closely in the chapter on religion.

country like a colourful mosaic, only loosely held together by a number of recurring motifs and the chapters describing arrival and departure.

Böll had taken care to revise and at times rework nearly all the chapters and added three, two of them entirely new, the first chapter, 'Arrival 1', and chapter 10, 'The Most Beautiful Feet in the World'. Parts of chapter 16, 'Not a Swan to be Seen', had already been included in the first article in the *Frankfurter Allgemeine Zeitung*, 'Der erste Tag' ('The First Day'). A further sign of careful revision becomes obvious when one looks at the articles in chronological order and the changed order of their appearance in the book.

As far as the newspaper articles are concerned – as is to be expected – a clear chronological pattern of stories emerges, first with Dublin and Böll's travels around Ireland from 1954 onwards, then with Achill-based content (with the exception of 'The Dead Redskin of Duke Street') from summer 1955 onwards. This is not the case, however, in the book. If one looks at the list of chapters, here presented with the dates of first publication of the articles on which the chapters are based and the order of first publication (or broadcast) in square brackets, it becomes clear to what extent Böll restructured and composed anew his Irish impressions:

1. Arrival I ('Ankunft I') [new chapter written for the book]
2. Arrival II ('Ankunft II', as 'Der erste Tag', 'The First Day', but with many changes: *Frankfurter Allgemeine Zeitung*, 24 December 1954, p. 39) [1]
3. Pray for the Soul of Michael O'Neill ('Bete für die Seele des Michael O'Neill': *Frankfurter Allgemeine Zeitung*, 26 February 1955, p. 32) [2]
4. Mayo – God help us (*Frankfurter Allgemeine Zeitung*, 7 July 1956, p. 41) [10]
5. Skeleton of a Human Habitation (as 'Skelett einer Siedlung': *Frankfurter Allgemeine Zeitung*, 16 July 1955, p. 40) [5]
6. Itinerant Political Dentist (as 'Gedanken eines reisenden Zahnarztes': *Frankfurter Allgemeine Zeitung*, 6 March 1956, p. 8) [9]
7. Portrait of an Irish Town (only 'Limerick in the Morning': radio, *NDR*, 25 March 1955, *Frankfurter Allgemeine Zeitung*, 26 March 1955) [3, 'Limerick in the Evening' written for the book]
8. When God Made Time ... ('Als Gott die Zeit machte ...': *Frankfurter Allgemeine Zeitung*, 19 July 1956, p. 8) [11]

9. Thoughts on Irish Rain ('Betrachtungen über den irischen Regen': *Neue Zürcher Zeitung*, 4 February 1956, p. 4) [8]
10. The Most Beautiful Feet in the World ('Die schönsten Füße der Welt') [new chapter written for the book]
11. The Dead Redskin of Duke Street ('Der tote Indianer in der Duke Street': Kulturkreis im Bundesverband der Deutschen Industrie (ed) *Jahresring* 55/56, Stuttgart [September] 1955, pp. 206-209) [7]
12. Gazing into the Fire ('Blick ins Feuer', as 'Torfklumpen im Kaminfeuer', ['Peat in the Hearth']: *Frankfurter Allgemeine Zeitung*, 26 August 1955, p. 6) [6]
13. When Seamus Wants a Drink ('Wenn Seamus einen trinken will...': *Frankfurter Allgemeine Zeitung*, 3 August 1956, p. 10) [12]
14. Mrs. D's Ninth Child ('Das neunte Kind der Mrs D.': *Aufwärts* 9, No. 8, 15 August 1956, S. 9) [13]
15. A Small Contribution to Occidental Mythology ('Kleiner Beitrag zur abendländischen Mythologie', as 'Auf einer kleinen Insel' ['On a Small Island']: *Frankfurter Allgemeine Zeitung*, 14 May 1954, p. 42) [4]
16. Not a Swan to be Seen ('Kein Schwan war zu sehen') [mostly new chapter written for the book]
17. In a Manner of Speaking ('Redensarten', as 'Es könnte schlimmer sein' ['It could be worse']: *Frankfurter Allgemeine Zeitung*, 8 January 1957, p. 8) [14]
18. Farewell (as 'Der Abschied von Irland fiel schwer': *Frankfurter Allgemeine Zeitung*, 9 March 1957, p. 38) [15].

A number of these articles were reprinted, sometimes with alterations, in other newspapers and journals and many chapters were read by Böll for radio broadcasts, mainly on the popular Berlin-based station *RIAS*.[10] Other articles on Ireland by Böll which did not appear in the *Irish Journal* (and

---

[10] For a longer list, see *KA 10*, p. 672, though this only notes the first broadcasts of the chapters and mentions only Böll as reader with an earlier reference that due to a lack of surviving material it is not possible to state whether on other occasions he was the reader or not (see ibid. p. 642). However, a radio review shows that at the same time that chapters were being broadcast by *RIAS*, read by Böll, in April 1957 (see p. 672) there was another broadcast by *NDR*, this time read by Heinz Reincke (cf. Bölls Reise nach Irland, in *Kölnische Rundschau*, 5 April 1957 [p. 20]). This indicates that there were several recordings within a short time, a clear indication of the popularity of Böll's Irish impressions. It is also interesting that the review mentions four chapters that include the descriptions of journey and arrival and that Irish folk music was played in the intervals between the chapters.

which, incidentally, carry far more conventional titles than those often favoured by him) include 'Am Rande Europas' ('On Europe's Fringe') [*Magnum*, Jg.2/1955, issue 10, p. 48] and 'Bilder aus Irland' ('Images from Ireland') [*Westermanns Monatshefte* 97 (1956), no.8, pp. 14-21], though parts of the latter story are to be found in Alfred Andersch's version of Böll's 'Irish Impressions' for the southern German radio station *Süddeutsche Rundfunk*.

The chapter on Limerick, now completed with a section on Limerick in the evening, has been moved from the third story to the seventh chapter; the fourth story, about the small island, appears as chapter fifteen. A few clusters of three can be found – travelling to Dublin and getting to know it (chapters 1-3), travelling to Achill and discovering it (chapters 4-6) and aspects of life on Achill (chapters 8-10 and 12-14), while chapters 7, 15 and 16 refer to trips around Ireland. Chapters 11 ('Dead Redskin of Duke Street') and 17 ('In a Manner of Speaking') deal in very different ways with the Irish use of language and imagination.

Events are not always viewed from the perspective of the first person singular. There is sometimes a more inclusive 'we' and in several chapters (10, 12, 13, 17) an omniscient third-person narrator reflects on time and language or describes, for instance, the doctor's wife waiting for her husband. The length of the chapters varies widely between three and twelve pages.

One can argue that Böll set out to destroy conventional patterns of travelogues, or at least that he went beyond them in not allowing the reader to know what to expect, forcing us to explore the notion that every chapter deals with a new situation, and not tying us down to preconceived ideas. Then again, the structure could be a homage to one of Ireland's finest authors and one whom Böll much admired – James Joyce. The commentary in volume ten of the Cologne edition of Heinrich Böll's work (published in 2006), which contains the *Irish Journal*, suggests that the framework for the book might well have been inspired by the outline of Joyce's *Ulysses*. A number of points support this claim: both books consist of 18 chapters (and Böll had decided on that number even before the final parts were written),[11] have two beginnings, start in the morning and cover – with a bit of imagination – one day. This is emphasised in the *Irish Journal* by the young woman lifting an orange milk jug into the room

---

[11] See *KA 10*, p. 649.

from the window sill in 'Arrival II' (p. 8) and the corresponding action in the finishing paragraph of the last chapter, 'Farewell': 'a young woman was just putting an orange milk jug out onto the window sill' (p. 119). In chapter four of each book a change of perspective occurs (from Stephen Dedalus to Leopold Bloom in *Ulysses*; from Dublin to the west of Ireland in the *Irish Journal*). Even the narrative style in the last chapter is reminiscent of Molly Bloom's famous monologue.[12] Böll knew *Ulysses* well. Indeed, according to his diary, he read it on his trip to Ireland in 1954.[13] Even in his early work Böll used composition schemes that were not immediately obvious and often went unnoticed.[14] To use *Ulysses* as one foundation for his own structure might well have appealed to Böll also as an underlying and very subtle championing of Irish literature.

A controversial title

The title, *Irisches Tagebuch* in German (literally 'Irish Diary') and in English *Irish Journal*, is a somewhat surprising one. Indeed this feature occasioned much discussion:

> The book's title, suggesting a traveller's tedious day-to-day jottings about strange peoples, landscapes, and mores, seems to belie the text itself, which is organized in topical chapters and not simply in temporal or spatial segments. 'Tagebuch' indeed! Why not, instead, 'Reise nach Irland,' [A

---

[12] For further textual examples of the affinity of the *Irisches Tagebuch* with *Ulysses*, see 'Entstehung', *KA 10*, p. 650.

[13] Information from Jochen Schubert, Böll Archive, Cologne.

[14] See, for example, Böll's letter to Gert Kalow, 7 November 1955 (see Böll, *Werke 1951*, Kölner Ausgabe volume 5, edited by Robert C. Conrad, Cologne: Kiepenheuer & Witsch 2004, p. 431, in the following abbreviated as *KA 5*), regarding his composition scheme for *Wo warst Du, Adam? (Where were you, Adam?)*: 'Mir scheint, daß Sie *Wo warst Du Adam* unterschätzen: ich habe darin ein neues, ganz bestimmtes Kompositionsschema zu erproben versucht: die Handlung nicht an einen Helden zu hängen – deshalb auch gleichgültig, daß er kapitelweise gar nicht auftaucht – sondern an völlig belanglose Gegenstände: Tisch, Hosen, Kuchen. Freilich nützt es wenig, solche Dinge, die bei der Lektüre hätten herauskommen müssen, nachträglich zu erklären.' [I think you underestimate *Wo warst Du Adam*: I have attempted using a new, very specific composition scheme: to attach the story-line not onto one hero – therefore it does not matter whether he appears or not in all chapters – but to entirely extraneous things: a table, a pair of trousers, a cake. But it is of no benefit having to explain things afterwards that should have been apparent while reading.]

Trip to Ireland] or 'In Irland,' or 'Irische Eindrücke/Notizen or Skizzen?' [Irish Impressions/Notes or Sketches][15]

Manfred Jurgensen similarly points out that if Böll had not chosen the title himself no one else would have come up with it; he suggests that it places conscious emphasis on personal experience.[16] Robert Conard argues that the title of the work 'is misleading. The book is neither a journal nor a diary, but a collection of eighteen stories connected by recurring themes, motifs, and linguistic patterns.'[17] Turning to the English translation, although 'diary' and 'journal' are to a large extent synonymous, 'journal' suggests more a log of an expedition whereas 'diary' indicates a more personal, suggestive account – which presumably is precisely what the original title was intended to convey.

At one stage Böll's chosen title for his collection of stories was that of one of the chapters - 'The Dead Redskin of Duke Street'.[18] This title had already been used for the radio feature. Another reason for contemplating it as the title for the book might have been the praise extended by one of Germany's foremost writers and critics at the time, Wolfgang Hildesheimer, who admired this story in particular. The other working title that was used often in correspondence between Böll and his publisher Joseph Caspar

---

[15] Cecile Cazort Zorach, Two Faces of Erin: The Dual Journey in Heinrich Böll's *Irisches Tagebuch*, in: *The Germanic Review*, 53/3, 1978, pp. 124-131, 124. Zorach goes on to declare that the title was chosen by Böll for its linguistic symmetry: 'two eight-letter words of identical syllabic stress. This simple balance of two sides anticipates the duality which marks the German's encounter with Ireland throughout the book. Furthermore, each of these two words taken separately incorporates tensions between two disparate elements found in the text itself.' She thought that implicitly hidden in 'Irish' was 'West German', that 'Tagebuch' already contained the tension between time and text, and that this tension could be found throughout the text.
[16] Manfred Jurgensen, *Das fiktionale Ich - Untersuchungen zum Tagebuch*, Bern: Francke 1979, pp. 264f. Similarly, Helmut Preuß observes that the *Irish Journal* is no diary in the traditional sense, nor a travel guide with precise information, but instead gives an impression of a country that remains elusive of general assessment: Helmut Preuß, Von der Kunst der Reiseschilderung in Heinrich Bölls *Irisches Tagebuch*, in: Eberhard Ockel (ed.), *Sprechwissenschaft und Deutschdidaktik*, Kastellaun: Henn 1977, pp. 244-255, 244f.
[17] Conard, *Heinrich Böll*, p. 74.
[18] *KA 10*, p. 650. See also the new edition of *Irisches Tagebuch*, edited by René Böll and Jochen Schubert (Cologne: Kiepenheuer & Witsch 2007) which shows a picture of the first draft of the cover – with the title 'Der tote Indianer in der Duke Street', p. 158.

Witsch was 'Irish Impressions',[19] at first glance probably the most suitable title as that is indeed what the book contains. It incorporates the personal perspective and allows for unrelated features. However, the final title formed a link with Böll's very first publications about his Irish experiences: 'Tagebuch aus Irland' [Diary from Ireland] was the subtitle of the first story published in 1954. The newspaper publications of chapters in 1955 and 1956 appeared with the byline 'from the Irish Journal by Heinrich Böll'.[20] It made Böll's a distinctly recognisable publication, standing out among the huge number of books about Ireland by virtue of its title alone – so much so, that when in 1996 a book about Ireland with the title *Mein irisches Tagebuch* [My Irish Diary] was published by Ralph Giordano, it was clear that it he wanted it to be seen in the tradition of Heinrich Böll's iconic depiction.

---

[19] See for example Böll's letter to Joseph Caspar Witsch, 1 September 1955, in Viktor Böll (ed.), *Das Heinrich Böll Lesebuch*, Munich: dtv 1984 (3rd edition), p. 120; also *KA 10*, p. 644.
[20] See Mayo – 'God help us', 'Skelett einer menschlichen Siedlung', 'Ambulanter politischer Zahnarzt', 'Als Gott die Zeit machte', 'Blick ins Feuer', 'Wenn Seamus einen trinken will' – as well as the final one in 1957, Abschied.

Chapter Seven

The Usage of Time— Past, Present, Future

> *Time present and time past*
> *Are both perhaps present in time future,*
> *And time future contained in time past*
> *If all time is eternally present*
> *All time is unredeemable*[1]

These opening lines of T.S. Eliot's poem 'Burnt Norton', the first part of his *Four Quartets*, seem to resonate strongly with Böll's understanding of time. To use another phrase from the poem, Ireland arguably became Böll's 'still point of the turning world': the centre of a revolving wheel, itself remaining in the same place but of crucial importance as the real source of movement. What Böll seemed to have found in Ireland was freedom from worldly attachments, from Eliot's (and arguably Böll's) perspective, a way to give value to human actions in time and thus to redeem time itself. Böll's use of time in the *Irish Journal* is a very specific one and is central to the book's unique portrayal of Ireland. One reviewer in Germany, Rolf Becker, repeatedly refers to time as the most important experience for Böll in Ireland, indeed the true essence of the book. He argues that the special relationship to time that Böll finds in Ireland is the very reason why Böll loves the country, namely that it implies a strong humanity, which is not to be found in Germany due to a perceived lack of time there.[2] This might have been the case, but, as James Reid points out, time plays a key role in all of Böll's work.[3] Reid argues that from Böll's earliest days he took a passionate interest in everything that was happening

---

[1] T.S. Eliot, 'Burnt Norton', *Four Quartets*, London: Faber and Faber 1944 (revised version 1979), p. 13.
[2] Rolf Becker, 'Weil nichts geschah', *Sonntagsblatt* (Hamburg), 5 May 1957 and *Kölner Stadtanzeiger*, 18 May 1957.
[3] J.H. Reid, 'Time in the Works of Heinrich Böll', in: *Modern Language Review*, 62/1967, pp. 476-485.

around him: 'the contemporary world was the material from which he constructed his novels, stories, plays and radio plays. "I am of my time, passionately of my time."'[4] This is reflected in all his novels, and a number of critics have pointed out that – at least following *Wo warst Du, Adam?* (1951) – these are all set in the year of their publication or in the year immediately preceding it.[5] 'All past is for him present in the present.'[6] Present time in his novels is recognisable through certain indicators, for example references to current affairs and political discussions. In Böll's own comments the concept of 'Zeitgenossenschaft' (strictly speaking 'contemporaneity', but also translated as 'contemporary') is mentioned frequently. This idea is double-edged. Firstly it has consequences for art in general, which is an expression of present time and firmly rooted in it, though some permanency is possible: 'I am not interested in whether art will last; I believe that art is made by contemporaries for contemporaries; there are unrecognised contemporaries and recognised ones, there is fleeting and there is permanent contemporary.'[7] Secondly it has implications for the author, who according to Böll is not freefloating but is bound to his surroundings and the experiences of his age group, in Böll's case a particularly unsettled generation which due to the war has not really grown up:

> [...tied] to time and times, to what a whole generation has experienced, digested, seen and heard, which in autobiographical terms has only rarely been anything like significant enough to be articulated in language; tied to the restlessness and homelessness of a generation which suddenly finds itself transferred into grandparenthood and still has not reached – how do they call it – maturity.[8]

---

[4] J.H. Reid, *Heinrich Böll*, p. 3.
[5] See ibid., p. 8; Hoffmann, *Heinrich Böll*, p. 136.
[6] Hoffmann, *Heinrich Böll*, ibid.
[7] [Für die Frage nach der Beständigkeit der Kunst interessiere ich mich nicht; ich glaube Kunst wird von Zeitgenossen für Zeitgenossen gemacht; es gibt verkannte Zeitgenossen, es gibt flüchtige und andauernde Zeitgenossenschaft.] Böll, Der Zeitgenosse und seine Zeit, *FAZ* 21 October 1961 (trans. Reid, *A German for His Time*, p. 3). Böll was writing about Picasso.
[8] [Gebunden an Zeit und Zeitgenossenschaft, an das von einer Generation Erlebte, Erfahrene, Gesehene und Gehörte, das autobiographisch nur selten annähernd bezeichnend genug gewesen ist, um in Sprache gefaßt zu werden; gebunden an die Ruhe- und Heimatlosigkeit einer Generation, die sich plötzlich ins Großvateralter versetzt findet und immer noch nicht – wie nennt man das doch – reif geworden ist]. Böll, *Frankfurter Vorlesungen*, Munich: dtv 1977, p. 8 and *KA 14*, p. 139.

If both author and art are dependent on time and contemporaries about whom and for whom the author is writing, obviously there will be a marked change when readership and characters are no longer congruent, as when writing about Ireland. If the war and Hitler were the defining experiences for Böll and his generation, then, as neither had a comparable impact in Ireland, his book about that country is not one where much of Böll's own background can be the basis, although of course it still plays a role for him as well as for his readers (a critic, who congratulated him after the publication of *Irisches Tagebuch* on leaving the 'smell of laundries' behind, received a withering answer in the form of Böll's essay 'Zur Verteidigung der Waschküchen'[9] ['In Defence of Laundries']).

Traditionally the defining experience of Ireland had been found in one particular aspect – the history of the English-Irish relationship. Given his emphasis on the contemporary, however, Böll found something else in Ireland; for him the uncharted environment became an opportunity to search, to be open to new things, and arguably also to experiment with the very ingredient that had always played such an important role for his writing – time. Past, present and future took on different meanings and shapes. Böll's enjoyment in playing with time in the *Irish Journal* is not surpassed in any of his other writing with the exception of his film about Ireland *Children of Eire*. One example is his description of almost illusory punctuality in the train which is precisely on time:

> [...] and the stationmaster smiles into the departing train as if to say: No, no, you're not dreaming, it's really true, it's really four-forty-nine, as my clock up there shows. For the traveler (sic) is sure the train must be late: the train is punctual, but the punctuality seems deceptive; four-forty-nine is too precise a time for it to be correct in these stations. It is not the clock that is wrong, but time, which uses minute hands. (p. 104)

Even as he arrives in Ireland the narrator comes across a one-line aphorism in the *Irish Digest* which indicates the importance of the past in juxtaposition with the present: 'The cemeteries [...] are full of people the world could not do without' (p. 10). This expression comes to sum up for him the substance of Ireland, which is presented as a conjunction of opposites: '[...] later on it seemed to me a kind of key to this strange

---

[9] In: Ferdinand Melius (ed.): *Der Schriftsteller Heinrich Böll*, Cologne/Berlin: Kiepenheuer & Witsch 1959, pp. 33-36. A 'Waschküche' was a common feature of houses in Germany, generally a room in the cellar where the laundry was done, the term 'sculleries' might come closest as 'laundries' conjure a less domestic setting.

mixture of passion and equability, to that temperamental weariness, that indifference coupled with fanaticism' (p. 10).

On several occasions past and present are mixed up, indistinguishable, almost reversed, as in a passage in 'Limerick in the Morning' from the first part of chapter 7, 'Portrait of an Irish Town':

> Moss shimmered green on ancient walls from the eighth, ninth, and all the subsequent centuries, and the walls of the twentieth century were hardly distinguishable from those of the eighth – they too were moss-covered, they too ruined ... (p. 43)

This corresponds to a passage reinforcing the image of dark ruins and poverty, in the second part of the chapter, 'Limerick in the Evening':

> King John's Castle reared grimly out of the darkness, a tourist attraction hemmed in by tenements from the twenties, and the tenements of the twentieth century looked more dilapidated than King John's Castle of the thirteenth ... (p. 50)

Further examples can be found in other chapters: in 'A Small Contribution to Occidental Mythology', 'the walls from the twentieth century are indistinguishable from those of the sixth century' (p. 98) and, a little earlier, when Böll describes the eighty-eight year old man on Hare Island as 'born before Rumania became what it has for years no longer been' and as a contemporary of Sun Yat-sen and Busoni, the narrator adds: 'all this merely to catch him in the frail net of time'. By characterizing time as a net, and a frail one at that, Böll emphasizes the arbitrary nature of history, in which some events or people are 'caught' and remembered. The image could be of a fishing net or perhaps a climbing net, with knots connecting apparently unrelated figures such as the man on Hare Island, the Chinese revolutionary and the Italian composer, and offering a structure for referral and remembrance.

While in a number of chapters time plays a significant role and takes on all kinds of shapes and forms (notably in 'Gazing into the Fire' where we hear about time embodied in cigarettes, leading to 'chopped-up time' being thrown away, p. 82) Böll devotes one chapter expressly to the subject ('When God Made Time ...'), where he ponders the links between time, punctuality and humanity:

> The man who has no time is a monster, a fiend: he steals time from somewhere, secretes it. (How much time must have been wasted, how

much must have been stolen, to make the unjustly famed military punctuality so proverbial: billions of stolen hours of time are the price for this prodigal kind of punctuality, not to mention the monsters of our day who have no time! They always seem to me like people with not enough skin ...) (p. 54)[10]

Here Böll combines a 'medieval' understanding of time (his description of time in Ireland was in fact used by a historian to emphasise the similarity of his understanding with that prevailing in the Middle Ages)[11] with a striking criticism of military order, probably with reference to noted Prussian virtues. It is ironic in this context that one of the many memories people in Achill have of Böll and his family is their punctual arrival at Mass on Sunday: 'You wouldn't need an alarm clock, you'd know the time when you saw the Bölls.'[12]

The critical view of strict time-keeping resurfaces in the chapter 'When Seamus Wants a Drink' where it is connected to alcoholism. There the regulations force Seamus to cycle for miles on a Sunday, as a traveller who is at least three miles from his own village may not be refused a drink. But worse, the strict adherence to closing time brings an 'influx of all those who are not drunkards but who have suddenly realized the pub is closing soon and they haven't done what they possibly wouldn't feel in the least like doing if it were not for this insane law: they haven't got drunk yet' (p. 88). It takes the tourists in the summertime to 'liberalize hard-and-fast time' – then 'time stands still, and rivers of dark beer flow through the

---

[10] A theological study by Hans Willy Hohn on time in the Middle Ages echoes Böll's comments and argues that time is not owned by man but by God who gave each creature 'his' time. If time is therefore a God-given substance of nature and of man then it is not only meaningless to measure the time of an object – for example with a clock, but it is a sin not to use it to God's given purpose, and even worse, to use the time of others for that. This interpretation means, according to Hohn, that time cannot be 'disposed of' as that would require time to pass neutrally, unchanged by God or nature. See Hans Willy Hohn, Zyklizität und Heilsgeschichte - Religiöse Zeiterfahrung des europäischen Mittelalters, in: Rainer Zoll (ed.), *Zerstörung und Wiederaneignung von Zeit*, Frankfurt: Suhrkamp 1988, pp. 120-142, 132.

[11] See Anton Gurjewitsch, *Das Weltbild des mittelalterlichen Menschen* (Munich: C.H. Beck 1980, p. 171), who argues that the medieval view of time was of slowly moving, unhurried, enduring time which was not saved. He then quotes Böll's comment on time in Ireland as characteristic of that medieval understanding of time: "When God made time, the Irish say, he made enough of it."

[12] Conversation with Mary Colohan, Achill, 28 August 2002.

whole summer, day and night, while the police sleep the sleep of the just' (p. 40).

The special role played by time is also notable in differentiation between past, present and future. Only for very few, such as Siobhan in 'The Ninth Child of Mrs D.', is the future secured; for most it is 'farewell and tears'. As a result no-one gives it any thought; it is negligible, 'for here the present counts for more than the future' (p. 96). Concern about what is to come is explicitly banished – 'I shouldn't worry'.[13] The result is 'improvisation instead of planning' (an approach generally favoured by Böll, as for example when he writes in chapter 4 of the train ride on credit), but the weighty present will be 'balanced with tears' when it comes to emigration (p. 96).

Böll hardly touches on the Irish past or English rule in Ireland, topics intrinsically combined and dwelt on at length by all other German writers about Ireland in Böll's time. A. E. Johann repeatedly talks about being taken aback when faced with the hatred towards Cromwell: 'his harsh deeds are still alive and present as if they had been committed only yesterday [...] In Ireland people hardly seem to know the difference between past and present.'[14] Enno Stephan proclaims that it is impossible to understand Ireland if one does not take into account the terrible past – Cromwell, William of Orange and the famine[15] – and Peter Grubbe looks at old castles and notes:

> In France, in Germany, in Spain ruined castles and their stories belong to the past. They have turned into history, have become memories. The wounds inflicted in their cause have long since scarred over. Here in Ireland they seem to bleed still. Here the ghosts of the slain seem even today to have found no rest. An invisible shadow lies over the rich, fertile green of the meadows and the pastures. A hidden sadness, a deep melancholy.[16]

---

[13] For example *Irish Journal*, pp. 27 and 110.
[14] A. E. Johann [Alfred E. J. Wollschläger], *Heimat der Regenbogen - Irland, Insel am Rande der Welt*, Gütersloh: Bertelsmann 1953.
[15] Enno Stephan, Eins Dritter Dublin, in: *Der Fortschritt* No. 33, p. 3 (part 1), 21 August 1953, in: *Der Fortschritt*, No. 34, p. 5 (part 2); 28 August 1953, in: *Der Fortschritt*, No. 35, p. 5 (part 3); 4 September 1953, in: *Der Fortschritt*, No. 36, p. 5 (part 4); 10 September 1953, in: *Der Fortschritt*, No. 37, p. 5 (part 5) and 18 September 1953, in: *Der Fortschritt*, No. 38, p. 5 (part 6), here second part.
[16] Peter Grubbe, *Die Insel der Elfen, Esel und Rebellen* (*The Isle of Elves, Donkeys and Rebels*), Wiesbaden: Brockhaus 1954, p. 81, translation Alison McConnell,

This view was not restricted to German writers of that time (or before: one of the most interesting of all German descriptions of Ireland is Richard Bermann's *Irland*, published in 1914, and delving heavily into the Irish past and its lingering shadows in the present). H.V. Morton, for example, wrote in 1930 along similar lines:

> Even educated Irishmen will talk about Cromwell's campaign as though it was the work of the present British Government. A wrong has never died in Ireland. Every injustice inflicted on Ireland since the time of Strongbow is as real as the last year's budget.[17]

In comparison with these elaborate and extensive reviews of the past, Böll is tight-lipped on the 'official' past at least. He does mention a number of decisive historical events: the Famine, the founding of the Free State (which according to Böll took place in 1923 (p. 111), a year later than was actually the case), and the signing of the Treaty in Limerick of 1691 when freedom of religious expression was promised, but later revoked by the English parliament, resulting in Limerick being called the city 'of the broken treaty' (p. 44).[18] Any background to that information is, however, missing and few German readers – at least until the start of 'the Troubles' – would have been in a position to realise the importance of the religious question in Ireland. Another scene is even more illuminating – a reference to the monument of an Irish patriot executed in 1799. The family is asked whether they have seen it and answer, 'yes, we've seen it' (p. 36), without any further curiosity displayed or information given – who was executed, why and by whom seems of no interest or relevance.

Although the general theme of history being preserved is strongly present in Böll's *Irish Journal*, it is significant that this is not on the level of official history but very much in the vein of storytelling and oral history among the 'ordinary' people.[19] In the chapter 'A Small Contribution to Occidental Mythology', he notes that 'in spite of radio and newspaper, news from the lips of the man you shook hands with, the man you had tea with, *that's* the kind that counts' (p. 98). Böll's first person narrator becomes

---

Belfast.
[17] H.V. Morton, *The Magic of Ireland*, London: Eyre Methuen 1978, p. 24 (originally published in 1930 as *In Search of Ireland*).
[18] Far more explicit is Max Senger's blow-by-blow account of events in 1690-91 in *Irland, die seltsame Insel*, Zurich: Büchergilde Gutenberg 1956, pp. 85f.
[19] See also Thorsten Päplow's *"Faltenwürfe" in Heinrich Böll's 'Irisches Tagebuch'*, Munich: Iudicium 2008, on Böll's focus on the individual as a form of literary history telling, especially pp. 149-153.

part of the ongoing 'mythologisation'; through a misunderstanding he becomes part of a heroic war story, with the probable result that tales will be told in 'fifty or a hundred years from now, of Rommel, of war, and of Henry' (p. 101).

Böll's description of Ireland can therefore appear in stark contrast to other German travelogues of his time and before, where Ireland's history tended to be among the main topics, intertwined more often than not with a lengthy catalogue of English sins against her neighbour. If one goes back further, to German publications on Ireland in the eighteenth and (early) nineteenth centuries, England was as it were the filter through which Ireland was seen from Germany; the pathway to Ireland went not only geographically but also culturally through England.[20] In both world wars, especially the first, Ireland had been a convenient subject of propaganda, giving rise to publications such as 'Germany's Victory, Ireland's Hope' (1915).[21] Böll may have wanted to avoid this blatantly political perspective, perhaps because he did not want readers to think that there might be any equivalence between England's treatment of Ireland and what Germany had unleashed not twenty years earlier, of which Böll reminds his German readership with references to Stalingrad and 'millions murdered and killed' (p. 101). The one time some of the key references to English-Irish history appear, it is tellingly in a juxtapositioned presentation when a lone Englishman (interestingly also called Henry) appears almost as a victim, as someone who suffers the fate of the exempted individual from a despised group:

> 'I don't know', he said, 'why I come back to Ireland every year; I don't know how often I've told them I never liked either Pembroke or Cromwell, and that I'm not related to them, that I'm nothing but a London office worker who has a fortnight's holiday and wants to go the seaside. I don't know why I come all this way from London every year to be told how nice I am but how terrible the English are; it's so exhausting. (p. 39)

---

[20] Doris Dohmen even argues that the German image of Ireland is always tied into the context of German-English relations and that the resulting polarisation is the defining focus for all German literature on Ireland (cf. *Das deutsche Irlandbild*, p. 189), arguably disregarding not only Böll's book but also a lot 'German-Irish' literature in his wake.
[21] Hans Rost, *Deutschlands Sieg – Irlands Hoffnung*, Stuttgart: Deutsche Verlagsanstalt 1915. See also Hans A. Walter, *Irland und wir, Deutschlands Kampf – Irlands Hoffnung* [Ireland and us, Germany's fight – Ireland's hope], Munich: A. Hertz 1915.

But it is only in this context of the individual Englishman who clearly cannot be blamed for long past injustices and cruelty, that Cromwell is mentioned – and crucially in the same context as complete misconceptions about Hitler – thereby implicitly making clear that from a German perspective there is enough to be dealt with in its own history and no referring back to or indeed blaming England for any atrocities.

What Böll achieved by essentially leaving England out was that there was suddenly, to all intents and purposes for the first time in popular awareness of his time, a direct route from Germany to Ireland. Ireland became attractive and interesting in her own right.

But there was another result of Böll's preference for the present over the past as one topic is left out that could hardly be explained without going into history: the ensuing casualty was Northern Ireland. There is no reference whatsoever in Böll's *Irish Journal* to the difficult political situation in the North. This is in fundamental contrast to all other German-language books on Ireland at the time. Even long before the Troubles started, other visitors (including the Swiss writer Max Senger) paid at least fleeting attention to Northern Ireland. A. E. Johann mentions Northern Ireland at first only to exclude it explicitly on the grounds that his book is not intended to be political, but even then he nevertheless still refers to it a number of times, while Peter Grubbe devotes more than a quarter of his book to the question. If Böll indeed intended, as is sometimes claimed, to create a utopia based on Ireland for Germany (a country also split at the time and experiencing different political systems) then arguably what he did was to create one of the island of Ireland for Ireland as well.

CHAPTER EIGHT

GERMANY: 'A CURSED COUNTRY'— BUT 'I AM STILL A GERMAN'

The question of past and present is also part and parcel of the role of Germany in Böll's work in general and in the *Irish Journal* in particular. James Reid, echoing Reich-Ranicki (see below), argues that all Böll's works 'are set firmly in the present and concern themselves with contemporary Germany – including even *Irisches Tagebuch,* which is aimed at a specifically German public and is in fact "ein verstecktes Deutschlandbuch"'.[1] As Böll wrote in German, there is of course no reason to assume that he would have had any other than a German public in mind – in fact, the longer than usual delay before the English translation appeared could be a sign that he was worried about the Irish readership (more on that later). The claim mentioned above that the *Irisches Tagebuch* concerns itself first and foremost with contemporary Germany calls for further examination. One of the lasting impressions in reviews of the *Irisches Tagebuch* is, as advocated especially by Marcel Reich-Ranicki, of 'a hidden book on Germany' ('ein verstecktes Deutschlandbuch'). As stated in the introduction, I have always thought this view rather simplistic as of course all travel books include inherently the individual background of the writer. One should recognise and accept that as an intrinsic feature of all travel writing, and then probe more deeply: does the book give us important new information on Böll's relationship with Germany? What else does it offer, for example in terms of literary achievement? To what extent is his description of Ireland a typical one; does it surpass the boundaries of general travel writing? In order to examine the treatment of Germany in the *Irish Journal,* it is a worthwhile

---

[1] J. H. Reid, Time in the Works of Heinrich Böll, p. 477. See also Conard, *Heinrich Böll,* p. 76: 'It is important to emphazise here, however, that the idyllic, romantic, and sentimental qualities in the *Irish Journal* serve a critical purpose: they are meant to enhance the narrative's criticism of Germany.'

exercise to look more closely at Böll's actual relationship with Germany, which is considerably more sophisticated than is often assumed.

For many German readers, Heinrich Böll was an author who stood up to the German State (and Church) when necessary, someone who could bitterly criticise abuses and air grievances, a constant champion of civil rights. But his often passionate engagement with politics and wrongs committed by the State was mingled with a certain kind of patriotism. In a speech of 1982, 'A few words on the comments constantly dinned into our ears', he called for the rediscovery of patriotism which for far too long had been changed into aggressive nationalism.[2] On another occasion Böll writes about belonging to a not very popular nation but not being ashamed of belonging to it.[3] When reading Léon Bloy's diary in 1942 he could not accept the collective guilt implied by Bloy's wish that all of Germany should die of hunger: 'Had I believed in German collective guilt I would have deserted and found a way to emigrate.'[4]

In an interview with René Wintzen in October 1976, published under the title *Eine deutsche Erinnerung* ('A German memory'), Böll declares:

> [...] in 1945 Germany was a cursed country, which people visited with disgust, as a soldier, a member of the occupation force or an administrator, and we felt that, of course. I at least felt it and developed some kind of pride, not a national pride, that would have been really not in character with me or with my experiences. But everything we heard, statements from former emigrants, statements from high-ranking officers of the occupation force between 1945 and 50, had this kind of condescension that we didn't like at all.
>
> This country was our home, destroyed, with its own language, and in this language we wanted to write, without feeling this condescension and also without ingratiation. It was very complicated, yes, but not particularly

---

[2] Böll, 'Ein paar Worte über ein paar Wörter, die uns da dauernd um die Ohren fliegen', in: Petra K. Kelly, *Um Hoffnung kämpfen - Gewaltfrei in eine grüne Zukunft*, Bornheim-Merten: Lamuv, 1983, pp. 7-11.

[3] [Da wir einer nicht sonderlich beliebten Nation angehören, uns dieser Angehörigkeit aber nicht schämen, analysieren wir unsere Erfahrungen gelegentlich.] Cf. Heinrich Böll, Attitudes and Anglo-Saxons. Essay about the English People. *The Sunday Times*, 24 February 1974 and Böll, Zum Beispiel Schuhe (1974), *KA 18*, pp. 274-278, 275.

[4] [Hätte ich an die deutsche Kollektivschuld geglaubt, ich wäre desertiert und hätte einen Weg in die Emigration gefunden.] Böll, Brief an einen jungen Katholiken, in: *Werkhefte Katholischer Laien*, 12/1958, no 8/9, pp. 208-215 und *KA 10*, pp. 441-458, 447.

painful, as I had already developed this pride in the prisoner-of-war camp. If you are for months treated as a 'fucking German Nazi' and kicked in your backside then you think, well, f... you, I am still a German and I will write.[5]

Even in his last major interview, conducted in June 1985 shortly before his death, he remembers: 'it was far from pleasant being German. It was virtually the most contemptuous description – German.'[6] Upon receiving the Nobel Prize for literature in 1972 he said he was grateful for the high honour which had been paid not only to him 'but also to the language in which I express myself and to the country of which I am a citizen'.[7]

---

[5] [Ein verfluchtes Land, man vergißt das heute, in Europa auch. Da gibt es also diese tüchtigen Deutschen, die aus einem Trümmerfeld einen neuen Staat gebaut haben, eine Wirtschaft, sogar eine Kultur, eine Literatur, eine Malerei, eine Architektur. Aber 1945 war Deutschland ein verfluchtes Land, in das man nur widerwillig fuhr, wenn man mußte, als Soldat oder Besatzungs- oder Verwaltungsbeamter, und das haben wir natürlich gespürt. Ich jedenfalls habe es gespürt und habe eine bestimmte Art von Stolz entwickelt, keinen Nationalstolz, das lag nun wirklich weder in meiner Person noch in meinem Schicksal. Aber alles, was uns so zu Ohren kam, Äußerungen von ehemaligen Emigranten, Äußerungen von hohen Besatzungsoffizieren zwischen 1945 und 50, hatte eine Art von Herablassung, die uns gar nicht gefiel.

Dieses Land war unsere Heimat, zerstört, mit einer eigenen Sprache, und in dieser Sprache wollten wir schreiben, ohne Herablassung und auch ohne Anbiederung zu spüren. Das ist sehr kompliziert gewesen, ja, aber nicht besonders schmerzlich, weil ich im Gefangenenlager schon diesen Stolz entwickelt habe. Wenn Sie so monatelang als fucking German Nazi behandelt werden und in den Hintern getreten, dann denken Sie, also nun leck mich mal am Arsch, ich bin trotzdem Deutscher, und ich werde schreiben.] Böll, *Eine deutsche Erinnerung - Interview mit René Wintzen*, in *KA 25*, pp. 292-465, 390.

[6] Böll's last major interview, with Margarete Limberg, 11 June 1985, 'Freedom is Fading Every Day', in *Heinrich Böll – On his Death – Selected obituaries and the last interview*, Bonn: Inter Nationes 1985, pp. 22-31, 23.

[7] [Ich danke der Schwedischen Akademie und dem Land Schweden für diese Ehre, die wohl nicht nur mir gilt, auch der Sprache, in der ich mich ausdrücke und dem Land, dessen Bürger ich bin.] Heinrich Böll, Rede zur Verleihung des Nobelpreises am 10. Dezember 12.1972 in Stockholm, in: Böll, *Werke 1971-1974*, Kölner Ausgabe volume 18, edited by Viktor Böll and Ralf Schnell in cooperation with Klaus-Peter Bernhard. Cologne: Kiepenheuer & Witsch 2003, pp. 176-178, 178 (in the following *KA 18*). See also Heinrich Böll's speech at the Nobel Banquet in Stockholm, December 10, 1972; http://nobelprize.org/nobel_prizes/literature/laureates/1972/boll-speech.html.

In Ireland he encountered only very mild criticism. Clodagh King recalled that in conversation with Böll she used to say: 'Oh those Germans they are terrible' (she believed he knew she was not totally serious). Böll's answer used to be, 'We are not too bad, really.'[8] Generally what is most suspect to Böll is Irish support for Germany, at times based on admiration of Hitler, possibly due to antagonism towards Great Britain ('my enemy's enemy ...'), and Böll's narrator in the *Irish Journal* comments accordingly: 'I'm tired of going to pubs in the evening. I always have to pull teeth, always the same ones. I'm sick of it' (p. 37).[9] 'Padraig', the almost proverbial Irishman now deprived of that particular tooth, is left wondering why he likes the Germans so much. '"You must like them", I said gently, "not *because of* but *in spite of* Hitler"' (p. 39). In earlier German descriptions of Ireland it is basically the rule that Ireland is fairly unknown in Germany: here, on the other hand, one feels that the Irish know little of Germany. German money seems unknown to train conductors and bank employees (the latter also having problems distinguishing between Germany East and West); in the post office there are problems when a puzzle is to be sent to

---

[8] Interview with Clodagh King by Jean Tansey.

[9] Arguably, this episode could also be read as a reminder for Böll's German readership that remnants or reawakenings of right-wing sentiments were being uttered again – at least in pub environments and after the consumption of some alcohol. While this might well be a possibility, Böll was not the only German traveller at the time who experienced this more or less overt admiration of Hitler. In Peter Grubbe's *Die Insel der Elfen, Esel und Rebellen* (*The Isle of Elves, Donkeys and Rebels*), published three years previously, this is far more developed and linked with an almost overwhelming admiration for anything German and a strong belief that the 'negative sides' which Grubbe hesitantly mentions such as the Gestapo and concentration camps were British propaganda (cf. pp 134-136). Peter Grubbe was actually a pseudonym, used by Klaus Volkmann, who started his double identity after the war, most likely to hide his involvement in atrocities during his wartime service in German-occupied Kolomea (Kolomyia) in Galicia in 1941-1942 and other places. In the late forties he became a correspondent for *FAZ* and later *Die Welt* in London; he returned to Germany in 1958. He wrote numerous books and produced several films, having established himself as a critical journalist and champion of the Third World. An attempt to bring him to justice in the 1960s was unsuccessful though his cover was blown in 1995 following articles in *taz* and *Die Zeit*. He died in 2002. It is unlikely that he was especially concerned with criticizing German war crimes and indeed gives up trying to correct his Irish counterpart.

Irish historian J.J. Lee also wonders how many Irishman believed, like Böll's Padraic, that the atrocities were inventions of British propaganda and argues that the censorship would have deprived 'the populace of much of this knowledge'. Lee, *Ireland 1912-1985 Politics and Society*, CUP: Cambridge 1989, p. 266.

Germany ('Limerick in the Morning'). All examples indicate a lack of contact, and in particular the small number of German tourists in Ireland at the time.

In terms of direct comparisons between Ireland and Germany in the *Irish Journal*, Ireland is shown more often than not in a far more positive light than Germany. A good example appears in the chapter 'In a Manner of Speaking':

> When something happens to you in Germany, when you miss a train, break a leg, go bankrupt, we say: It couldn't have been worse; whatever happens is always the worst. With the Irish it is almost the opposite: if you break a leg, miss a train, go bankrupt, they say: It could be worse (...) With us – it seems to me – when something happens our sense of humor and imagination desert us; in Ireland that is just when they come into play. (p. 109)

Here (even more in the English translation than in the German original) as in other places, Böll includes himself and his family in the criticism. In the episode 'Mayo - God help us' the narrator is afflicted by worries rather than being able to adopt the carefree disposition of the Irish people. In the chapter on the deserted village on Achill, 'Skeleton of a Human Habitation', the abandoned houses are described as being left in peace: 'not even the children try to pull down walls or doorways; our children, when we suddenly found ourselves in the village, tried it immediately, to raze it to the ground.' (p. 33)

In order to judge how far Böll's book is exceptional either in referring back to his home country or in regarding aspects of Irish life as superior to German ones, we can compare it with other contemporary descriptions. Even a quick search yields numerous examples of comparisons of Ireland with Germany along the same lines as Böll's, if anything more explicit in their praise for Ireland and criticism of German conditions. Enno Stephan expresses his delight that 'suddenly one has time, work is not urgent. A rhythm of life that is foreign to us and unfamiliar. But this is what creates the magic of this country. People are not so terribly ambitious and dedicated to work as at home'.[10] A. E. Johann and Grubbe single out

---

[10] [Man hatte plötzlich Zeit, die Arbeit eilte nicht so sehr. Ein Lebensrhythmus, der uns fremd und ungewohnt ist. Aber gerade er, meine ich, macht den unsterblichen Zauber dieses Landes aus. Man ist nicht so schrecklich strebsam und in seine Arbeit verbissen wie bei uns zulande], Stephan, Eins Dritter Dublin, part 5, in: *Der Fortschritt*, 10 September 1953.

Ireland as a positive example not only in comparison with Germany but with the whole of Europe where, according to Johann, people might have been equally 'open, hospitable, talkative and in the truest sense humane' (as he found them in Ireland) before they were 'swallowed up by technology, anonymity, money matters and urbanisation',[11] while Grubbe also sees the Europe of his day as a place of haste and speed, the noise of machinery, glaring advertising, increasing industrial production – a sad comparison to Ireland where there is still time for conversation and individualism.[12]

These opinions are far from new; H.V. Morton expressed similar views towards the end of his travels in Ireland in 1930: 'She [Ireland] is the only European country, with the exception perhaps of Spain, which is not dehumanized by industrialism.'[13] It can therefore be safely concluded that Böll's is actually neither a specifically German perspective nor one based solely in the 1950s, but rather a frequently voiced criticism in the context of industrialisation. The somewhat limited interpretation of the *Irish Journal* as primarily a criticism of Germany may in this context say more about the critics than about Heinrich Böll.[14]

Overall the not surprising verdict, therefore, would be that all German travel literature about Ireland at the time (or basically at any other) consists of 'hidden books on Germany', and that similar remarks apply to any author's country of origin. Böll himself certainly seems not to have been aware of an unduly didactic approach towards his readership. He claims that his descriptions of Ireland are quite different from his writings on Germany insofar as they are without bias, without an agenda:

> A comparison must also be made between what I have written about Ireland and what I have written about Germany. I think it would then be quite clear that *Children of Eire* and *Irisches Tagebuch* are thoroughly

---

[11] [ehe sie von der Technik, der Vermassung, der Geldwirtschaft und der allgemeinen Verstädterung verschlungen wurden], Johann, *Heimat der Regenbogen*, p. 206.
[12] Grubbe, *Die Insel der Elfen*, pp. 208f.
[13] H.V. Morton, *The Magic of Ireland*, p. 160.
[14] Similarly, in Senger, *Irland die seltsame Insel*, there are many comparisons between Ireland and Switzerland – consumption of beer (p. 15), multilingual issues (p. 41), statistics for population, import and export, debt and income (p. 93), and the respective neutral status of Switzerland and Ireland (p. 149).

friendly in tone, indeed sweet, and this is absolutely genuine, arising out of the author's complete sympathy with and for his subject.[15]

---

[15] Böll, 'A reply to critics of *Children of Eire*', *Hibernia* (Dublin), No. 29, March 1965, p. 15.

Chapter Nine

Irish People, Traditions and Landscape

Throughout the *Irish Journal* Böll's descriptions of the Irish are positive. The Irish are portrayed as the only people in Europe who never set out to conquer: instead they travelled to all corners of the world to spread the Holy Gospel.[1] The people encountered seem to come from all walks of life: young families with children, emigrant workers back on a visit home, a waitress, beggar and bank manager, train conductors, priests, acquaintances in a pub, a post office worker, a lost accountant and a talkative policeman, a doctor and his wife.

It seems that particularly the women tend to have a friendly smile when they see the narrator, starting with the young woman who lifts an orange milk jug into the room on the morning of 'Arrival II' (p. 8)[2], continuing with the 'tousled tea goddess' (p. 9) and finishing with the very last sentence, describing the corresponding scene which frames the book: 'a young woman was just putting an orange milk jug out onto the window sill. She smiled at me and I smiled back' (p. 119). The 'laconic, almost mute flirtation' in 'Mrs. D's Ninth Child' is carried out with few words and many smiles (p. 92), the picture of the Madonna smiles (p. 45) and 'even the monuments were smiling' (p. 118). The 'doctor's young wife' waits anxiously for the return of her husband and the woman with the 'most beautiful feet in the world' is an example of the strong local women who raise a family in harsh conditions. To show women as friendly (and pious) is not especially unusual for Böll. Such portrayals appear in many of his novels (Käte Bogner in *And Never Said a Word*, Edith Schrella in *Billiards at Half-past Nine* and Marie in *The Clown*, to mention but a few).

---

[1] See *Irish Journal*, p. 7. However, William O'Keeffe rightly pointed out to me that this was a half truth at best and that the Irish before Christianisation (and possibly for quite a while after it) were active raiders and slave traders – St. Patrick himself came to Ireland first as a slave.

[2] The next smile is bestowed on the traveller by the young girl pouring his tea, p. 9.

Indeed one literary critic has expressed the view that like angels Böll's female characters surpass reality in personifying the principles of humanity.[3]

This appears to be a fairly narrow view of women, to which, however, the role of mother of many children is added in the epilogue. Here the extent of Böll's sorrow about the arrival of the contraception pill[4] further exposes a biased viewpoint which takes only a limited account of the possible problems connected with the many children. He admits to not having to worry about it from a father's point of view, but seems unaware that there could be worries or downsides from a mother's perspective. Here he only sees occasion to praise: 'Honor (sic) and glory are due to the Irish women who bring such lovely children into the world' (p. 126). There seems to be no awareness of potential problems for women arising from the patriarchal and Church-ruled Irish society, only sadness about the reduction of the number of children and the disappearance of nuns from the newspapers (p. 124). In contrast to Böll's impressions are those of another German traveller to Ireland at the time, Peter Grubbe, who points towards a very conservative, strictly male-dominated way of life, which is, for example, a long way from giving equal pay for equal work and where any such ideas are viewed with distrust.[5]

Böll's description of Irish men is more diverse and multi-faceted: they are dreamers, escaping through drinking, who spend their last penny in betting shops, but still spare some for ice cream for the children. They appear as friendly priests and poetic policemen, drunken heroes and pious beggars. In some ways the portrayal of men in the *Irish Journal* follows a pattern that is recognisable in other works – they can be desperate, often unable to function or deal 'with activities known as family, occupation, honor, society' (p. 15). More is expected of them than they can actually achieve.

---

[3] Hans Joachim Bernhard, 'Es gibt sie nicht, und es gibt sie', in: Renate Matthaei (ed.), *Die subversive Madonna: Ein Schlüssel zum Werk Heinrich Bölls*. Cologne: Kiepenheuer & Witsch 1975, pp. 58–81, 66ff. Bernhard mentions Olina in *The train was on time*, Edith Schrella in *Billiards at Half-past Nine* and Leni Pfeiffer in *Group Picture with a Lady*.

[4] 'And a certain something has now made its way to Ireland, that ominous something known as The Pill – and this something absolutely paralyzes me: the prospect that fewer children might be born in Ireland fills me with dismay (...) and to know that The Pill will succeed where all the Majesties of Great Britain have failed – in reducing the number of Irish children – seems to me no cause for rejoicing.' (p. 122).

[5] Grubbe, *Die Insel der Elfen*, p. 60.

Here Böll does not exclude himself. He points to the interrelation of expectation and anticipation and fulfilment, the make-believe and role play on both sides of the gender game as he perceives it:

> [...] my family was waiting trustfully for me at the bus stop. There was hunger in their eyes, almost a yearning, the anticipation of powerful masculine, powerful paternal aid, and I made up my mind to do something which is the basis of the myth of masculinity: I made up my mind to bluff. (p. 24)

Böll deconstructs the myth by displaying both sides as fulfilling the mutual expectations of their specific gender roles. The family arrangement is described as a helpless father, three tired children, and two dejected women, one a friend of the family – on one side the 'powerful masculine' who is not powerful at all, and who squanders the final resources in 'a grandiose gesture', on the other the women and children who seem to expect nothing less, regardless of whether or not it is appropriate in the circumstances.

Böll is particularly fond of Irish children. As mentioned before, he is fascinated and delighted with the huge number of them (something that is also a strong feature in the film *Children of Eire*). Their apparent carefree cheerfulness is mentioned several times, for example on the way to Limerick: 'For over a hundred miles the car drove through Irish schoolchildren, and although it was raining, and many of them were barefoot, most of them poorly dressed, almost all of them seemed cheerful.' (pp. 41f.)

Although in contrast to many other travel writers Böll abstains generally from claiming any special Irish national characteristics,[6] he obviously takes the Irish people for a happy population, happier anyway than they

---

[6] However, he did write an essay about the English people. In a review of J.B. Priestley's *The English* for *The Sunday Times*, Böll speculated how nationalities and differences within regions are recognisable. He argues that it could be apparent non-issues such as shoes or gestures that make people of a certain country recognisable – in the case of England the specific colouring, variations and combinations of yellow, brown and pink, in clothes, wrapping, fronts of a row of houses and house decorations, spring and autumn colours, parks with bold trees and daffodils – seemingly unimportant things such as stirring sugar in tea – and indeed, tea itself. Cf. Heinrich Böll, Attitudes and Anglo-Saxons. Essay about the English People, and *KA 18*, pp. 274-278.

think themselves,[7] and it is not difficult to see why, especially in the cinema episode in the chapter 'When God Made Time ...' – everything is shared, everyone talks with everyone else and his dream of a 'classless society' has 'become reality' (p. 55). That this was actually the case is obviously questionable but probably the degrees of class distinction were hard to see for an outsider. The happiness Böll found in Ireland was most probably due to the discovery of mutual tastes and aided by the general friendliness he encountered. The travelling narrator marvels at the 'endless line-ups in front of the movies' and ponders that in the mornings the Irish seem to 'crowd into and around the churches, and in the evening appararently into and around the movies' (p. 11), a combination of religion and dream that he, who had spent one of his first ten hours in Ireland in a church himself, thoroughly approves. The whole approach to life, the non-judgemental view of poverty, the seemingly egalitarian society, the ability to wait and to savour the moment, is admired[8], and he happily agrees with Padraic that the Irish are charming people (adding in a qualifying way, that they are fully aware of it), while being able to keep pace when it comes to drinking pints (p. 40).

Alcohol and pubs are portrayed as an important part of daily life in Ireland. Pubs are frequently mentioned, as places where light-hearted banter as well as serious discussion (about Hitler, for example) takes place, and they are a hiding place or the last port of call after the betting office or the church ('Limerick in the Evening'). To have a beer seems regularly incorporated in a working day, as for example when the postman is coming and is to be kept company over a beer ('The Ninth Child'). The surprise visitor on a rainy night enjoys a whiskey with his hosts while even in the cinema 'somewhere out of the dark comes the promising squeak of a cork being pulled out of a whisky (sic) bottle' (p. 54). The frequent mention of drinking gives an impression of alcohol playing a crucial role in everyday Irish life. At times there seems to be a certain almost poetic desperation (among the men) that can find relief only in the 'private drinking booth with the leather curtains' (p. 14; Böll describes it in German more emphatically as an 'Einzelsäuferkoje' – a 'snug for a solitary drunkard'): 'here the drinker locks himself in like a horse; to be alone with

---

[7] '"I think," I said, "that you are happier than you know. And if you knew how happy you are you would find a reason for being unhappy. You have many reasons for being unhappy, but you also love the poetry of unhappiness."' *Irish Journal*, p. 37.
[8] In this context Böll's essay 'Anekdote zur Senkung der Arbeitsmoral' ('Anecdote on lowering work morale') is also significant, as will be discussed in chapter 17.

whisky and pain, with belief and unbelief, he lowers himself deep below the surface of time, into the caisson of passivity' (p. 14f.). In its extreme form, when alcohol is consumed only in order to get drunk in an attempt to prove oneself, it becomes one of the few things Böll expressly criticises (women are excluded from this criticism - 'No wonder there is no room in these pubs for women, the busy ones of this earth: here the man is alone with his whisky', p. 15).

> This urge to drink, to be generous, has something childish about it, it is like furtive cigarette-smoking of those who vomit as furtively as they smoke – and the final scene, when the policeman appears at the door on the dot of eight, the final scene is pure barbarism: pale, grim seventeen-year-olds hide somewhere in the barn and fill themselves up with beer and whisky, playing the senseless rules of the game of manhood, and the landlord – the landlord fills his pockets, heaps of pound notes, jingling silver, money, money – but the law has been kept. (p. 89)

The main criticism here in 'When Seamus Wants a Drink' is directed less though at the people drinking than at the unfeeling attempts to regulate customs and force a legalistic approach to counter the clearly questionable rituals of male teenagehood, where the only winner is business for the pub owner.

Viewed geographically, the Ireland described by Böll is patchy, consisting of Dublin and the West, here ranging from Limerick in the mid-west to Achill and Sligo in the north-west; Galway and Connemara do not feature, and nor does Donegal. The traditional tourist destinations such as Kerry and Cork are completely left out, as are the south-east, the north-east, the area surrounding Dublin – and as mentioned before, Northern Ireland. Böll himself had intentions of writing about the south, which he had visited on his first trip and described in a letter home as 'really overwhelmingly beautiful',[9] but although he travelled around Ireland in order to get more material and 'do Ireland justice'[10] he must have decided against using it. As to why, we can only speculate – perhaps it did not provide enough creative impetus, or, as also implied by the unusual format of his book, he wanted to avoid arousing expectations of a 'complete' picture of Ireland which could never be fulfilled.

---

[9] Letter 7 October 1954, in: Böll, *Rom auf den ersten Blick*, p. 65.
[10] Letter to his publisher Joseph Caspar Witsch, 27 July 1956, *KA 10*, p. 648.

Overall, Ireland is not portrayed as a strange or very romantic place. A glance at the titles of contemporary travel writing in the 1950s shows how unusual this was: Max Senger's *Irland die seltsame Insel* ('Ireland, the Strange Island'), Peter Grubbe's *Die Insel der Elfen, Esel und Rebellen* ('The Isle of Elves, Donkeys and Rebels') and A. E. Johann's *Heimat des Regenbogens* ('Home of the Rainbow') were in good company and part of a long history. A romantic view of Ireland was popularised in 1831 by the aforementioned Pückler-Muskau's *Briefe eines Verstorbenen* which appeared in translation only a short while later as *Tour in England, Ireland and France: in the years 1826, 1827, 1828 and 1829, with remarks on the manners and customs of the inhabitants and anecdotes of distinguished public characters*. The idea of Ireland as a strange and remarkable place goes back further, to classical writers such as Strabo and Pomponius Mela, later Gerald of Wales, who was sent to Ireland by Henry II in 1185 and later wrote his influential *Topographia Hibernia*, and including late medieval texts such as *Fortunatus*.[11] Böll, however, does not appear to be part of this tradition, which can still be found in many publications following his book, for example in Giordano's *Mein irisches Tagebuch*. Böll was more interested in creating a contemporary piece of art, using techniques and reference points previously unfamiliar to his German readers in the context of Ireland, as we will see in the next chapter.

---

[11] For more detailed information on traditional views of Ireland see for example John Hennig's writing in *Exil in Irland – John Hennigs Schriften* edited by G. Holfter, H. Rasche, Trier: WVT 2002, Joseph Th. (Joep) Leerssen, *Mere Irish & Fíor Ghael – Studies in the idea of Irish nationality, its development and literary expression prior to the nineteenth century*, Amsterdam/Philadelphia: John Benjamins 1986; Patrick O'Neill, *Ireland and Germany – A Study in Literary Relations*, New York: Peter Lang 1985; Andreas Oehlke, *Die Iren und Irland in deutschen Reisebeschreibungen des 18. und 19. Jahrhunderts*, Frankfurt a.M. et al: Peter Lang 1992; Dohmen, *Das deutsche Irlandbild* and G. Holfter, *Erlebnis Irland,* Trier: WVT 1996.

CHAPTER TEN

A MULTIMEDIA EXPERIENCE
THROUGH DIFFERENT ART FORMS

The comparison with other books on Ireland makes clear how special Böll's portrayal is. His is not the conventional mix of personal thoughts and experiences of Ireland within a carefully sequenced geographical and chronological structure furnishing contemporary facts and figures, ranging, in Giordano's popular book, for example, from case studies on the often disadvantaged and marginalized Traveller community[1] to the dates and conditions of the angling season in Ireland[2]. Böll, on the other hand, carefully selects almost random aspects that take his fancy, more often than not the ordinary everyday encounters rather than the special. He presents only occasionally his thoughts on his experiences; often he suppresses his personal reactions and becomes only the eye or ear transmitting what it sees or hears. In a strongly sensory description, he relays the smell of peat and the warmth of the fires in houses. Often he acts as a painter and seeks to present an image or an impression for the viewer's benefit, asking us to form our own judgement. A recent publication of essays on Böll's oeuvre uses for the title a double meaning Böll himself used as a self characterisation of the main character in *Ansichten eines Clowns*: 'Ich sammle Augenblicke'.[3] This could be translated as 'I collect moments' but 'Augenblicke' literally means 'blinks of the eye' – and both elements, the visual and the fleeting are at the forefront of his presentation of Ireland.

His style is imaginative and lyrical, and at times he abandons descriptions of real situations and moves into outright fiction, as in 'The Dead Redskin of Duke Street' or in the last chapter, 'Farewell'. Here traces of inner

---

[1] Ralph Giordano, *Mein irisches Tagebuch*, Munich: dtv 1999, pp. 154f. (First edition: Cologne: Kiepenheuer & Witsch 1996).
[2] Ibid., p. 193.
[3] Werner Jung, Jochen Schubert (eds), *'Ich sammle Augenblicke' – Heinrich Böll 1917-1985*, Bielefeld: Aisthesis 2008.

monologue can be found and motifs from earlier chapters are brought together in an almost surreal journey 'on a gently slanting roller coaster' through Dublin and Irish history, or, as Böll writes, 'through the no-man's-land between dream and memory, across Dublin threatened by the chasms around our bed which stood in the middle of the room' (p. 113). In this voyage of imagination, the former approach of getting to know Ireland with all senses is reversed, in a noisy accretion:

> Everything we had looked at was now looking at us: lions roared at us, gibbons leaped across our paths, we were carried up the giraffe's long neck and down again, out of his dead eyes the iguana reproached us for his ugliness; the dark water of the Liffey, green and dirty, went gurgling past us, plump seagulls screamed. (p. 114)

Böll does not paint only one picture of Ireland, but many; he gives not a photographic reproduction of the 'official' Ireland with information on current politics, special events or famous personalities of the time, but instead tells stories about everyday situations with an ageless and timeless quality: a young girl 'with the eyes of Vivien Leigh', working in the post office on the Atlantic coast, and her painfully shy admirer; Seamus in search of a drink outside the three-mile zone on a Sunday (now a dated situation, but for decades reality for beer-thirsty Irish people); conversations about the weather between a policeman and a car driver; the experience of heavy rain; musings about turns of speech; people in church, praying for the horses they backed to win. In fact, Böll's *Irish Journal* is both a book about his actual experiences in Ireland as a traveller as well as a testimony to his literary abilities to fictionalise his impressions and to create a piece of art out of these ingredients. As he expresses in answer to a reviewer, Georg Rosenstock: 'I have written the book, not a word too much, not a word missing, as a piece of art'[4] and he reiterated that six weeks later: 'For me one thing counts: whether my book passes as a piece of art'[5]. In the following we will accordingly look at the role that different art forms, specifically literature, painting and music, play in this artistic endeavour.

As discussed previously, Irish literature played an important role for Böll from his youth onwards and this is strongly reflected in the *Irish Journal* which is interspersed with numerous intertextual references, often quite casual ones.[6] It is telling that the narrator in the *Irish Journal* defends

---

[4] Letter from Böll to Georg Rosenstock, 24 June 1957, *KA 10*, p. 697.
[5] Ibid., letter from Böll to Georg Rosenstock, 4 August 1957, p. 700.
[6] One of the few book-length studies on this, Päplow's *"Faltenwürfe" in Heinrich*

Ireland passionately soon after his arrival in an argument with another German, with reference to Irish literature, specifically Joyce and Yeats (p. 11). Even before that, the names of many writers (not all Irish but all with Irish backgrounds) are given and form a sort of welcoming committee: 'all came rushing to meet me as bookkeepers, innkeepers, greengrocers – Joyce and Yeats, McCarthy and Molloy, O'Neill and O'Connor'[7] - in short, the literary names have become ordinary, or, another possible interpretation, even bookkeepers, innkeepers and greengrocers have literary connotations in Ireland.

This rather unusual portrayal of Irish literary giants is continued even when the narrator in the *Irish Journal* seeks explicit encounters with them. A little later, one of his first excursions in Dublin is to Jonathan Swift's grave in St. Patrick's Cathedral, where his heart 'caught a chill' (p. 13). William Butler Yeats's grave is visited in another chapter, 'No Swan to be seen' (p. 103); the title refers to Yeats's poem *The Wild Swans at Coole*.[8] Böll attempts (perhaps not very successfully, but with intertextual significance in the German text)[9] to translate the famous quote on Yeats's grave taken from the poem *Under Ben Bulben*: 'Cast a cold eye, on life, on death, Horseman pass by', and is reminded of the chill at Swift's tomb. Both graves are comfortless. In Drumcliff there are no swans but only rooks, circling around the old church tower. It rains, and nature does not lift the spirits of the narrator: 'The ferns lay flat on the surrounding hills, beaten down by the rain, rust-coloured and withered. I felt cold' (p. 108). The surroundings are as dead as Swift and Yeats. Böll does not simply leave St. Patrick's Cathedral: he flees, and only when he has almost exited does he realise that he was not alone: 'there was someone in the church after all: the cleaning woman; she was washing down the porch with lye, cleaning what was already clean enough' (p. 13). Later, on the way to Drumcliff the taxi driver is surprised when he hears the destination of the narrator: '"To Drumcliff Churchyard" – "But nobody lives there."' Böll's

---

Bölls 'Irischem Tagebuch' (Munich: Iudicium 2008), focuses on the numerous intertextual references to Irish authors (as well as some German ones, as Päplow shows).

[7] See *Irish Journal*, pp. 8f. See also Päplow, *'Faltenwürfe' in Heinrich Bölls 'Irischem Tagebuch'*, p. 75.

[8] W.B. Yeats, *Selected Poetry*, London: Pan Books 1990, pp. 64ff. (first published in a collection in 1919).

[9] See Georg Rosenstock's review 'Manche Länder muß man dreimal sehen', *Die Welt*, 8 June 1957 and his letter to Böll 30 June 1957, *KA 10*, p. 700. For the inter- and intratextual references see Päplow, pp. 50-52.

alter ego is not sure: '"Maybe," I said, "but I'd like to go there"' (pp. 106f.). Once there, he realises the truth of the driver's assessment, and declines the offer to go on to Innisfree, another popular destination for Yeats fans and immortalised in the poem 'The Lake Isle of Innisfree'. If 'Innisfree' stands for the longing for somewhere else, a home, some simple place away from hectic, noisy life, one could argue that the narrator does not need this now and if one takes into account Böll's personal circumstances at the time another interpretation is also possible – that he is indeed longing for home, but his actual home in Germany and specifically his family, to whom he writes a letter: 'I still don't know whether I will go to Sligo on Saturday: it is probably very lonely there and I fear – because I would so much like to be with you all – this loneliness.'[10] It is a strong testament to his interest in Yeats that Böll overcomes his fears and undertakes the long journey from Dublin to Sligo. His literary presentation of it, however, seems to indicate that he did not find what he was looking for when visiting the graves: his attempt to contextualise the writers and their literature apparently fails. Päplow argues convincingly that this actually refers to his intention not to be reduced to mere travel writing but to open up several levels of dialogue and create multifaceted meaning.[11] In any case, despite the examples he gives of attempts to engage with Irish writers and numerous though often implicit intertextual references, Böll does not refer extensively in the *Irish Journal* to the Irish literature which he otherwise so greatly appreciated. In fact, another visit to a literary monument, the house where Oscar Wilde was born, is described in the newspaper version of 'Arrival II'[12] but is left out of the book. Comparison with other travel literature of the time shows by numerous examples that Böll was not the only one with a strong liking for and extensive knowledge of Irish writers, but that in other Ireland books this preference is far more explicit and deferential. Max Senger, for instance, quotes nearly six pages of Jonathan Swift.[13] Even more influential was another form of Irish literature: nearly all German books about Ireland since the nineteenth century referred also to Irish fairy tales which were closely linked to the strong oral tradition that existed in Ireland into the twentieth century. In Germany the recording of fairy tales had started early. When

---

[10] [Ich weiß noch nicht sicher, ob ich samstags nach Sligo fahren soll: es ist sicher einsam dort, und ich fürchte mich – weil ich gerne mit Euch zusammensein möchte – vor dieser Einsamkeit.] Böll, *Rom auf den ersten Blick*, p. 66.
[11] Päplow, pp. 55f.
[12] 'Der erste Tag', *FAZ*, 24 December 1954, where it is the very first thing the traveller encounters upon his arrival in Ireland.
[13] Senger, *Irland die seltsame Insel*, pp. 102-109.

the Brothers Grimm translated Thomas Crofton Croker's *Fairy Legends* in 1825 it signified the beginning of an immense interest in Irish fairy tales, which found, as we saw earlier, a delighted follower in the young Heinrich Böll. However, there is no trace of this early enthusiasm in his book about Ireland.[14]

While the explicit connection with Irish literature might be less pronounced than one could have expected and fairy tales are left out altogether, poetry and fantasy still play a major role in Böll's Irish impressions, in the form of the 'lived poetry' of the drunken hero in Limerick or as the fantastic story of the 'Dead Redskin of Duke Street', told by a policeman during a traffic check. His actual job is humiliating for the garda: he is 'the descendant of a king, the grandson of a poet, the great-nephew of a saint' (p. 75), and is keen to engage in long conversations. The 'official exchange' is therefore mainly concerned with the endless possibilities available in the topics of weather and relatives ('If you multiply the number of relations by their age and then multiply this result by 365, you have roughly the number of possible variations on the topic of weather') (p. 77), and develops further into a bizarre journey in which a dead Redskin in war paint falls down on Duke Street. The narrator begins 'to suspect that the policeman was not the grandson of a poet but a poet himself' (p. 78). And finally, when attempting to sum up changes and what Ireland means to him in the epilogue, added in 1967, Böll prioritises literature above everything else that embodies Ireland for him: 'I have also read a great deal of Irish writing, and this utterly un-uniform unity that is Ireland has spoken to me most clearly of all through its literature' (p. 123). In his opinion, Irish poets played a decisive part in releasing Ireland from its long oppressor ('scraping away the first stone from under the pedestal of that other empire'); being motivated not by political fanaticism but rather by a dream – and fraternity with the poor, as Böll shows by quoting words of a monument for Thomas Kettle:

> Died not for flag, nor king nor emperor,
> But for a dream, born in a herdsman's shed

---

[14] Ironically, as J.H. Reid points out, one of Böll's early poems, 'Gericht über das Märchen' (from 1937, KA 1, p. 101) pits fairy tales against the cinema, the latter portrayed as a cheap form of convention triumphing over individual fantasy (cf. J.H. Reid, Nur 'Gesellenstücke' – Zum Frühwerk Heinrich Bölls, in Werner Jung, Jochen Schubert (eds), *'Ich sammle Augenblicke' – Heinrich Böll 1917-1985*, Bielefeld: Aisthesis 2008, pp. 9-29, 27f.). This view had clearly changed twenty years later.

And for the secret scripture of the poor. (Epilogue, p. 123)

In Böll's oeuvre imagery and acoustics generally play a dramatic role. In an interview with Gabriele Hoffmann he pointed out that art influenced him more than literature; that one should not only compare literature with literature but also art, music and literature with each other.[15] This is underlined by his habit of creating drawings of his literary compositions, with different colours for motives and people, arguably not only as a structural aid but also as a way to establish a creative distance to his narrative, possibly even an attempt to transpose literature into art.[16] In a recent publication which shows a number of different sketches for his major works in an interesting print edition, René Böll refers to this important part of his father's writing process and argues that he did it 'in order to see the entire book "at a glance". It made the composition all the more clearer'.[17] In this publication, René Böll also points out that a watercolour paint set was a constant companion of his father, whether at his desk or on his travels.[18] In the *Irish Journal* this interest in the exploration of other art forms is explicitly expressed within Böll's writing, as in the following quote which expresses his fascination with painting, colours and forms:

> If anyone ever tried to paint it, this skeleton of a human habitation where a hundred years ago five hundred people may have lived: all those gray triangles and squares on the green-gray slope of the hill; if he were to include the girl with the red pullover who is just passing along on the main street with a load of peat on her back, a spot of red for her pullover and a dark brown one for the peat, a lighter brown one for the girl's face, and then the white sheep huddling like lice among the ruins – he would be considered an unusually crazy painter: that's how abstract reality is. (p. 32)

Böll in fact did try painting in Ireland. The watercolour painting, part of the 'Heinrich Böll Life and Work' exhibition that was shown around the

---

[15] Hoffmann, *Heinrich Böll,* p. 230.
[16] Ibid., p. 159. See also p. 161 about things Böll describes again and again: 'music, colours and especially smells'. René Böll pointed me also towards the important role music played in the letters his father wrote to his mother during the war as well as to his father's high regard for Beethoven, see for example his poem 'Beethoven', *KA 1*, p. 92.
[17] René Böll, Shapes Taking Form, in *Ansichten - Die Romanskizzen Heinrich Bölls – In View: Heinrich Böll's Novel Sketches,* Berlin: Heinrich Böll Stiftung 2010, pp. 8-10, 8.
[18] Ibid.

world, is entitled *Blick auf die Keel Bay/Achill Island/Irland* (View over Keel Bay). It shows the view that he would have had from the house they rented in Keel, the beige driveway (with some grey and brown dots) to the house with the stone pillars on either side and the cast iron gate, green grass and plants on both sides of this driveway, at its beginning on the bottom left corner of the painting a deckchair in yellow and red. A white house is shown on the left without a roof, a beige sky takes up the top third with some grey clouds. The hills, the Minaun Heights, on the left are presented in as many shades of green as the grass in the front garden (poetic licence as the hills are really more brown than green), the sea in between these green parts is bluish green. The last hills, on the middle of the right edge of the painting, are lower and black, looking almost like back teeth. The view is also remarkable as except for a roofless house on the left there are hardly any houses obstructing the view onto the sea; only two rooftops are depicted in the picture (in stark contrast to a photo Böll took of his actual view).

It is easy to imagine this as the daytime picture of the following literary portrait in the *Irish Journal* of an evening at the seaside that has its own darkish beauty and is presented as if in several dimensions: 'Azure spreads over the sea, in varying layers, varying shades; wrapped in this azure are green islands, looking like great patches of bog, black ones, jagged, rearing up out of the ocean like stumps of teeth ...' (p. 56). Further examples of strong imagery and the generous use of colour can be found on every page. At times it seems to overwhelm the narrator, who is almost incapable of adequate description: 'The greenness of these trees and meadows defies description; they throw green shadows into the Shannon, their green light seems to reach up to the sky where the clouds have gathered round the sun like patches of moss' (p. 97). But although one can almost see the 'forty-two shades of green', the traditional description of Ireland and its 'national' colouring, it is not the predominant impression – in Böll's literary sketches white, grey and brown are just as strong, and occasionally a vivid stroke of red or dark blue as in the passage quoted above, is etched onto the picture as well. Even when he reinforces the green, it is not necessarily as a colour of splendid copiousness and fertility but can be depressing and connected with two of the main topics in the *Irish Journal*, poverty and emigration:

> [...] yes, Ireland is green, very green, but its green is not only the green of meadows, it is the green of moss [...] and moss is the plant of resignation, of forsakenness. The country is forsaken, it is being slowly but steadily depopulated, and we – none of us had ever seen this strip of Ireland [...] –

we felt a little apprehensive: in vain the women looked left and right of the train for potato fields, vegetable plots, for the fresh unresigned green of lettuce, the darker green of peas. (p. 24)

Böll's attempts to transpose visual art into literature in the *Irish Journal* were appreciated by some critics, especially in the US when the translation appeared in 1967: 'The author is an original creative artist, and his impressions are unique and entertaining, with the same sort of persuasiveness as those of Pissaro or Monet.'[19] Arguably one could compare him with Joyce in this respect. While Joyce's *Chambermusic* expressed his musical interest, Böll, instead of turning to music, chooses a painter's approach, creating mosaics full of colour.

This art is not however confined to colours or quiet painting, but is a film, a radio feature with a soundtrack created by braying donkeys and old squeaky bikes that complement the picture:

Donkeys bray in the warm summer night, passing on their abstract song, that crazy noise as of badly oiled door hinges, rusty pumps – incomprehensible signals, magnificent and too abstract to sound credible, an expression of limitless pain and yet resignation. Cyclists whir by like bats on unlit wire steeds, until finally only the quiet peaceful footsteps of the pedestrians fill the night. (p. 58)

Just as before with the landscape that seemed to be painted by an 'unusually crazy painter' showing 'how abstract reality is' the symphony of sounds surrounding the narrator are 'too abstract to sound credible' (ibid) – Ireland is hard to convey and can not be presented as 'realistic', as it would not be believable.

While there is a vivid description of sounds, what is noticably absent in the *Irish Journal* is music. Given Böll's earlier statement indicating how important music was for him and the central position that traditional music held in Irish social life (and as featured in numerous travelogues of Ireland), this is remarkable.

So why is there not even a reference to fairy tales in the *Irish Journal* or a word about traditional Irish music? Possibly for the same reasons that Böll reduces the usual leading role of history and does not endeavour to undertake longer excursions into other aspects of Irish literature – because

---

[19] R.L. White, *Heinrich Böll in America 1954-1970*, Hildesheim: Olms 1979, p. 136, quoting Anonymous, Briefly Noted, *New Yorker*, 7 October 1967.

Böll intended through the sewing together of patchwork impressions of Ireland to create his own piece of art (as emphasised so strongly in his correspondence with Rosenstock), a contemporary image, yet one containing future and past; one which relied on a multi-media presentation that crucially did not include many of the traditional elements. Instead, everyday conversations, everyday sounds and everyday scenes and observation are woven together in deceptively simple language to give a tender and moving account of Ireland, without hiding some of the darker aspects. In Böll's multimedia version of Ireland a peaceful image is conjured up, yet his description contains suffering – none more central than that brought through emigration resulting from poverty and lack of economic opportunity in Ireland.

Blick von meinem Fenster (View from my window). Photograph by Heinrich Böll.
© Samay Böll.

Blick auf die Keel Bay/Achill Island/Irland, painting by Heinrich Böll. This image is a copy from the exhibition 'Heinrich Böll - Life and Work' (colours faded) as the original was lost with the collapse of the Cologne City Archive. © Samay Böll.

Chapter Eleven

Poverty and Emigration

One of the more controversial aspects of the *Irisches Tagebuch* was the way it described poverty.[1] A number of things should be taken into account when considering this theme, firstly the socio-economic situation in which Böll found himself after the war. He and his family had suffered actual hunger, and now he would have regarded with distrust Germany's rapid rise in prosperity, the beginnings of the 'economic miracle'. The universal unspoken desire in Germany to forget what had happened under Hitler and to work a way out of rubble and poverty, both metaphorically and in reality, was something he saw with regret all around him, and he defended passionately the so-called 'Trümmerliteratur', dealing with that period:

> When at the end of the fifties a critic praised him for finally leaving the 'environment of the poor' behind him and for the fact that his books were finally free of the kitchen sink and social indictment, Heinrich Böll wrote his essay: 'In defense of the kitchen sink'. He was indignant that such false praise should be possible in a world which 'stinks of exploitation', a world 'in which poverty is no longer a stage in the class war nor a mystical homeland but only a kind of leprosy ...'[2]

His personal background, a strongly austere Catholic upbringing, helped shape Böll's views. The intellectual openness of converts in the Chesterton mould appeared to Böll like a fresh wind, and the French writer Léon Bloy, whom he discovered in the mid-1930s, was immensely important to

---

[1] Böll was criticised in this regard for example by Germany's foremost critic Marcel Reich-Ranicki during the TV programme *Im literarischen Kaffeehaus*, 21 December 1967.

[2] Heinrich Vormweg, 'Heinrich Böll is Dead – An Obituary', in: *Heinrich Böll – On his Death – Selected obituaries and the last interview*, Bonn: Inter Nationes 1985, pp. 14-16, 14 (German version in *metall*, No. 15, 26 July 1985). The term used here, 'kitchen sink' is a very free translation of 'Waschküchen', but conveying the same meaning to a large extent – the place where domestic work was done (see also p. 66).

him, as was Dostoyevsky, whom he read first at around the same time.[3] Bloy's text the *Blood of the Poor* had a powerful influence on Böll and his view of poverty. In 1952 Böll wrote in a review of the German translation of Bloy's work that for Bloy poverty was not only pleasing to God but the actual way of God, that 'for him [Bloy] poverty was not only one path but the only path to human dignity.'[4]

Böll's engagement with the question of poverty and the influence and importance of money was lifelong. In his Nobel address delivered on 2 May 1973 in Stockholm, 'An Approach to the Rationality of Poetry', he declared that the greatest 'crime' of the American Indians was that they had no concept of the value of gold or of money. It seems generally accepted that for Böll money was part of the 'unholy trinity',[5] but this topic has not been much studied.[6] Money is one of Böll's leitmotifs[7] (and especially explosive for him in conjunction with the Church): it is the main theme or a decisive factor in several of his novels (in *House without Guardian* for instance the word 'money' is spelled in italics almost throughout). Böll's article on Dostoyevsky stresses the importance of

---

[3] Dostoyevsky's importance for Böll is underlined in 'Wenn ich danken müßte' ('If I had to say thanks'), a fragment from 1938, in which he names Dostoyevsky and Chesterton as his main literary influences: *KA 1*, pp. 282-283. On Bloy see also Gerhard Sauder, Heinrich Bölls Léon-Bloy-Lektüre – Ursprünge eines radikalen Katholizismus, in: W. Jung, J. Schubert (eds): *'Ich sammle Augenblicke' - Heinrich Böll 1917-1985*, Bielefeld: Aisthesis 2008, pp. 31-48, especially pp. 39-47.
[4] Heinrich Böll, 'Jenseits der Literatur - Über deutsche Ausgaben Léon Bloys', *Werke 1952-1953*, Kölner Ausgabe volume 6, edited by Árpád Bernáth, Cologne: Kiepenheuer & Witsch 2007, pp. 92-99 (commentary pp. 601-613), p. 97. In the following abbreviated as *KA 6*.
[5] Paul Konrad Kurz, *Apokalyptische Zeit – Zur Literatur der mittleren 80er Jahre*, Frankfurt a.M.: Josef Knecht 1987, p. 128.
[6] Michael Olson's dissertation, 'Money and Love in the Novels of Heinrich Böll: The Marriage Theme in His Fiction between 1953 and 1985' (UCLA 1989) being a laudable exception.
[7] Hans Werner Richter's memories of Böll, 'Liebst du das Geld auch so wie ich?' ['Do you love money as much as I do?'] (in Hans Werner Richter, *Im Etablissement der Schmetterlinge*. Munich: Hanser 1986, pp. 63-78) seem to give a somewhat different emphasis and have been repeated several times recently by Christian Linder in an attempt to argue that there was a carefully hidden side to Böll (cf. Christian Linder, *Das Schwirren eines heranfliegenden Pfeils. Heinrich Böll – Eine Biographie*, Berlin: Matthes & Seitz 2009). However, given the context of Richter's story, Böll's reported comment could be interpreted in a number of ways, ranging from joke to irony and sarcasm – from an author Richter admits he never quite understood (cf. Richter, pp. 72, 75f.).

money: according to Böll, Dostoyevsky hardly wrote a note or a diary entry in which it did not appear. The ambiguities in the relationship with money arguably refer not only to Dostoyevsky but to Böll himself: 'Money is as abstract as real, it is dirty, pure and divine. It is nothing if you can't get anything for it and everything that one can get for it.'[8] Böll acknowledged that his experience of the Great Depression led to lifelong anxiety, which would have been reinforced by his postwar situation. Later, when more financially secure, he did not forget those in less fortunate circumstances, though he generally insisted on his assistance being kept quiet. This is evident, for example, in Marcel Reich-Ranicki's remarks in his obituary of Böll:

> [...] if I mention it now it is only because I am one of many: Helping others was natural to him and he never spoke of it. Only once did he tell me how he had succeeded in rescuing a citizen of a totalitarian state and bringing him to the Federal Republic in his car with a German passport he had forged himself [...] countless people all over the world owe him so much; many owe him their lives.[9]

To be among the poor was not only an empty phrase for Böll: he had a strong feeling of belonging with the unfortunate, even in the most difficult circumstances. During the war he wrote to his mother about a possible promotion to officer status for which he was eligible and which greatly tempted him as it would have made his life much easier, but he could not bring himself to sit on a horse, proud and clean, with the dirty exhausted mass of soldiers at his feet: 'somehow I belong far more and far more intimately to the masses, who have to suffer, more, a thousand times more than those on horseback.' He sees it as close to a betrayal of their suffering if he became an officer, 'as if the dirt down there didn't seem good enough for me anymore'.[10]

---

[8] [Geld ist so abstrakt wie wirklich, es ist schmutzig, rein und göttlich. Es ist nichts, wenn man nichts dafür bekommen kann, und alles, was man dafür bekommen kann] in: Manès Sperber (ed.), *Wir und Dostojewskij. Eine Debatte mit Heinrich Böll, Siegfried Lenz, André Malraux, Hans Erich Nossack*, Hamburg: Hoffmann und Campe 1972, p. 70.
[9] 'Writer, Jester, Preacher', in: *Heinrich Böll – On his Death*, pp. 10-13, 11. René Böll has indicated that Reich-Ranicki might have confused things here: at a lecture in Achill on 30 April 2011 he described the rescue of Jaroslava (Slavi) Mandl, smuggled out by Böll in his car that he had specially adapted with the help of a magician so that she could hide.
[10] Böll, *Briefe aus dem Krieg 1939-1945,* Letter 19 July 1942, p. 399.

As in the passage quoted earlier, one of the first and most abiding of Böll's impressions of Ireland, as he makes clear from the very first page of the first chapter, was that poverty was neither disgrace nor honour but was irrelevant. In the second chapter the narrator notices 'these ragged, barefoot children', and the third chapter starts with the contrast between the cold and clean St. Patrick's Cathedral and the surrounding desolation, including the first Irish beggar he meets:

> [...] beggars like this one are only to be found otherwise in southern countries, but in the south the sun shines: here, north of the 53rd parallel, rags and tatters are something different from south of the 30th parallel; rain falls on poverty, and here an incorrigible aesthete could no longer regard dirt as picturesque; in the slums around St. Patrick's, squalor still huddles in many a corner, many a house, exactly as Swift must have seen it in 1743. (pp. 13f.)

In the *Irish Journal*, poverty is most pronounced in the descriptions of cities, especially Dublin and Limerick. This dichotomy between urban and country life becomes explicit in Andersch's radio version of 1955: 'Dark and tragic Dublin seems [...] but quiet and gentle is the country.' A dark, desolate image is painted by Böll in his descriptions: 'Darkness hung over Dublin: every shade of gray between black and white had found its own little cloud, the sky was covered with a plumage of innumerable grays: not a streak, not a scrap of Irish green [...] In the slums dirt sometimes lies in black flakes on the windowpanes.' (p. 14) Limerick is portrayed similarly: 'Dark clouds came up from the Atlantic – and the streets of Limerick were dark and empty.' (p. 43) In contrast with the grey and black environment are only the 'painfully white milk bottles that seemed destined for people long dead' and the seagulls, 'splintering the gray of the sky, clouds of white plump gulls' (ibid). In this place the poverty is such that even a safety pin is too expensive – string is cheaper and 'when there's no more string, the fingers will do, thin, dirty, numb children's fingers' (p. 47). This description evokes Dickensian scenes; Böll is clearly not giving any romanticised version of poverty.[11]

---

[11] And it is clear evidence that he does not perceive it as 'appealing' as Conard seems to think: 'Ireland's poverty and drinking, its restrictive religion and the people's predilection for the gab, for example, appear as appealing.' (R. Conard, *Heinrich Böll*, p. 76). See also Irish academic Una Carthy who takes issue with assessments such as Conards in her article Heinrich Böll – Redensarten, in: J. Morrison, F. Krobb (eds), *Prose Pieces*, Konstanz: Hartung-Gorre 2008, pp. 159-168, 165.

What he is giving, though, is some hope, the indication that even at this level of poverty generosity exists, in the unlikely form of 'a dark, bloodstained drunk'. He is the man 'who lives poetry instead of writing it' by paying 'ten thousand per cent interest' for six drops of vinegar poured by a poor boy on his chips, when the boy is accused by the saleswoman of ruining her. She stands for the cold lack of mercy that exists towards the desperate need of the poor – similar characters are included in many of Böll's novels, most commonly members of the establishment and very often Catholic members of the so-called better society or even the clergy. In Böll's Ireland, however, the Church still functions as a reminder of other values, as in the confrontation between the drunk and the woman, when the drunk reminds her that it is time for the evening service and she starts crying, a possible indication that at least a part of his meaning has reached her (p. 49). Böll's message that outer appearances are deceptive, that they have no relevance to true humanity, is underlined by his comment when his companion fears for their safety in a poor neighbourhood:

> My companion was trembling; he was the victim of the most bitter and stupid prejudice of all: that people who are badly dressed are dangerous – more dangerous than the well-dressed ones. He ought to tremble in the bar of the Shelbourne Hotel in Dublin at least as much as here, behind King John's Castle in Limerick. If only they were more dangerous, these ragged ones, if only they were as dangerous as those in the bar of the Shelbourne Hotel who don't look dangerous at all. (p. 48)

In this environment betting shops prosper, offering a last desperate hope to the men who are willing to risk part of their unemployment benefit. Böll captures the tenseness and desperation by his use of italics and the frequent repetition – almost like a litany – of the words 'Crimson Cloud *has* to win'. 'Crimson Cloud' symbolises the hopes which will be disappointed;[12] it appears in opposition to, albeit in close affinity with, 'the crimson Sacred Heart'.

Church or a successful bet are the only carriers of hope, and as each fails to fulfil the hopes invested in them (the churches being cleared at night despite some last fervent prayers for Crimson Cloud's success) a visit to the pub afterwards seems the only way to quench the grief: it is the attempt

---

[12] See *Irish Journal*, p. 51: 'Ruins from the time of the Rebellion, boarded-up houses that are not yet ruins, the sound of rats moving around behind the black boards, warehouses cracked open and left to the disintegration of time, green-gray slime on exposed walls, and the black beer flows to the health of Crimson Cloud, who is not going to win.'

to escape into oblivion described earlier in the second episode in Dublin. The children endlessly playing marbles, 'clicking against the worn steps of the pub, against the worn steps of the churches and bookies' offices' (p. 51), bring all the failed institutions onto one level, and indicate the permanence of the situation.

In 'A reply to the critics of *Children of Eire*' Böll addresses the topic of poverty, tellingly referring to the West of Ireland:

> I have to say something on the topic of poverty, the one literary subject that is most open to misinterpretation. I believe that even the poorest inhabitant of a village in the West of Ireland is richer than he knows: he has his house, his turf, his potatoes, milk, butter and eggs, he owes allegiance to no master, ht (sic) enjoys magnificent air and scenery and he is free – I personally consider him richer than the occupant of a two-roomed flat with all mod. cons. in any industrial city, and others, simply because there is no place for them elsewhere, coop themselves up in two-roomed flats in industrial suburbs.[13]

Another 'blow-in' who came from Germany to Ireland in 1937 and moved to Achill in 1946 remembers things differently and disagrees to a certain extent with Böll:

> It was not quite like he described it. At the time he came in we were behind the time [...] He saw the world with different eyes, we were living here, working, while he was in the clouds, saw it as romantic, but it was a hard life. We had no water or electricity, no gas, I had to get water from the tank, there wasn't much time for sitting and chatting.[14]

She also remembers that there was a very good community spirit: neighbours looked after one another, and people helped with hay and turf. The topic of poverty was raised in an interview with Marcel Reich-Ranicki and Hans Mayer on the occasion of Böll's fiftieth birthday.[15] Reich-Ranicki, Germany's foremost literary critic of the time, criticised what he saw as Böll's admiration of poverty, mentioning a recent trip of his own to Ireland and the poverty he had encountered in Dublin. Böll's answer is a nearly classic Irish one: he argues that Dublin is not Ireland, and that only in Dublin could one find real poverty. Ireland itself he sees as rich in many

---

[13] Böll, 'A reply to the critics of *Children of Eire*', in *Hibernia*, March 1965, p. 15.
[14] Conversation with Elisabeth Sweeney, Achill Island, 28 August 2002.
[15] *Im Literarischen Kaffeehaus,* transcription available in the Böll archive, Cologne.

ways. He admits, however, having transferred to Ireland without reflection the German post-war optimism that developed out of thankfulness for some bread, for survival; he had not taken into account the Irish history and Irish sensitivities.

One could argue that Böll was not alone in some respects in having a vision of Ireland as retaining a way of life without materialism and following the way God meant people to live. The idea sounds like an echo of a speech by one of the most influential, though somewhat controversial, Irish figures in the twentieth century, Eamon de Valera, given on St. Patrick's Day eleven years before Böll set foot in Ireland for the first time:

> The Ireland that we had dreamed of would be the home of a people who valued material wealth only as a basis of right living, of a people who were satisfied with frugal comfort and devoted their leisure to things of the spirit; a land whose countryside would be bright with cosy homesteads, whose fields and villages would be joyous with the sound of industry, with the romping of sturdy children, the contests of athletic youths, the laughter of happy maidens, whose firesides would be forums for the wisdom of serene old age. It would, in a word, be the home of a people living the life God desires that men should live.[16]

The historian Joe Lee convincingly argues that this dream-Ireland never really existed; the 'contests of athletic youths' took place, if at all, on English building sites, and the laughter of the young girls was the bitter-sweet laughter of a narrow society liberated by emigration.[17] Diarmuid Ferriter, however, argued recently that it could also be understood as a statement showing de Valera's ideals and ambitions, emphasising the need for a nation to move in a positive direction, and 'for there to be a scepticism about the idea that material gain would solve all of a country's problems.'[18]

Emigration is a central topic of the *Irish Journal* and is mentioned in nearly every chapter. The only possible escape from poverty seems to be to leave for good, even if this means travelling as far as Australia, like the man who is the topic of conversation between the narrator and an elderly lady at the end of the Limerick chapter. Emigration connects the very

---

[16] Address by Mr de Valera, 17 March 1943. This can be listened to on *RTE* radio http://www.rte.ie/laweb/ll/ll_t09b.html (last access: 14 April 2011).
[17] J. J. Lee, *Ireland 1912-1985*, pp. 334f.
[18] Diarmuid Ferriter, *Eamon de Valera and broadcasting*, 12 October 2007, *RTE 1*, http://www.rte.ie/laweb/ll/ll_t09_main_a.html (last access: 15 April 2011).

different forms of poverty that according to Böll exist outside the cities. While poverty is also a common experience there, forcing people such as Aedan McNamara ('The Most Beautiful Feet in the World') to work for three quarters of every year in England, or leading to permanent emigration to the US or Australia, poverty outside the cities is described as having a different quality. There is no hopeless dragging on in the squalor of a desolate and forlorn environment. Life is hard, but people live surrounded by a 'beauty that hurts' (p. 66).[19] However, the reality of emigration and the narrowness of society are clearly equally present in Böll's portrait of Ireland.

Emigration is one of the very few aspects of Ireland and Irish society where Böll gives facts and figures:

> a hundred years ago Ireland had some seven million inhabitants, Poland probably had just as few at that time, but today Poland has more than twenty million inhabitants and Ireland scarcely four million, and Poland – God knows – has certainly not been spared by its powerful neighbours. This dwindling from seven to four million among a people with a surplus of births means a great tide of emigrants. (p. 110)

Böll's preoccupation with this theme is not surprising and is indeed a reflection of the situation around him. Twentieth century Irish emigration reached a peak in the years between 1951 and 1961. With a population of nearly three million (not including Northern Ireland) and a surplus birthrate of nearly 135,000, the period 1951-1955 saw 200,000 people emigrate, about 40,000 per year. Between 1956 and 1961 this annual rate increased to 42,000. The north-western counties were especially affected. The population in Connacht decreased between 1951 and 1956 from nearly 472,000 to 446,000, despite a considerable surplus birthrate. Between 1956 and 1961 it decreased by another 27,000.[20] Mayo was the

---

[19] In a short article about the views of the Atlantic from Westport in the evening and life on the islands from 1955, Böll similarly mentions that it is 'unbearably beautiful' but continues with a more pessimistic portrayal, arguing that to live there would mean living in a paradise that was to be paid for in hunger – that could be accepted by oneself but could not be dictated as a price to six or seven children. Heinrich Böll: Am Rande Europas, in: *Magnum*, 2 /1955, issue 10, p. 48.
[20] Hans Happe, *Irland und die Emigration - Die Bedeutung des Auswanderungsphänomens*, Aachen: Rader 1987, p. 111, quoting Census of Population 1981, Table 1 - Population of each Province at each Census since 1926: Marriages, Births and Deaths registered. Natural increase and estimated Net Migration in each Intercensal Period since 1911.

county with the second highest rate of depopulation,[21] and Achill Island was particularly hard hit: while its population stayed relatively stable between 1946 and 1951 (4918 in 1946, and 4906 in 1951), by 1956 it had decreased to 4493 and in 1961 there were only 4069 inhabitants, a drop of nearly 20% within only one decade. The trend continued – in 1966 there were only 3598 people left on the island.[22]

The phenomenon of emigration was noted in nearly all travel descriptions of Ireland at the time, often with statistics and an analysis of the economic impact,[23] but Böll manages to give the reader a glimpse of the actual suffering and heartbreak experienced by emigrants and their families by describing the situation of individuals rather than relying only on statistics.

---

[21] Census 1981, Table 9, Average Rate of Estimated Net Migration per 1,000 of average population from each County in each Intercensal Period since 1951 and Happe, *Irland und die Emigration*, p. 113.
[22] McNally, *Achill*, p. 178.
[23] See for example Johann, *Heimat der Regenbogen*, p. 84; Grubbe, *Die Insel der Elfen,* p. 64 or Stephan, Eins Dritter Dublin, second part, 21 August 1953.

CHAPTER TWELVE

RELIGION

> *He was a real Christian, a believing Catholic and that is why he wrangled all his life with the Catholic Church, which he officially left at the end although – paradoxical as it may sound – he was never separated from it.*
> —Marcel Reich-Ranicki[1]

> *He lashed out against Catholicism, the elegant priesthood, the worldly weakness of ecclesiastical power, not because he was un-Catholic but undoubtedly because he was too Catholic.*
> —Joachim Kaiser[2]

At the very end of 'Arrival I' and the beginning of 'Arrival II' Böll repeats the traditional and long cherished description of Ireland as 'the isle of saints' (pp. 6 and 7).[3] Ireland is further described as the only country in Europe that did not take part in conquering others, instead

---

[1] Reich-Ranicki: Writer, Jester, Preacher, pp. 10f. On the theme of Böll and the Church in general see also Melanie Helm, *Spes contra spem – Ansätze zu einem Kirchenbild der Zukunft bei Heinrich Böll*, Münster et al: Lit 2005.

[2] Joachim Kaiser: 'The Suffering and Greatness of Heinrich Böll – on the death of a distinguished writer' in: *Heinrich Böll – On his Death – Selected obituaries and the last interview*, Bonn: Inter Nationes 1985, pp. 17-21, 19 (German version in *Süddeutsche Zeitung*, 17 July 1985).

[3] Another German in Ireland, John Hennig, who wrote extensively and with considerable insight about Irish-German relations, followed up the development of the image of the 'island of saints' and came to the conclusion that it was a cherished belief founded on the mistranslation of the Irish word *noibh* (really meaning 'honourable' or 'venerable') as 'canonized saint' - a fact that was happily exploited by later generations of Irish monks on the continent from the 10th century onwards. See Hennig: *Studien zur Geschichte der deutschsprachigen Irlandkunde bis zum Ende des achtzehnten Jahrhunderts*, in: *Deutsche Vierteljahrsschrift für Literaturwissenschaft und Geistesgeschichte* (= *DVjs*) 35, 1961, pp. 221-233, 223f.

all they sent out was priests, monks, missionaries who, by strange detour via Ireland, brought the spirit of Thebaic asceticism to Europe; here, more than a thousand years ago, so far from the center of things, as if it had slipped way into the Atlantic, lay the glowing heart of Europe. (p. 7)

If Ireland was to be the 'glowing heart of Europe' then maybe it is fair to say that Irish Catholicism was the glowing heart of Böll's Ireland. Böll finds a country that is characterized by being the 'oldest and most faithful daughter' of 'our gracious mother the Church', where the people 'live closer to Heaven than anyone else in Europe' (Epilogue, p. 124). However, though religion and the Church permeate his portrayal of Ireland and are on the whole positively portrayed, there is also an often overlooked reservation in his descriptions.

Upon his first arrival (described in 'Arrival II') the narrator is startled by his first encounter with the strong presence of the Church in Ireland. In the *Irish Journal* we read about the narrator hearing 'a sudden roar, a sound almost like thunder' which turns out to be 'the powerful opening bars of *Tantum ergo*' and the narrator finds himself left with 'the impression of an overwhelming piety' (p. 9f). He is clearly moved, particularly when thinking about the situation in Germany, where, he writes, one could see as many people only after Easter Mass or at Christmas (these sentiments are echoed by Böll in his letter home: 'Really, it is very astonishing, surprising and reassuring to see, how much the Irish are truly religious')[4]. However, in the *Irish Journal* the passage continues with the observation that he had not yet forgotten 'the confession of the unbeliever with the sharp profile' from the ferry trip over, who told of the need to pretend to be religious, of the pressures from the family and community. This encounter is described in 'Arrival I'. Nevertheless, in a discussion with a German compatriot ensuing shortly afterwards in 'Arrival II' the narrator defends Ireland against the accusation that everything is dirty and expensive. The narrator defends Ireland 'passionately, [he] fought with tea, *Tantum ergo*, Joyce and Yeats' (p. 11), obviously using the piety symbolised through the *Tantum ergo* as one of his arguments.

How can this seemingly inconsistent approach to Irish devoutness be explained? It helps to look at the development of the *Irish Journal* and the earlier publications. The first published form of 'Arrival II', the newspaper

---

and Gisela Holfter, Hermann Rasche (eds): *Exil in Irland – John Hennigs Schriften zu deutsch-irischen Beziehungen*, Trier: WVT 2002, pp. 145-159, 148.
[4] Böll, *Rom auf den ersten Blick*, letter 7 October 1954, p. 64.

article 'The First Day' of 1954, does not contain any reference to the unbeliever with the sharp profile described in 'Arrival I'. Also missing in the original article 'The First Day' is the inclusion of 'so many sharp profiles', indicating that the unbeliever is not alone but one of many. Given that the chapter 'Arrival I' was written only for the book publication some two years later than 'Arrival II', this is not very surprising, and one could argue that this is merely one of Böll's methods of injecting more coherence into the publication, bringing in connecting elements between the chapters. But there is more to it. What Böll is underlining here, in a very subtle way, is that Irish piety is and was very impressive for him, but that he is also aware that there is more than meets the eye and that there is a darker, unhappier side to it. The episode he describes in 'Arrival I' seems to encapsulate Böll's own experience of Ireland: from cold and windy surroundings the narrator is invited to find a warm haven by an Irish priest, a kind and gentle representative of both Ireland and the Church. In this newly found protected sphere (which can be interpreted as Ireland as a whole) he is witness of (not participant in) the conversation between returning emigrant and priest. And by listening in his shelter, he is learning more and more about the hidden, darker side to religion in Ireland, the piousness and the almost ostentatious belief so admired by him initially. It clearly shows that some of the returned emigrants on a visit home, who seem devoutly kneeling church-goers, do not believe in God, having lost their faith as they have seen 'how many loose women *Kathleen ni Houlihan* has sent to London, the isle of saints' (p. 4). The 'isle of saints' is a term of bitterness here, used to provide a contrast with the sin of prostitution – however, not meant as criticism of the women but rather the unholy place that forces its children out, to fend for themselves with whatever means they have. Still, when coming back they have to pretend to believe as they cannot afford to expose the hypocrisy, cannot disappoint and hurt their parents and grandparents. The attempts of the priest to point out other countries' deadly occupations by exporting ideas of suicide, machine guns and nuclear weapons (hygiene and automobiles are also mentioned; it is not quite clear whether they are as negative as the other products), fail to convince the returning emigrant, who is well used to these arguments, having a brother and two cousins who are priests – adding that they are the only ones in the whole family who have cars, the ones therefore marked as better-off, wealthier. If this were to be interpreted especially negatively, one could argue that these relatives have sold themselves to the Church, but as Böll mentions priests as one of Ireland's main export products this seems unlikely, though the implied criticism of their worldly wealth lingers.

Böll's narrator is only the silent outsider, listening but not joining in the conversation or indeed the criticism of the Church, delivered by a girl with a light clear voice and 'a sharp profile' (p. 4), revealed by the 'glowing cigarette' (p. 5). An indication of where Böll's sympathy lies is the portrayal of the girl as smoking, given the importance of cigarettes in Böll's novels and their frequent connection with the 'goodies' rather than the 'baddies' – indeed, Böll is probably one of the very few writers about whom one can write dissertations, purely on the use of cigarettes and smoking. The author of one such MA thesis argues that smoking was closely connected to Böll's demand to rehabilitate the ordinary, the everyday and construct places of humanity,[5] and that tobacco was a decisive characteristic, a necessary indulgence and an indispensible provision of life.[6] Here the 'glowing cigarette' of the disbeliever, mentioned twice (p. 5), acts almost as a counterbalance to the 'glowing heart' of Europe, the seemingly peaceful, ascetic place that did not conquer but brought Christianity. Later, Böll portrays another uneasy relationship between poverty and religion when it comes to the extreme forms of poverty in 'Limerick in the Evening' (another part of the *Irish Journal* written for the book alone). The narrator comes to realise that Limerick, 'the most devout city in the world' (p. 44), is also the place of 'scepticism flowering in hard, sad eyes: melancholy shining in blue eyes [...] thorns around the rose, arrows in the heart of the most devout city in the world' (p. 46).

The contrast between his first story of 1954, where he expresses amazement and delight about the overwhelming Irish participation at Mass (also in terms of sheer acoustic presence, as it tricks the narrator into believing in imaginary trains approaching), and the inclusion in the 1957 book publication of 'the confession of the unbeliever', a harsh reminder that hypocrisy exists even in the 'glowing heart of Europe', shows his growing awareness of the multi-faceted nature of Church affairs and religion in Ireland. That Böll had become well aware of problems in Ireland is also clearly evidenced in his exchange of letters with Georg Rosenstock, who in his review of the *Irisches Tagebuch* in 1957 had regretted Böll's lack of heart and believed that Ireland needed three visits before it was understood,[7] not realising that Böll had indeed visited Ireland

---

[5] Alexandra Lisbeth Jähn, Tabakgenuß als Kommunikation – Vom Rauchen, Reden und Schweigen bei Heinrich Böll, MA thesis, Universität Bayreuth 1995, p. 123.
[6] Ibid., p. 1.
[7] Georg Rosenstock, Manche Länder muß man dreimal sehen, *Die Welt*, Berlin, 8

three times. Böll subsequently wrote to Rosenstock[8] (as far as is known the only time he ever entered into a sustained discussion with a critic – in fact, they later met in Ireland and became quite friendly), firstly saying that 'showing more heart simply could not be permitted and less "criticism" would have been shameless towards the reader'.[9] After pointing out that he had indeed been to Ireland three times and spent altogether ten months there, Böll continues that his book would have become as bitter as Swift and Joyce had he been in Ireland longer, but this seemed not appropriate for him as an foreigner: 'Therefore I also consciously omitted some elements of Irish life – clericalism for example – as I felt it to be outside my area of expertise.'[10] In the next letter he goes further and writes that he is sorry and regrets that he omitted Irish clericalism ('which I don't find amusingly funny'), but that he did it intentionally and reiterates that he omitted it so as not to get involved as a foreigner in domestic problems.[11]

While this correspondence leaves no doubt that Böll was very aware of certain problems connected with the Irish Church, even if he does not more explicitly focus on them in the *Irish Journal,* there is equally much evidence of his positive feeling towards the omnipresent signs of religious life, indicated for example by churches being filled with people from all walks of life. In his article 'Reise nach Polen' ('Trip to Poland', also published in 1957) he refers to a phenomenon that in Western Europe 'only still exists in Ireland and in English cities populated by the Irish: workers in the churches.'[12] In the *Irish Journal* the narrator encounters beggars, children with their hurley-sticks and dark-haired beauties. That

---

June 1957.
[8] Georg Rosenstock was a German doctor who had met and married an Irish woman while being held prisoner of war in the Channel Islands and who had moved to Ireland in 1948.
[9] Letter from Böll to Rosenstock, 13 June 1957, 'Mehr Herz zu zeigen, als ich in diesem Buch gezeigt habe, dürfte einfach unerlaubt sein – weniger 'Kritik' zu zeigen, wäre dem Leser gegenüber einfach schamlos gewesen.' *KA 10*, p. 693.
[10] Ibid. 'So habe ich auch bewußt einige Elemente des irischen Lebens – Klerikalismus etwa – ausgelassen, weil ich mich nicht zuständig fand'.
[11] Böll to Rosenstock, 24 June 1957: 'Es tut mir leid, ich bedaure es aus Gründen der Wahrhaftigkeit, daß ich den irischen Klerikalismus, den ich keineswegs amüsant-komisch finde, ausgelassen habe; doch habe ich gerade dieses Problem ausgelassen, bewußt, um mich als Ausländer nicht in innere Probleme zu mischen.' *KA 10*, pp. 696f.
[12] Böll, Reise durch Polen, in: *KA 10*, pp. 171-180 (commentary pp. 624-629), here p. 176.

the Church has an impact on all aspects of life becomes obvious also during his trip to Limerick when the whole town is deserted during a weekday which turns out to be the Feast of the Rosary. Only when the church door opens does the town fill with life again – 'even the post office was opened, and the bank opened its wickets' (p. 45). Obviously religion in Ireland is not a matter for women and children alone, it affects everyone and all professions. Seemingly a true Church of the people therefore. But which Church? Was there only one in Ireland?

A clear contrast emerges between the coldness of St. Patrick's Cathedral that appears to him 'so clean [...] so empty of people and so full of patriotic marble figures' (p. 13), a sentiment that he repeats a few pages later, adding 'and so beautiful', and the other church 'full of people, full of cheap sentimental decoration, and although it wasn't exactly dirty it was messy: the way a living room looks in a family where there are a lot of children' (p. 16). This scene is also echoed in Böll's letter home on 14 October 1954 though with a strongly partisan sentiment, which is carefully removed in the *Irish Journal*: 'It is terrible that the huge, beautiful, old churches (St. Patrick's and Christ Church) are Protestant, while the Catholic churches are new and 'kitschy', never totally clean and generally full'.[13] In the book there are only hints that the two churches belong to different confessions, which would have been an easy explanation for the difference in popularity and looks – in the descriptions of St. Patrick's there is a reference that it smelled only of mould 'as in every church where for centuries no incense has been burned' (p. 13). In Ireland people would have been well aware that St. Patrick's, founded in 1191, was one of the main churches of the Protestant Church of Ireland. For German readers on the other hand that might well not have been clear at all. It would have been obvious enough from the descriptions of the saints' statues, the halo around Mary's head etc that the crowded church was Catholic, but unsuspecting German readers might well take St. Patrick's for a church that had become more of a museum, an eminent old Cathedral, simply not so popular or without a parish. Tellingly, the beggar who had been outside the front of St. Patrick's Cathedral, waiting for gifts there, moves to the other church once he has received a cigarette and a bit of money from the narrator, and now donates some of his money with the help of a school boy – it is the Catholic churches where the poor are at home.

---

[13] [Schrecklich ist, daß die großen, schönen, alten Kirchen (St. Patrick und Christ Church) protestantisch sind, sauber und groß und vollkommen leer, während die katholischen Kirchen neu und kitschig, nie ganz sauber und meistens voll sind], *Rom auf den ersten Blick*, p. 59.

All priests that are encountered in the *Irish Journal* are Catholic priests, holding a rosary, and nuns often feature as well. Böll's omission of Protestant religion in Ireland would have led many readers to assume that there are only Catholics in Ireland. It also enables Böll to leave out the connected problems. Northern Ireland is not referred to at all in the *Irish Journal*. No direct information is given about the century-long struggle of the Irish Catholic Church for emancipation, which would have given important background to an at least partial explanation of the immense role of religion.

Priests tend to be portrayed very positively in the *Irish Journal*: even when challenged or when discussing controversial themes they remain patient, speak quietly and in a friendly way, they offer a seat to lost tourists such as the narrator (see Arrival I, p. 3) and interfere when children are about to be hit (see 'Not a Swan to Be Seen', p. 103) – the reality of the time, particularly regarding the issue of punishing children was very often a different one. The fact that Ireland holds the world record for ordinations of new priests is also one that seems to be put forward with satisfaction by Böll (see 'Arrival 1', p. 2).

The immense political influence of the Church in Ireland is referred to in the chapter 'When Seamus Wants a Drink ...', when Seamus 'probably also curses' the clergy who 'stubbornly cling to this incomprehensible law' (p. 87) that allows alcohol on a Sunday only to someone who has travelled for more than three miles, causing Seamus to have to cycle a considerable distance for just one beer. Böll continues with some further examples, though only in brackets, as if this is only additional but not important further information, and adds that the clergy also has the final say when it comes to licences, deciding on closing time and dances. This list could obviously be extended considerably. For a foreign reader, even brief reference to the historic role might have helped to explain this situation.

Another aspect of Irish society at the time with a close link to the Irish Church is that of censorship. Whereas in Böll's *Irish Journal* the topic is disregarded (and in the film only obliquely referred to, when he states that many Irish writers had to emigrate) in other German travel descriptions of the time it is widely discussed and at times comes in for criticism.[14] Given Böll's admiration for Irish writers, one wonders whether he was not worried about the censorship of their work. Eoin Bourke rightly points out that Böll's own

---

[14] See Johann, *Heimat der Regenbogen*, p. 44 and Stephan, Eins Dritter Dublin.

books would not have found favour with Church authorities (though this would have affected mostly his later books – for his early works he clearly tried hard to avoid any direct clashes with the official Church, even checking, for example, with the authorities in the Cologne diocese whether some of his writing in *The bread of those early years* was in line with Catholic teaching)[15]:

> Böll writes that the Irish are a people who relish religion to the utmost. But whoever would have preferred not to savour it was force-fed. Wherever priests and nuns appear in Böll's *Irish Diary* – and they do so repeatedly – they are seen nodding gently and sighing softly as persons do who are humble, compassionate and kindly. But those of us who had the bad luck to go through puberty in those same 1950s encountered a different kind of clergy: authoritarian, narrow-minded, anti-intellectual, artful, pampered and power-hungry. Their never-ending tirades against the sinfulness of the human body instilled in us a preventive guilt complex even before we had time to be innocent. The Church Index of forbidden books read like a guide to the best Irish and European literature. If Böll's own critical stance against the Church had been known, he, too, would have been placed on the list of forbidden books.[16]

Rachel McNicholl agrees with this assessment: '... he [Böll] apparently only noticed the velvet glove and not the iron fist concealed and with which the Catholic church in Ireland managed to rule, directly or indirectly, almost every facet of private and political life in the fifties'.[17]

As we now know, privately he had acknowledged the problematic nature of clericalism as early as 1957 in his correspondence with Rosenstock (and indeed was ready to fight with him if Rosenstock was not prepared to admit the problem).[18] However, publicly the closest Böll came to

---

[15] See Böll, *Werke 1981-1984*, Kölner Ausgabe volume 22, edited by Jochen Schubert, Cologne: Kiepenheuer & Witsch 2007, p. 463 (in the following abbreviated as *KA 22*), referring to Vilma Sturm's memoirs *Barfuß auf Asphalt* (published 1981), where she recounts her first meeting with Böll while she worked for the Catholic Institute for Media Information in Cologne (my thanks to Markus Schäfer for the reference).
[16] Eoin Bourke, *Das Irenbild der Deutschen*, Tübingen: Schriftenreihe des Deutsch-Irischen Freundeskreises in Baden-Württemberg e.V. 1991, p. 14. Thanks to Eoin Bourke for providing this translation.
[17] Rachel McNicholl, 'Heinrich Böll's Other Ireland', in: John L. Flood (ed.), *Common Currency – Aspects of Anglo-German Literary Relations since 1945*, Stuttgart: Hans-Dieter Heinz 1991, pp. 71-86, 73.
[18] See the aforementioned letter of June 1957 and his letter of 4 August 1957:

condemning aspects of the Irish Catholic Church was in his epilogue to the English translation 'Thirteen Years Later' where the final sentences are Böll's answer to criticism of this kind, underlined in the German version by Böll's use of italics for 'Catholic':

> For someone who is Irish and a writer, there is probably much to provoke him in this country, but I am not Irish and have sufficient grounds for provocation in the country about which and in whose language I write; in fact the Catholic provocation in the country [in] whose language I write is enough for me. (Epilogue, p. 127)

So Böll obviously admits to having concentrated on the positive aspects but argues that it is his right (and possibly duty) as a foreigner – he can (and certainly did) criticise his own country and the German Catholic Church, whereas in Ireland he is freer to search for and find his utopia (which does of course entail an implicit criticism of Germany). In an interview of 1975 he explains further that for him Ireland has become something like his second home, but the difference between your second and your real home lies in precisely your involvement with, for example, Church questions.[19] In this context it is important to remember that basically all of Böll's bitter portrayals of the Catholic Church are of the *German* Catholic Church, which is for Böll an important prerequisite for both his right and duty to get involved. This is reinforced by another statement he makes: 'The guilt of the Catholic Church in Germany, and everything that I find problematic about it is foremost concentrated on the

---

'Should you believe that clericalism is no problem in Ireland we will need to fight" [Sollten Sie glauben, der Klerikalismus sein [sic] in Irland kein Problem – so werden wir uns über diese Frage schon raufen müssen], *KA 10*, p. 700.

[19] Cf. Heinrich Böll u. Christian Linder, *Drei Tage im März*, Cologne: Kiepenheuer & Witsch 1975, p. 60: 'Irland war wirklich so etwas wie eine zweite Heimat, ist es zum Teil noch. Aber das nehme ich sofort zurück, denn natürlich weiß ich, daß es keine zweite Heimat gibt, entweder man emigriert oder behält seine Nationalität – ich bin Deutscher, schreibe deutsch. Wenn man sich irgendwo zu Hause fühlt – und ich fühle mich in diesem unserem Land zu Hause, habe das Gefühl, daß ich hierhin gehöre –, dann muß man sich auch einmischen oder eingemischt werden in das politisch-gesellschaftliche – und in Irland sehr wichtige religiöse – Leben, und insofern bin ich natürlich in Irland ein Fremder, immer Tourist geblieben.' See also Conard: 'Why does Böll mythologize this little republic? Why doesn't he see what is wrong with Ireland as he does so clearly with Germany, the reader may ask. The answer is simple. Böll is a German citizen; he lives in the Rhineland. He is a guest, a visitor in Ireland and, therefore, chooses to see the island with a friendly eye', in *Heinrich Böll*, Boston: Twayne 1981, pp. 77f.

Federal Republic of Germany'.[20] What particularly annoyed Böll was the Church's agreement with and fostering of economic development but, worse, the Church's participation in and dependence on State finances in the form of the Church tax, automatically deducted by the state from anyone who was registered as Catholic or Protestant. In his eyes, German Catholicism was little more than 'in effect an obedience-Catholicism', that threatened excommunication when criticised.[21] He left this specific German Catholic Church in January 1976, but continued to feel a German and a Catholic.[22] It was the contrast with this German Church that formed Böll's description of the Irish Church and in particular his perception of the Irish way of life, which allowed one to be anticlerical and Catholic at the same time, and where being excommunicated was nothing special.[23] Ireland is for him the famous exception to the rule, a country where despite the dominance of Catholicism, 'strikes thrive just as in other places obedience' (Epilogue, p. 125).

We need to keep in mind also that even within Ireland there is by no means consensus about the past experiences with the Catholic Church. Irish travel writer Dervla Murphy, for example, refers to the historian and journalist Louis McRedmond whose experience of a Catholic childhood in a small town convinced him that 'in Ireland the Church *is* the people, and if the people seem priest-ridden to outsiders it is because they want them to be so', to which Murphy adds, 'My own experience certainly confirms this'.[24] Today, following clerical sex scandals and the development of a more secular and pluralistic Ireland, the critical voices have become much stronger and louder. But possibly Böll's deeply rooted connectedness with

---

[20] Im Gespräch: Böll mit Heinz Ludwig Arnold, Munich: Boorberg 1971, p. 21, quoted in: *Querschnitte – aus Interviews, Aufsätzen und Reden von Heinrich Böll*, edited by Viktor Böll and Renate Matthaei, Cologne: Kiepenheuer & Witsch 1977, p. 173.
[21] Interview with Erich Kock, WDR, 3rd TV channel, 10 April 1977, in: *Querschnitte*, p. 177.
[22] Cf. Heinrich Böll, Über Religion und Kirche – Interview von Robert Stauffer, broadcast on *Deutschlandfunk*, 12 January 1982, later published in *Konkret*, No. 6, 28 May 1982, pp. 115-117 under the title 'Die Kirche fault'. See also Heinrich Böll, *Werke – Interviews III 1980-1985*, Kölner Ausgabe volume 26, edited by Jochen Schubert, Cologne: Kiepenheuer & Witsch 2010, pp. 147-155, 147. In the following abreviated as *KA 26*.
[23] Cf. Heinrich Böll, Brendan Behan, in: *Werke 1963-65*, Kölner Ausgabe volume 14, edited by Jochen Schubert, Cologne: Kiepenheuer & Witsch 2002, pp. 401-404. In the following abreviated as *KA 14*.
[24] Dervla Murphy, *A Place Apart*, Harmondsworth: Penguin 1979, p. 25.

Catholicism can still be found in Ireland, but it has become a much more private relationship than what Böll found and rejoiced in on his first trip to Ireland in 1954.

CHAPTER THIRTEEN

RECEPTION IN GERMANY

> *This little masterpiece of a thoroughly humane way of writing transports its readers into a country of poverty, of anarchy, of Catholicism and of humour, in other words into a Böllian Utopia, which was different from normal day dreams insofar as it was reality.*
> —Alfred Andersch[1]

When examining the reception of the *Irish Journal* we need to bear in mind the existing general interest in Germany towards Ireland at the time. This needs to be seen in the context of a general interest in other countries, the rapid acceleration of tourist travel, especially to countries such as Italy and Spain that offered not only sunshine but less negative reaction towards German tourists than in those countries that had suffered more during the war. Ireland would have appealed in that context, too. As mentioned in chapter four, there was competition between the newspapers for Böll's Irish stories even before the first story appeared. Furthermore, articles appeared in several media outlets, often being reprinted in several newspapers or used as radio programmes, some read out by Böll himself. Other radio programmes were newly composed features on Ireland in their own right, for example one arranged by Alfred Andersch in May 1956. With this ongoing promotion of Böll's Irish writing for over two years, it is not surprising that the book enjoyed immediate attention. Accordingly, the reviews upon publication were numerous, literally hundreds can still be accessed in the Böll Archive in Cologne – and overwhelmingly positive. Again and again the book was seen as a declaration of love for

---

[1] Alfred Andersch, Einleitung, in Patrick Warner, *Irland*, Frankfurt/Berlin/Wien: Ullstein 1977, p. 9. [Dieses kleine Meisterwerk einer durch und durch humanen Schreibweise versetzte seine Leser in ein Land der Armut, der Anarchie, des Katholizismus und des Humors, mit anderen Worten in eine Böllsche Utopie, die sich von gewöhnlichen Wunschträumen aber dadurch unterschied, daß sie Wirklichkeit war], thanks to Ian Wallace for helping with the translation.

Ireland;[2] it was characterised as 'a poem dedicated to Ireland and the Irish, dedicated to poverty and belief, the bitter and the sweet'[3] and seen as 'without doubt the most beautiful tribute to this island of the saints that has ever been made by a German'[4]. Only a few reviews still refer to Ireland as a country 'we hardly know'[5] or state that Ireland was 'for us Germans [...] one of the least known countries of our continent';[6] though Böll is praised for 'discovering Catholic Ireland for German literature [...] one wonders how long it took for this discovery. Was England the wall that hid Ireland from us?'[7]. Again and again, one reviewer after another praised the language and style.

There were only a few dissenting voices. Interestingly, the two most notable ones came from reviewers who lived in Ireland or had spent a lot of time there, Enno Stephan and Georg Rosenstock. The latter though, despite his reservations, was clearly impressed with Böll's writing. Enno Stephan complains about a lack of explanations, the incorrect spelling of Guinness (lacking one 'n') and argues that Böll concentrates too often on the darker sides of Ireland. He even declares:

> [a]nd finally it is a hard decision, whether the following sentence on p. 72 [p. 52 in *Irish Journal*] is still poetic or simply pseudo-poetic word diarrhea: Limerick slept, under a thousand rosaries, under curses, floated

---

[2] See for example Robert Haerdter, Meerumglänzt, in: *Gegenwart* 12, No. 7, 1957, p. 210f.; Christian Ferber 'Mehr als eine Liebeserklärung', *Die Welt*, 2 June 1957; Franz Taucher, Geliebte grüne Insel, *Deutsche Zeitung und Wirtschaftszeitung*, 5 June 1957; Hans Dieter Hüsgen, Liebe zu einem kleinen Land, *Trierische Landeszeitung*, 28 July 1957; Friedrich Rasche, Große Liebe zur Grünen Insel – Heinrich Bölls *Irisches Tagebuch*, *Göttinger Presse*, 3 October 1957, *Braunschweiger Presse*, 2 October 1957 and *Hannoversche Presse* 27 October 1957.
[3] Curt Hohoff, Bölls *Irisches Tagebuch* – Ein Autor hat sich freigeschwommen, *Rheinischer Merkur*, 12 July 1957 (also IT Materialien, p. 166). This review, specifically Hohoff's remark that Böll almost overcame his resentment, that 'the smell of the scullery and cheap tobacco is gone', caused Böll to write the aforementioned 'Zur Verteidigung der Waschküchen' [In Defence of Sculleries] two years later.
[4] Georg Hermanowski, Die Insel der Heiligen, *Die Anregung* 9, 1957 (supplement), also IT Materialien, pp. 185f.
[5] Anon., *Autobus Kurier*, Heidelberg, VIII, 21 November 1957.
[6] Ha, *Delmenhorster Zeitung*, 29 June 1957.
[7] Wolfgang Grözinger, Der Roman der Gegenwart – Erzähler des Gemeinsamen, in: *Hochland*, 50, 1957/58, pp. 578-585, 578.

on dark beer; watched over by a single snow-white milk bottle, it was dreaming of Crimson Cloud and the crimson Sacred Heart.[8]

However, even Stephan is not entirely negative and finishes his review with the statement: 'Böll's 'Irisches Tagebuch' is a very nice book but for someone who knows Ireland it is also a very annoying book'.[9]

Böll's Ireland account also enjoyed critical acclaim by fellow writers.[10] German author Carl Zuckmayer called it one of the 'most beautiful and worthy books written in the last fifty years'[11] (conveniently printed on the back of all dtv paperback editions). Alfred Andersch, one of Germany's foremost writers after 1945, said: 'Apart from the Irish authors, there has been nobody in recent years who has influenced the image which we Germans have of Ireland and the Irish more than Böll'.[12] And another of the main German writers after the Second World War, Arno Schmidt, contemplated emigrating to Ireland and exchanged letters with Böll on the topic.[13]

In the GDR, the *Irish Journal* appeared in 1965; it was published by the Leipzig Insel publishing house and seems to have been read with enthusiasm. Christa Wolf, one of the foremost authors of the GDR, praised the book as having no national arrogance but rather something 'permanent' about it.[14] In one of the relatively few GDR books on Ireland,[15] Reinhard

---

[8] Enno Stephan, Heinrich Böll: Irisches Tagebuch, *dpa-Buchbrief*, 9 September 1957, in: Heinrich Böll, *Irisches Tagebuch*, Mit Materialien und einem Nachwort von Karl Heiner Busse, Cologne: Kiepenheuer & Witsch 1988, pp. 197-199, 199.

[9] ['Bölls *Irisches Tagebuch* ist ein sehr schönes Buch, aber für den, der Irland kennt, auch ein sehr ärgerliches Buch'], ibid. Less drastic but also critical of Böll's imagery is Rainer Nägele, *Heinrich Böll – Einführung in das Werk und die Forschung*, Frankfurt: Athenäum Fischer Taschenbuch 1976, pp. 134f.

[10] Cf. Holfter, *Erlebnis Irland*, pp. 147–154.

[11] Carl Zuckmayer, Gerechtigkeit durch Liebe, in: Marcel Reich-Ranicki (ed.), *In Sachen Böll*, Cologne: Kiepenheuer & Witsch 1968, pp. 67-71, 67.

[12] Alfred Andersch, Einleitung, in: Patrick Warner, *Irland*, p. 9.

[13] See G. Holfter, Fasziniert von Irland – eine Untersuchung über die Begeisterung für Irland bei deutschen Schriftstellern in den 50er bis 70er Jahren von Heinrich Böll bis Arno Schmidt, in: Hasso Spode (ed.), *Goldstrand und Teutonengrill - Kultur- und Sozialgeschichte des Tourismus in Deutschland 1945 bis 1989*, Berlin: Verlag für universitäre Kommunikation, Berichte und Materialien 1996, pp. 137-145.

[14] Cf. Karl Heiner Busse, Nachwort – Nicht Stolzenfieber noch Einbildungshusten, in: Heinrich Böll, *Irisches Tagebuch – Mit Materialien und einem Nachwort von Karl Heiner Busse*, Cologne: Kiepenheuer & Witsch 1988, pp. 222-233, 229.

Ulbrich's comprehensive and amusing *Irland – Inseltraum und Erwachen* (Ireland – Island Dream and Awakening), published in 1988, a year before the wall came down, a quote from Böll's book is used as a preface and numerous intertextual references remind the reader of the *Irish Journal*.[16] But Böll's impressions also had relevance for those who were not able to visit Ireland during GDR times and enabled them to nourish a dream of it which then actually came true 'after long years of state ordered abstinence from travels to the west' as Ramona Maurer writes in 1993:

> 'My' Ireland was born out of a mixture of Irish music, which is actually much more full of nuances than the continental pub visitor would believe. It was born out of eagerly soaking up the diary entries of the founding father of enthusiasm for Ireland, Heinrich Böll, and out of many failed attempts to read James Joyce's *Ulysses*.[17]

The book was also the impetus to travel to Ireland for other writers such as Erich Loest, who wrote a humorous account of how Ireland had changed in the thirty years since Böll's earliest visits; he is especially impressed by metre high fuchsia bushes and remarks that Ireland has obviously changed in the meantime.[18] Ralph Giordano takes a different approach in *Mein irisches Tagebuch* ('My Irish Journal').[19] Unlike Loest, who seems to be in Ireland mainly because of Böll, Giordano has his own ongoing passion for Ireland and knows the island, including its northern part, very well.[20] While he does choose the title 'My Irish Journal' obviously to refer to Böll and explicitly pays homage to him in the text (especially in the chapter on Achill), Giordano presents his picture without many comparisons or intertextual references: regarding the considerable part on Northern Ireland

---

[15] Cf. Holfter, *Erlebnis Irland*, pp. 249–263 and Frank Thomas Grub, ‚Bei mir regnet's schon': Irland aus DDR-Sicht, in: Monika Unzeitig (ed.), *Grenzen überschreiten – transitorische Identitäten*, Bremen: edition lumière 2011, pp. 67-80.
[16] Reinhard Ulbrich, *Irland - Inseltraum und Erwachen*, Leipzig: F.A. Brockhaus 1988.
[17] Ramona Maurer, Wo die felsigen Berge sanft in den Atlantik fallen – Impressionen aus einem Traumland, *Mitteldeutsche Zeitung*, 24 July 1993.
[18] Erich Loest, Schon kichert die nächste Wolke – Eine Irland-Reise – dreißig Jahre nach Heinrich Böll', *Süddeutsche Zeitung*, 19/20 October 1985.
[19] Giordano, *Mein irisches Tagebuch*, pp. 313-415.
[20] See also my article on the German perception of Northern Ireland, 'Nordirland hat ein Superklima' – Ein Beispiel der Darstellung und Beurteilung von Gewalt in der Literatur, in: Robert Weninger (ed.): *Gewalt und Kulturelles Gedächtnis. Repräsentationsformen von Gewalt in Literatur und Film seit 1945*, Tübingen: Stauffenburg 2005, pp. 207-215.

his description stands on its own anyway, as Böll never refers to the North in the *Irish Journal*.

Overall one can summarise that there is still considerable interest in the book in media and literary circles. Most numerous are references to Böll in Ireland and his *Irish Journal* in newspaper articles, especially on any anniversaries to do with Heinrich Böll.[21] In a quarter-annual German magazine, the *irland journal* (!), Heinrich Böll and references to the *Irish Journal* feature often.[22] In addition, even in the last fifteen years numerous radio programmes[23] and TV documentaries[24] have been produced. Especially the fiftieth anniversary of the book's publication in 2007 stirred up a lot of publicity,[25] supported strongly by Böll's publisher Kiepenheuer

---

[21] Some examples are: Walter Gerlach, Im Bild des Auslands das Heimatland getroffen: Auf den Spuren des *Irischen Tagebuchs* – 30 Jahre nach seinem ersten Erscheinen, *Börsenblatt* 36, 5 May 1987; Elfriede Pollety, '... wenn er auch nur 765 Meter hoch ist' – Wallfahrt auf den Croagh Patrick – Erinnerungen an Heinrich Bölls 'Irisches Tagebuch', *Straubinger Tagblatt*, 31 July 1993; Michael Netzhammer, Tagebuch einer anderen Zeit – Auf den Spuren des Schriftstellers Heinrich Böll: Eine Reise an die irische Westküste, *Badische Zeitung*, 31 May 1998.

[22] Christian Ludwig, editor and main stakeholder in *irland journal* who is also director of Gaeltacht Reisen, a German travel agent specialising in Ireland, has had a long interest in Heinrich Böll. He was the driving force behind the attempt to establish a Heinrich-Böll-Academy with the intention of creating a multipurpose conference centre and spa in Mulranny in the former Rail Hotel in the mid-1990s. While these plans were not realised he is still strongly committed to emphasising the importance of Heinrich Böll for Irish-German relations and German tourism to Ireland. A recent example is the travel brochure within the *irland journal* in the XXII, 1/11 2011 edition with the headline 'Mit Heinrich Böll nach Irland' [With Heinrich Böll to Ireland] – indicating the perceived added attraction of Ireland due to its connection with Böll.

[23] To mention only two of the more recent ones: Mosaik - Das Kulturmagazin: 50 Jahre "Irisches Tagebuch" von Heinrich Böll, *WDR* (West German Radio), 3 September 2007; Heinrich Bölls grüne Insel – Eine Spurensuche in Irland, *Nordwestradio*, 16 March 2008.

[24] The best so far is probably *Zwischen den Heimaten / A Second Home: Heinrich Böll in Ireland* by Wibke Kämpfer, see chapter eighteen Reverberation.

[25] See for example Uwe Wittstock, Wiedersehen mit Bölls grüner Insel, *Die Welt*, 15 March 2007, Christiane Zwick, Böll in Irland - Ansichten einer Insel, *Frankfurter Allgemeine Sonntagszeitung*, 22 April 2007 or Regine Reinhardt, Der Blick auf Böll hat Bestand – und verrät so viel über uns Deutsche, *irland journal* XVIII, 1.07 2007, pp. 138-143 (as well as a number of other Böll-related articles in the same edition).

& Witsch and also Tourism Ireland. The latter produced a CD *Grüß die Lieben in Mayo – Auf Heinrich Bölls Wegen durch Irland* with readings from the *Irish Journal* and an audio feature about Böll in Ireland by Jule Reiner. Kiepenheuer & Witsch reissued the *Irisches Tagebuch* with the epilogue 'Dreizehn Jahre später' (Thirteen years later) as previously published with the English edition, edited by René Böll and with an afterword by Jochen Schubert. It contains many photographs of the Böll family and information on the background to the creation of the book. This followed volume 10 of the *Kölner Ausgabe* published in 2005 which contains the *Tagebuch*.

A new development is that the interest in the *Irish Journal* is now also being maintained and extended by literary endeavours that are deeply influenced by it but attract a new readership which in turn finds its way back to Böll. The two main 'culprits' in this case are Irish author Hugo Hamilton with a book currently published only in German, *Die redselige Insel* (The Island of Talking. An Irish Journal Fifty Years after Heinrich Böll), and German *Spiegel* journalist Markus Feldenkirchen, with *Was zusammengehört* (What belongs together).

Hugo Hamilton's *Die redselige Insel – Irisches Tagebuch* is a unique update of Böll's book, not a recreation. Published in 2007 in time for the 50th anniversary of the publication of *Irisches Tagebuch* in the form of a renewed trip around Ireland in Böll's footsteps, Hamilton's book created a following and admiration in its own right. The cover tells us that fifty years on, Hamilton follows Böll's footsteps and travels around the green island, showing that though much has changed, much has stayed the same. For the benefit of the potential tourist, traditional images are then used to describe the Irish landscape, mixed in with some colourful descriptions that already give the reader an inkling that this book is not only a retelling of well-known stories but a new literary approach. Hamilton is a writer who, thanks to his German mother and a lot of time spent in Germany, commands a unique point of view among Irish writers – he is able to look at Ireland with both German and Irish eyes with some authority.

Quite apart from the many thematic and structural similarities that can be found between the books, the true legacy picked up by Hamilton is the literary approach, the rendering of remembered encounters as artistic vignettes, the transformation of reality into a poetic truth. Like Böll, he presents a country made up of individuals, their settings imaginatively sketched in with colourful strokes. He takes many pieces out of Böll's mosaic but forms his own, adding current Irish issues and his own mixed Irish-German heritage to his approach.

Another even more recent literary addition to the long list of publications influenced by the *Irish Journal*, is Markus Feldenkirchen's first novel *Was zusammengehört* (What belongs together), published in 2010. It has already enjoyed critical acclaim and created quite a stir in the Irish-German community in Germany, with readings in the Irish Embassy in Berlin and for Irish-German Societies. *Irish Times* journalist Derek Scally also mentioned it several times and interviewed the author.[26] Bringing together an Irish-German love story with German reunification, Catholic Ireland and the current banking crisis, with numerous references to Heinrich Böll thrown in, the novel does not lack ambitious frames of reference. A successful but lonely banker, Benedikt, is sent to Ireland to investigate rumours of reckless banking practices and is reminded of his first love by a letter (that he only opens at the very end of the novel). As a boy Benedikt had fallen in love with Victoria, an Irish girl he met on his class trip to Killarney in 1989, while the Berlin Wall comes down at home. The class trip is organised by teacher Hubert Boell (spelled with oe) who, as a dedicated Hibernophile at first seems to ironically play with the literary link, but soon afterwards Heinrich Böll and the *Irish Journal* feature explicitly, culminating in a crash course on Böll's influence:

> All Germans who since came to Ireland, had a copy of Böll's *Journal* with them, for many of them it was the reason that made them come to Ireland. They followed Böll's footprints and worshipped his book as others worshipped the Bible.[27]

The *Irish Journal* is referred to repeatedly and quotes from it are sprinkled throughout the text (even Böll's novel *The Clown* with its different versions has a key role). Indeed, the Irish heroine of the story, Victoria, Benedikt's first love, shows that the *Irish Journal* even impacted on her when she identifies herself with the woman portrayed in the chapter 'The Most Beautiful Feet in the World'. At their last meeting before her separation from Benedikt, Victoria declares somewhat dramatically: 'I want to be your Mary McNamara' (p. 296).

---

[26] Derek Scally, From Germany to Ireland with love – still, *Irish Times*, 2 December 2010. See also Derek Scally's Berlin Diary, *Irish Times*, 12 February 2011.
[27] Markus Feldenkirchen, *Was zusammengehört*, Zürich: Kein & Aber 2010, p. 40.

Accordingly it is not surprising that many literary reviews recommend the (re-)reading of the *Irish Journal*.[28]

Overall one can argue that the *Irish Journal* still functions in Germany as an almost automatic response to all things Irish – when 'Munich's smallest pub', O'Connelly'S (sic), was opened in May 2010 in one of the 1052 new flats at the Olympic Village in Munich, it started a programme with cultural activities on Wednesdays with a reading from Heinrich Böll's *Irisches Tagebuch*.[29] As this is an initiative by students and artists in their twenties one can safely say that even among the younger generation in Germany, Böll and the *Irish Journal* still have currency.

---

[28] See for example internet reviews such as Wolfgang Niedecken, Logbuch 2 October 2010, http://www.bap.de/start/aktuell/logbuch/berlin-brandenburger-tor or the review http://www.amazon.de/gp/cdp/member-reviews/A1DVHWQJR86JZ8 or Arno Hjuuge, 7 November 2010 http://www.amazon.de/gp/cdp/member-reviews/A1LSD44Q1YZ1HY?ie=UTF8&display=public&sort_by=MostRecent-Review&page=2 (all accessed 21 April 2011).

[29] http://oconnollys.wordpress.com/ (accessed 6 June 2010).

CHAPTER FOURTEEN

RECEPTION IN IRELAND

But what about the book's reception in Ireland? Hugo Hamilton has stated that while the Germans loved it, the Irish hated it.[1] Given Hamilton's own engagement with Böll this was possibly a tongue in cheek comment. There has been a very diverse and at times surprising reaction to the *Irish Journal* which shows no signs of letting up.

Initially, following the first publication of *Irisches Tagebuch* in 1957, feedback in Ireland was not very widespread, which is not surprising given the language barrier. There must, however, have been a certain awareness of both the author and his writing. On at least three occasions during 1956, short stories by Böll were translated and broadcast on BBC Radio Three and the Irish audience was informed about this in their daily newspapers.[2] There also seems to have been a preview, or reprint of one of the essays that appeared in the *Frankfurter Allgemeine Zeitung* (*FAZ*) in a bulletin issued by the German Embassy in Dublin. As indicated by Georg Rosenstock, it was read by many German-speaking Irish people, 'intelligent Dubliners (not really lacking in culture or taste)' and they were far from enthusiastic in their response.[3]

Furthermore, there had been a number of references to Böll and his writing on Ireland, notably in the *Irish Times*. As early as 1956 Desmond Fennell wrote from Germany, where he had met Böll, that judging from the frequency with which they had been mentioned to him in conversation, Böll's articles on Ireland in the *FAZ* had made a deep impression on many

---

[1] Hugo Hamilton, The loneliness of being German, *The Guardian*, 7 September 2004.
[2] Cf. *Irish Times*, 3 May 1956, p. 5: 'Dr. Murke's Collection of Silences' Short story by Heinrich Böll; *Irish Times*, 7 July 1956 (with programme for 8 July): 'The Man With The Knives', by Heinrich Böll, translated from German by Richard Graves; *Irish Times*, 8 November 1956, p. 6: 'The Balek's Weighing Machine': A short story by Heinrich Böll.
[3] Böll, *KA 10*, p. 694.

German readers.[4] Three years later Fennell mentions in his 'Letter from Germany' that *'Irisches Tagebuch* has been the most-read book on Ireland in Germany over the past two years'. Fennell also wrote a review about it in 1958 under the title 'Ireland in the Rain', referring to Böll's lengthy stays in Achill and the earlier publication of some chapters: 'Irish people living in Germany know that these articles have been very much talked about'. Fennell finds much to praise ('Details have been observed with great attention and the pictures painted have a wealth of accurate and evocative background. The style is often novelistic, symbols are used with effect') but also indicates that from the Irish perspective not everything was as would be expected:

> These pictures are for the most part true ones. It is no criticism of the book to remark that the Ireland shown here is the Ireland that interests German readers, the Ireland that is "different". This is inevitable. What is to the author's credit is that we find no romantic fantasy-making. But we might find the main themes overdrawn or in need of balancing out with other aspects and topics of Irish life which the author does not mention.

> The constant themes of the book are emigration, deserted country sides, the unimportance of time, the omnipresence of religion, rain. There is a lyrical composite portrait of Limerick city in the morning and evening. The Dublin of small lodging houses, crowded churches and the slums around St. Patrick's Cathedral is dealt with sensitively, perhaps a trifle morbidly. [...] The Ireland which this book shows has no fairs nor race meetings nor hurling finals, no prelates nor industrialists. It is a gentle, melancholy, shabby Ireland with religion everywhere, beautiful landscapes and men and women of character. In this book, as in his novels, the author shows preference for things and people that are marginal and never quite successful.[5]

Terence de Vere White, who was at the time the literary editor of the *Irish Times*, provides a further indication that the impact was far greater in Germany than in Ireland. In his report of his visit to Germany in 1967 he stresses that the one name that came up in every conversation was Heinrich Böll. Unfortunately de Vere White had not read anything by him, and worse still did not know about Böll's relationship to Ireland:

> What caused me no little embarrassment was having to confess that I had never read and did not know that he had written a book about Ireland. I had

---

[4] Desmond Fennell, 'Heinrich Böll in Ireland', *Irish Times*, 23 June 1956, p. 7.
[5] D[esmond] F[ennell], 'Ireland in the Rain', *Irish Times*, 19 April 1958, p. 8.

never seen it. He lives some of the year on Achill Island, where he has a house. Perhaps everyone knows this. It was news to me.[6]

And there were certainly negative responses, notably by Conor Cruise O'Brien, who in a review of the English translation in 1967 labelled the *Irish Journal* a 'ghastly little book' and accused Böll of idealising 'everything that is most wishy-washy in the Ireland he thinks he has seen', and – more understandably given the changes in the ten years since the first publication, but not quite fair in overlooking this – disapproves of the fact that Böll 'naturally laments any signs of progress'.[7] Sean O'Faolain, though, had a different perspective. He published his comments under the title 'A land that bewitches' in the *New York Book Review* on 13 August 1967, remarking: 'No man can jump off his own shadow, and no German can stop being a bit of a moralist and a bit of a sentimentalist ...'. His overall verdict was positive:

> A sympathetic, understanding, unprovocative book, the most pleasant compliment I can pay it – not one that can be paid to many travel books about my beloved country – is that it is likely to give equal pleasure to both, the -philes and the -phobes. And, as one would expect of so good a writer, it has Style.[8]

There have since been negative comments of the style of writing. Rachel McNicholl echoes earlier criticism of the writing style by Enno Stephan and argues that even if one could accept Böll's proclaimed innocence as excuse for 'rose-tinted perceptions of Irish piety and for romanticisation of many features of Irish life, however, it can hardly excuse the "gushiness" of the text at a linguistic or stylistic level'.[9] She critically contrasts his writing on post-war Germany ('extremely sparse, compact and unsentimentally moving') with that on Ireland where he 'waxes painfully lyrical and pathetic at times'.[10] In this context it should be noted that the *Irish Journal* received mixed reviews within English-language academic

---

[6] Terence de Vere White, 'Supply and Demand', *Irish Times*, 11 March 1967, p. 10.
[7] Conor Cruise O'Brien, In Quest of Uncle Tom, *New York Review of Books*, 14 September 1967.
[8] Sean O'Faolain, A land that bewitches, *New York Times Book Review*, 13 August 1967, pp. 3 and 30.
[9] Rachel McNicholl, Heinrich Böll's Other Ireland, in: John L. Flood (ed.), *Common Currency - Aspects of Anglo-German Literary Relations since 1945*, Stuttgart: Hans-Dieter Heinz 1991, pp. 71-86, 73f.
[10] Ibid., p. 74.

criticism in general. In *The Narrative Fiction of Heinrich Böll – Social conscience and literary achievement*, edited by the late British academic Michael Butler and published by Cambridge University Press, the *Irish Journal* is not mentioned even once.[11] James Reid maintains in his volume *Heinrich Böll: A German for his Time* that '*Irisches Tagebuch* today is remarkable mainly for its period charm'[12] and that Böll's analysis of Irish society 'was hardly profound, nor politically perceptive; it is meaningful only in the context of his attitude to his own country.'[13]

Yet there are many reviewers who took a more positive view. Northern Irish academic T.W. Woodland, who taught German at Magee College in Derry, praised the book a few years after the German publication, calling the *Irisches Tagebuch* 'a brilliant introduction to a fascinating subject'. He even acknowledges an increased awareness of his surroundings thanks to Böll: 'The 'Sicherheitsnadel' did not attract this reviewer's attention until after he had read Böll'.[14] Eda Sagarra shows how Böll's description fitted into the context of earlier travel literature of Ireland.[15] Fergus Pyle reviews a new edition of the *Irish Journal* in 1983[16] and approaches it

> with some scepticism and not a little wonderment to see how it would hold up since I read it years ago in a battered DTV copy, and I was astonished to find how much of the clearminded rhapsody I had forgotten, the entrancement and the inherent doubt. He was tolerant of our non-religious foibles to the point, sometimes, of ecstasy, but he wasn't carried away by them. The gentle humour and the poetry have worn well'.[17]

Pyle finds he reads the book with a certain nostalgia, provides an overview of themes and quotes a number of passages from the *Irish Journal* (implicitly not expecting readers to have read it) and reminds the reader

---

[11] Michael Butler (ed.), *The Narrative Fiction of Heinrich Böll – Social conscience and literary achievement*, Cambridge: CUP 1994.
[12] J.H Reid, *Heinrich Böll: A German for his time*, Oxford: Berg 1988, p. 115.
[13] Ibid., p. 117.
[14] T.W. Woodland, *Irisches Tagebuch* by Heinrich Böll, in: *German Life and Letters* 13/1 (1959), pp. 62-63.
[15] Eda Sagarra, Die 'grüne Insel' in der deutschen Reiseliteratur. Deutsche Irlandreisende von Karl Gottlob Küttner bis Heinrich Böll, in: Hans-Wolf Jäger (ed.), *Europäisches Reisen im Zeitalter der Aufklärung*, Heidelberg: Winter 1992, pp. 183-195.
[16] Heinrich Böll, *Irish Journal: A Traveller's Portrait of Ireland*, Secker and Warburg.
[17] Fergus Pyle, Ireland trough German eyes, *Irish Times*, 16 April 1983.

'that the benighted land that Boll (sic) saw was distilled through a kind of poetic instinct that enhanced what was before his eyes.'[18]

But it is not only journalists and academics who continue to refer to Böll. Possibly quite surprising is the strong awareness of Böll and his *Irish Journal* among Irish politicians and diplomats. At the 9th Limerick Conference in Irish-German Studies in 2007 on 'Heinrich Böll and Ireland – 50 years *Irisches Tagebuch*' contributors included the then Minister for the Environment, Heritage and Local Government John Gormley, Dr Martin Mansergh, Fianna Fáil TD as well as Irish diplomats David Donoghue and Seán Ó'hUiginn, the latter three contributing to the academic publication that arose from the conference.[19] Accordingly it is not unexpected to find also Irish President Mary McAleese referring to Heinrich Böll on a state visit to Germany in 2008: 'In the mid-twentieth century Heinrich Böll fired the German imagination with his beautiful word-sketches of the west of Ireland'.[20]

What about the reception of the *Irish Journal* among Irish writers or artists? Is there evidence that Böll and the *Irish Journal* spurred artistic imagination among Irish writers, comparable to the German situation? Again, a diverse picture emerges. Following on from Sean O'Faolain's overall positive verdict, Eilis Dillon found Böll's description of Ireland also attractive and thought he had found 'the exact refuge he needed' and 'where his temperament is matched by most of his neighbours: material matters are not taken too seriously but ideas can keep people talking until

---

[18] Ibid. Pyle is also surprised that the new edition does not include further updating than the Epilogue from 1967 and adds: 'The uninstructed reader (I mean, of course, in the wider audience overseas) would have to search for clues that the idiosyncratic and exotic place that he describes is as dead as Adenauer's Germany or the France of General de Gaulle'.
[19] See Martin Mansergh, Heinrich Böll and Ireland. 50 Years Irisches Tagebuch: Political Connections and Developments in Comparison, pp. 9-11; David Donoghue, Heinrich Böll and a Changing Ireland, pp. 33-36 and Seán Ó'hUiginn, Heinrich Böll's Irisches Tagebuch Fifty Years Later, pp. 37-42, all in: G. Holfter (ed.), *Irish-German Literary and Cultural Connections. 50 Years Heinrich Böll's 'Irisches Tagebuch'*, Irish-German Studies V, Trier: WVT 2009. Likewise the current Ambassador Dan Mulhall has a keen interest in Böll and the role of the *Irish Journal* as well as expertise in Irish-German historic links.
[20] Remarks Mary McAleese at an Irish community reception, Berlin, 26 February 2008, http://www.president.ie/index.php?section=5&speech=474&lang=ire (accessed 21 April 2011).

the dawn'.[21] This feeling that Böll and the Irish were close to being soul mates however was not shared often. In Brian Friel's short story 'The Saucer of Larks', two Germans, a "Herr Grass" and "Herr Henreich" (not too difficult to read as references to Günter Grass and Heinrich Böll) are notably different in temperament to the Irish sergeant accompanying them.[22] Irish poet Michael O'Loughlin also shows diametrically opposed experiences in his poem entitled 'Heinrich Böll in Ireland', written in 1985, which was included in the 1996 anthology *Another Nation*:

> We slept through it. A stray bomber,
> A black sheep strayed from the pack
> Came crackling in out of the watching darkness
> Later, some stumbled across our shores
> In search of a green poultice
> For wounds we couldn't have understood.
> There, at last, a small destiny, ours.
> This also; the skyways criss-crossed
> By peaceful jets, their passengers reading
> In magazines about the
> Most profitable
> Industrial
> Location
> In Europe[23]

O'Loughlin manages in very few words to create a 50-year overview of the most important German-Irish links. Böll, though only mentioned in the title, serves as a prominent German link to Ireland. O'Loughlin invokes the horrors of the Second World War, through which Ireland slept in an apparently innocent neutral slumber, except for the 'stray' German bombs on Dublin (Belfast did not fare so lightly). He portrays Ireland as a place

---

[21] Eilis Dillon, The urgency of Heinrich Böll, in: *Commonweal*, 9 March 1973, p. 13, cf. Caítriona Budhlaeir, Critical and experimental approaches to translations of Heinrich Böll's prose into Irish, MA thesis University of Limerick 1996, pp. 34f.
[22] Brian Friel, The Saucer of Larks, *The New Yorker*, 24 September 1960, p. 109. There are not really any intertextual references to the *Irish Journal* or Böll's relationship with Ireland. Friel only playfully uses the names and describes the Germans as employees of the German War Graves Commission, in Ireland to find the grave of a German airman, killed during the war, preoccupied with their duty rather than their beautiful surroundings, in contrast to the more perceptive Irish Garda.
[23] Michael O'Loughlin, *Another Nation*, Dublin: New Island Books 1996, p. 28 (the poem was first published in *Diary of a Silence*, Ravenart Press 1985). Thanks to Dermot Bolger for referring me to this poem.

of shelter for Germans such as Heinrich Böll, who were trying to find a place and destiny free of guilt, but he also heralds the changes that Ireland underwent since the 1950s and to which Böll also referred to in 'Epilogue - Thirteen years later'.

In a similar vein but far more critically, Jim Smyth writes in his introduction to the Irish artist Dermot Seymour for his entry in the 2005 volume *Contemporary Art from Ireland* under the title 'A load of old Boellix':

> Heinrich Böll has a lot to answer for. Böll discovered an Ireland in the 1950s and 1960s which probably never existed; or if it did it was an Ireland the Irish were trying to forget. But it was an Ireland the Germans desperately wanted to believe in, a place, in the words of Böll's *Irisches Tagebuch*, where they could "play truant" from Europe, among the "bog farmers, peat cutters and fishermen". Things have changed and Dermot Seymour knows it. His west of Ireland is one of sulphurous skies, dazed and bewildered animals and unstable landscapes.
> Heinrich would not like it.[24]

Here the *Irish Journal* seems to be viewed as a catalyst for the creation of art out of sheer opposition. Overall though we find there has been no shortage of references and articles to Böll and his *Irish Journal* in the Irish media and among writers. Francis Stuart believed that Böll was well known in Ireland due to his Irish Journal and his presidency of the International PEN and that his recognition as a Catholic writer may have helped, too[25] - but more often than not, references to Böll pointed to the large impact he had in Germany with his writing on Ireland. *Irish Times* journalist Derek Scally wrote somewhat ambiguously that 'Heinrich Böll's slim volume of sly beauty has frozen an ideal of Ireland in millions of German minds'.[26] Don Morgan, son of the late comedian Dermot Morgan and himself a result of an Irish-German union, wrote an article about his German grandparents where Böll also features:

---

[24] Jim Smyth, A load of old Boellix, in: *Contemporary Art from Ireland*, edited by European Central Bank, Frankfurt 2005, p. 62.
[25] Francis Stuart, Shadow of the Nazis, in: *Sunday Tribune*, 3 March 1985. He himself seems to have made contact with Böll already in the mid-1950s. Stuart's papers in the Southern Illinois University Carbondale Special Collections contain a letter from Böll to Stuart from 1955, expressing his hope to see him in Cologne.
[26] Derek Scally, 'Berlin as the new Achill – despite Böll', *Irish Times*, 1 March 2008, p. 15.

His trip to Ireland had one far-reaching consequence. Many of the young in post-war Germany were inspired by the images of an uncomplicated idyll in the north Atlantic. Armed with dog-eared copies of the book, they followed Böll to Ireland, and have continued to do so. Many, particularly in the 1970s, married Irish men and women, staying here for good.[27]

There remains a strong awareness of Böll and his impact. Böll's depiction of Ireland merited entries in such standard reference works as J.J. Lee's *Ireland 1912–1985* and Peter Somerville-Large's *Irish Voices: 50 years of Irish life*,[28] who used it to demonstrate the effects of censorship and the perception of Hitler in parts of Irish society. But there seems uncertainty whether this awareness extents to the general Irish readership. In an *Irish Times* article in 2002 on Achill Island by Brendan Ó Cathaoir one can find a detailed introduction to Böll himself and his *Irish Journal* (Brendan Ó Cathaoir calls it 'an affectionate picture of the country in the mid-1950s'),[29] and Böll becomes a role model. Ó Cathaoir expresses his hope that 'the maximum number of emigrants or their children will return, and that those fortunate enough to own a holiday home will develop some of Böll's appreciation of this enchanting island'.[30] However, given the detailed introduction to Böll that seems to have been necessary, one is left to assume that to most Irish readers Heinrich Böll was only peripherally known, if at all.

Probably the same can be said about the translation of the *Irish Journal* into Irish that was undertaken by Seán Sabhaois and appeared in 1988 as *Dialann as Éirinn*. The translation has not met with critical approval. Alan Titley maintains it 'must surely be, at least in parts, one of the most execrable translations ever made'.[31] Caítriona Budhlaeir echoes this

---

[27] Don Morgan: An Irishman's Diary. In: *Irish Times*, 21 July 2010, p. 15. Morgan also went around Dublin with the German dtv edition of *Irisches Tagebuch*, retracing the steps of Böll, gaining enough material for an article of almost a whole page including five photos of himself (and one of Böll) at different places of relevance in the book. See Don Morgan, In The Rare Old Times, *Irish Examiner*, 21 May 2010, p. 17. Thanks to Hermann Rasche for this reference.
[28] J.J. Lee, *Ireland 1912-1985*, Cambridge: CUP 1989; Peter Somerville-Large, *Irish Voices – 50 years of Irish life 1916-1966*, London: Chatto & Windus 1999.
[29] Brendan Ó Cathaoir, An Irishman's Diary, *Irish Times*, 17 June 2002, p. 13.
[30] Ibid.
[31] Alan Titley, Turning Inside and Out: Translating and Irish 1950-2000, in: *The Yearbook of English Studies*, vol 35, 2005, pp. 312-322, 317.

assessment: 'The translation of *Irisches Tagebuch* is essentially quite weak and shows lack of experience on the part of the translator'.[32]

Arguably, a new English translation would also be desirable. Irish academic Eda Sagarra asks: 'Why don't we see it [the *Irish Journal*] in English translation in our bookshops? How many people have actually read it?' and answers herself that the problem has at least partly to do with the quality and availability of translations.[33]

To a certain extent this is also the answer to the question of how the *Irish Journal* has been received in Ireland. It has received a lot of attention, both positive and negative, and it does appear frequently as a frame of reference. Not only Irish journalists, writers and academics but also diplomats and academics engage with it, and it is likely to have ongoing relevance. But it does not have the appeal of a bestseller among the general public as it does in Germany. A new translation might alleviate this somewhat as the translation by Leila Vennwitz now seems at times dated and the American spelling further indicates a translational shift, removing the description further from the direct experience of the Irish reader. But a number of other aspects are as likely to play a role in this context.

Irish readers are unlikely to find what German readers and tourists seemingly still succeed in finding, because for them the overall happy and

---

[32] Caítriona Budhlaeir, Critical and experimental approaches to translations of Heinrich Böll's prose into Irish, MA thesis University of Limerick 1996, p. 86. Her assessment of other translations of Böll's works (such as Klopfzeichen) by Gabriel Rosenstock, Georg Rosenstock's son, is far more positive. As part of her MA, Budhlaeir translated Böll's 'Anekdote zur Senkung der Arbeitsmoral' herself. Regarding Böll's reception in Irish also see Éilis Ni Anluain, Ceacht Heinrich Böll dúinn, in: *Irish Times*, 20 June 2007.

[33] Eda Sagarra, Heinrich Böll – Father of German Tourism in Ireland, in: G. Holfter (ed.), *Irish-German Literary and Cultural Connections. 50 Years Heinrich Böll's 'Irisches Tagebuch'*, Irish-German Studies V, Trier: WVT 2009, pp. 13-17, 17. See also Florian Krobb and Sabine Strümper-Krobb, Übersetzung und Rückübersetzung: Bölls *Irisches Tagebuch*, in: Gisela Holfter, Hans-Walter Schmidt-Hannisa (eds): *German-Irish Encounters – Deutsch-irische Begegnungen* Irish-German Studies 2, Trier: WVT 2007, pp. 185-195.

On the positive side it should be noted that in May 2011 a new edition was published by American publisher Melville with an insightful introduction by Hugo Hamilton, which at least makes the translation by Leila Vennewitz easily available again.

simple life portrayed does not present an alternative in the same way as it has done to German readers – and the impressions of the Irish readers (whether personal memory or historical awareness) of the times described some fifty years ago are probably quite different anyway. They are also unlikely to develop the same emotional attachment that so many German readers in Böll's footsteps clearly have, both to the *Irish Journal* and to Ireland, because a description of one's own country is of course interesting but it is interesting because one wants to see how one is portrayed. The writing style can cause delight, fond memories of earlier times can be evoked, but in the end for the Irish reader his or her own assessment of Ireland is always going to be the decisive one and Böll's viewpoint is correspondingly less persuasive. Other places are arguably always more interesting than one's own backyard and one's own history, they are more likely to allow dreams and the sense of the possibility of freedom from aspects of home one has become disillusioned with.

CHAPTER FIFTEEN

THE *IRISH JOURNAL* IN CONTEXT

Sheer numbers demonstrate and help explain the huge influence of the *Irisches Tagebuch*. The dtv paperback edition alone has sold 1.3 million copies to date and the *Irisches Tagebuch* holds the enviable position of being the first volume in this hugely successful series.[1] It also continues to be among the three best selling books by Böll.[2] Taking into account the editions of his publisher Kiepenheuer & Witsch and special art publications,[3] it seems safe to estimate more than two million copies have been sold in German alone. The book has been translated into at least 17 languages.[4]

---

[1] dtv, the successful 'Deutscher Taschenbuch Verlag' (German Paperback Publisher) was founded in 1961. Böll's publisher, Kiepenheuer & Witsch was part of the new publishing house and in charge of dtv was Heinz Friedrich, one of Böll's oldest friends in the business (for more details see *KA 13*, p. 271). All this certainly helped in *Irisches Tagebuch* being chosen as the very first volume of the dtv series.

[2] Thanks to Mr Rudolf Frankl, director of marketing, Deutscher Taschenbuch Verlag Munich, for providing this normally well guarded information. He also confirmed my guess that the *Irisches Tagebuch* is – with the exception of Böll's *Ansichten eines Clowns* and *Die verlorene Ehre der Katharina Blum,* which are often compulsory texts for school children in Germany – Böll's best selling book, by a considerable margin (emails 6 July 2005 and 19 March 2008). In 2011 the publishing house celebrated its 50th anniversary by taking Austrian, German and Swiss booksellers on a trip to Ireland, as the *Irisches Tagebuch* was not only the first book in its programme but is now also the best selling one. See Hauptverband des Österreichischen Buchhandels, Mit dtv nach Irland, 9 June 2011, http://www.buecher.at/show_content.php?sid=94&detail_id=4296.

[3] For example the edition of *Irisches Tagebuch* with water colour paintings by the internationally renowned German artist Walter Dahn, Cologne: Kiepenheuer & Witsch 1996.

[4] Among them are Czech, Danish, Finnish, Norwegian, Swedish, French, Dutch, Italian, Spanish, Turkish, Chinese, Catalan, Hungarian, Polish, Bulgarian and, of course as mentioned, Irish. Information thanks to Nicole Koch, Kiepenheuer & Witsch, 9 May 2008.

So what is it - a typical Böll book, a typical (German) Ireland book, a book about Germany – or a book unlike any other? Regarding the position in Böll's oeuvre, Bernd Balzer, the editor of the first edition of Böll's works, called the *Irish Journal* a unique phenomenon or a 'Unikat'.[5] However, other literary scholars have expressed the opinion that it is entirely congruent in terms of topics and style with his other works.[6] So where does the *Irish Journal* fit in the context of Böll's other work, where can we find similarities, what is different and how can we characterise his writing about Ireland? Arguably, one could draw a line from his early writings and his letters home from the war, to the *Irish Journal*. All of these writings sprang foremost from an urge to write for the enjoyment of writing and the need to communicate. These elements still played a crucial role later when he started writing full-time, but what also became part of his work was a missionary aspect that concentrated not only on religion (which had been present from his earliest writing as a teenager), but was born out of his experiences during the war and the political environment afterwards. Both his background and these experiences contributed strongly to his development into the writer who coined the slogan 'Einmischung erwünscht', which is only inadequately translated as 'involvement desired'. This involvement meant for Böll a lifetime of writing – about Germany and for Germany. When he said once in an interview that Ireland was his second home he qualified that immediately and argued that there was no such thing as a second home, ultimately he always remained a tourist as the difference between being at home somewhere or not was precisely whether one was involved in everything or not.[7]

Guilt and innocence are intriguing concepts in this context as well. Guilt especially has proved to be a strong catalyst for many German authors since World War II. Böll did not believe in collective guilt, but in the epilogue to the *Irish Journal* 'Thirteen years later' written in 1967, he indicates that both innocence and guilt could initiate writing, but the innocence he had regarding Ireland had gone, he now knows 'a certain amount, one might even say a lot, about it, yet it is not by any means enough; my innocence is a thing of the past, and still my guilt, my knowledge, are inadequate.'[8] Regarding Germany, this was different.

---

[5] Balzer, *Das literarische Werk Heinrich Bölls,* p. 213. Zorach argues in 'Two Faces of Erin' that it occupies 'a somewhat ambiguous place in Böll's oeuvre', p. 124.
[6] Cf. Robert C. Conard, *Heinrich Böll,* p. 79.
[7] Cf. Böll, Linder, *Drei Tage im März,* p. 60.
[8] Böll, *Irish Journal,* pp. 122f.

Böll actually wrote at length about other countries – not as a writer but as a correspondent from the war, mostly to his fiancée and later wife Annemarie. Some of Böll's descriptions of his French surroundings while stationed there as a soldier probably bear most resemblance to his writing in the *Irish Journal*, though on a far smaller scale and lacking the cohesion and interwovenness of his Irish writing. But they do contain precise images, already more than mere outlines.[9]

In the *Irish Journal* the sketches have became an artform, to some extent literally so that there is no other work by him that uses colours to the same extent, no other work in which more or less unconnected vignettes present a larger image of another country. Böll presents astute descriptions of important parts of everyday Irish life – conversations with poetic policemen about the weather, the experience of the sometimes 'absolute, magnificent and frightening' Irish rain, the pubs as social meeting places, skeletons of abandoned villages as witnesses of poverty and emigration amidst peaceful surroundings. His observations take the form of personal encounters and adventures, a few times also as stories about individuals such as Mary McNamara in chapter ten, Seamus in chapter thirteen and Siobhan in chapter fourteen, illustrating particular aspects of Irish life through intimate and sympathetic comments, crucially hardly ever in broadsweeping statements about 'the Irish', a term used only a handful of times and then not with reference to fixed characteristics but in the context of holding a world record in tea drinking (p. 2) or the habit of adding 'God help us' whenever Mayo is mentioned (p. 25). The large spectrum of captured vignettes presents a very colourful imagery, including such darker explorations as the evening episode in Limerick, and all delivered with powerful poignancy, in a simple but never simplistic style.

The *Irish Journal* is strongly rooted in Irish geographic, literary and social experiences, while not disguising Böll's particular German perspective and background. Emigration, one of the main themes that is contained in almost every chapter, was clearly not one of the foremost topics in Germany (and certainly not for economic reasons) but indisputably a situation that very many Irish families of the time had to face. All his later literary works were firmly set in concrete, contemporary Germany – unlike the timeless Ireland he presents in the *Irish Journal* – and generally

---

[9] See William O'Keeffe, Western Approaches: Heinrich Böll in Normandy and Ireland, in: Gisela Holfter (ed.) *Heinrich Böll's 'Irisches Tagebuch' in Context*, WVT: Trier 2010, pp. 89-98.

contain clear criticism of German society and the clergy. In Ireland, being a guest, he felt he had no right to be critical.

The mixture of fictional (see for example the chapter on 'The Dead Redskin of Duke Street') and non-fictional elements also sets the *Irish Journal* apart. In this context a statement made during the famous lecture series Böll gave in 1964, *Frankfurter Vorlesungen*, is of special interest as he referred specifically to the *Irish Journal*:

> You are welcome to ask questions regarding my own work but I am not sure whether that is really of interest to you; while writing there is a mix of consciousness and unconsciousness, in constantly changing relations – and when I presented the over fifty meanings of 'poein' this wasn't a philological joke – it is not only not that easy but actually nearly impossible to give reliable information about the development of a story or a novel – it is not even possible when the writing has a seemingly – I stress seemingly – real background – as for example my book on Ireland – especially then you are dealing with difficulties that are comparable with the ones you have when dealing with painting portraits.[10]

Taking the old question of fact and fiction out of its usual literary context and putting it into the realm of art is once more a reminder of Böll's main aim – to produce a piece of art – and nowhere in his written work more than in the *Irish Journal* did he come closer to portraying something as if with the stroke of a brush. We should also remember that while Böll was not only a Nobel Prize winning novelist, he also wrote numerous though lesser known, essays, speeches and journalistic articles. Yet, this particular colourful blend of fact and fiction is not found elsewhere in Böll's work. So overall, the verdict is that, yes, in many ways the *Irish Journal* is something quite special among Böll's books.

---

[10] Commentary *Frankfurter Vorlesungen* (1964), *KA 14* (pp. 139-201), pp. 567-568, 568 [Sie dürfen mir getrost Fragen stellen, was meine eigene Arbeit betrifft, aber ich weiss nicht, ob das für Sie interessant ist; es mischt sich beim Schreiben Bewusstes mit Unbewusstem, mischt sich (in) ständig wechselndem Mischungsverhältnis – und wenn ich Ihnen die mehr als fünfzig Bedeutungen von poein aufzählte, so war das kein philologischer Scherz – es ist nicht nur nicht so einfach, sondern fast unmöglich, gewissenhaft Auskunft über die Entstehung einer Geschichte oder eines Romans zu geben – es ist nicht einmal möglich, wenn das Geschriebene einen scheinbar – ich betone scheinbar – realen Hintergrund hat – wie etwas mein Buch über Irland – gerade dann entstehen Schwierigkeiten, denen vergleichbar, die beim Porträtmalen entstehen].

But the *Irish Journal* is not unique only among Böll's work, it is also unique among German-speaking descriptions of Ireland. There is certainly no shortage of such travelogues about encounters with Ireland and the Irish. The book's outstanding success sets it apart, starting right from the point of publication and continuing through more than five decades, an appeal unblemished despite all the changes Ireland – and Germany – have gone through.

As we saw before, the usual Irish attractions for German visitors, music and literature, both by writers such as Yeats, Swift and Wilde and in the form of fairy tales, are not presented in the usual travel literature fashion. The special position of Böll's *Irish Journal* becomes even more obvious if one follows John Hennig's dictum that the history of Ireland's place in German literature is of interest from three principal view-points: 1) the preservation in Central Europe of the Irish missionary and monastic tradition; 2) the foundation of German interest in the language and the antiquities of Ireland; 3) the development of German political interest in modern Ireland.[11] This lists historical, academic and political contact in the form of religious mission, Celtic studies and Ireland as a propaganda tool for Germany during the wars. Again, none of these three traditional stalwarts is pivotal to Böll's portrayal. While Böll does mention the Irish missionaries as those who made Ireland 'the glowing heart of Europe' in 'Arrival II' there are no further references to St. Kilian, St. Gall, St. Columban or the numerous other Irish monks and missionaries on the continent. There is no discernible interest in the Irish language and no political interest. From the tradition of German travel descriptions of Ireland both the romantic tradition, including the strong emphasis on Irish fairy tales, and the ubiquitous references to England and Irish history are missing.

Though the form, based upon his travels and the descriptions he gives of them, clearly belongs to the genre, it also presents a very unusual version of travel literature, changing the format of the narration and dispensing with a clear temporal or spatial progression (with the exception of the opening and closing chapters). The literary claim as well as the lack of interest in touristic descriptions are key to the success and resonance of the book.[12] By combining individual stories that were nearly all already

---

[11] John Hennig, Mile-stones of German-Irish Literary Relations, in: G. Holfter, H. Rasche (eds), *Exil in Irland – John Hennigs Schriften zu deutsch-irischen Beziehungen*, Trier: WVT 2002, pp. 174-177, 174.
[12] See also Zorach, Two Faces of Erin, p. 130: 'his journal, while not a perfectly

acclaimed in their own right, thereby allowing the reader to pick up the book at different chapters and never claiming to portray a complete picture, Böll has managed to allow his readers the space to add their own impressions. Thus, readers through the decades can contemporise his portrayal with their own experiences and conceptions. This is helped further by the concentration to a considerable extent on everyday life, as seen by an outsider from Germany. This concentration on everyday life in the *Irish Journal* was an unusual feature for a travelogue in the 1950s, but it still serves German tourists today as an introduction to Ireland, even if Ireland has changed nearly beyond recognition in the more than fifty years since the texts were written.

As a direct comparison to the *Irish Journal*, it is illuminating to look at a 'counter product' – Irish author and poet Monk Gibbon's *Western Germany*, published in 1955.[13] Starting from the Preface, where he quotes Michel de Montaigne on travels in Germany, Gibbon proceeds to explain that he hopes to spare the reader the regret expressed by Montaigne in the 16th century by providing what the former had lacked – a book telling the reader about the best things to be seen. Gibbon continues to quote other famous travel writers such as François-René de Châteaubriand. He also includes references to German literature such as Goethe's *Werther* in the context of visiting Frankfurt and the Goethehaus, describes famous paintings and generally provides a learned introduction to a different culture – precisely what Böll does not do.

The final question that remains is whether the *Irish Journal* is foremost a book about Germany or about Ireland – here it might be useful to look at

---

sober account of sights and sounds of Ireland, remains a travel book, still far removed from fabulous yarns like 'Der tote Indianer'. Through the proverbial broadening acquired in travel, the narrator has expanded the contours of his own writing; still venturing beyond intial attempts to read isolated signs and landmarks, he learns to put these signs together into coherent wholes, creating contexts and connections from his own imagination where none offers itself to his immediate perception. In thus creating narrative continuity out of splinters of personal experience, Böll has overcome the chaotic and episodic quality plaguing many travel books, while still retaining the rich diversity and dynamism which marks the best travel literature. The reader, as he travels through the text, is led to expand his own perspective on writing, to abandon limited notions about the travel sketch, story, or journal, and to learn to read a new textual geography while he is learning to understand a foreign land.'

[13] I would to like to thank Dan Mulhall for referring me to Monk Gibbon's account of Germany.

the reception of the *Irish Journal* also in countries other than Ireland and Germany. Overall reviews were generally positive and the frame of reference overwhelmingly Ireland. In his review French translator and academic Henri Plard places Böll in the context of a broad spectrum of European and Irish writers, mentioning Joyce, Synge, Ernst Jünger, Kurt Tucholsky and Camille Bourniquel and even John Ford's film *The Quiet Man*, and praises Böll's slim volume as one from which more can be learnt than from many pretentious in-depth studies.[14] Only a qualified welcome came from the *Allgemeine Zeitung* in Windhoek, however, with its criticism of Böll's 'unmotivated jibes at Hitler and National Socialism'. The reviewer declared that he did not mean to defend the latter but he nevertheless found it annoying to have to read about it constantly and that Böll should rather have mentioned the Irish-English relationship, if any such thing at all.[15] It seems that the urge of revisionism was strongest in the former colonies – or could just be expressed more freely there.

Walter Widmer (father of Swiss writer Urs Widmer) refers in the *Basler Nachrichten* to the earlier 'known' chapters and readings on the radio by Böll in the previous winter which enhanced his anticipation of the book. He calls the book admirable, beautifully narrated and a poetic piece of art 'filled into the finest details with warmth and humanity'.[16] Another Swiss review also praises the book:

> Poor, happily unhappy Ireland, place of escape for reflection, country where the silence is paid for with poverty, where the road still belongs to the pedestrian, country full of human character – a poet has created a monument for you out of colourful, well placed and warm words. He might have only seen one side of this diverse country – but what he saw has become a precious gift for us.[17]

In the US, a country with its own perception of and a strong link with Ireland, the reception was generally very positive and reviews surprisingly numerous (in fact, the reviews of Sean O'Faolain and Conor Cruise O'Brien already quoted both appeared in New York rather than Dublin). In R.L. White's study *Heinrich Böll in America 1954-1970* one can find

---

[14] Henri Plard, Heinrich Bölls *Irisches Tagebuch*, *Allemagne d'aujoud'hui* 5, No. 4/5 (1957), pp. 220f.

[15] Anon., 'Heinrich Böll *Autobus Kurier*, Heidelberg, VIII, 21 November 1957 *Irisches Tagebuch*', *Allgemeine Zeitung* (Windhoek), 28 July 1957, IT mit Materialien, pp. 187f.

[16] Walter Widmer, Ein bedeutsames Tagebuch, *Basler Nachrichten*, 7 June 1957.

[17] Anon., Das Land ohne Selbstmörder, in: *Atlantis*, 29/7, Zurich, July 1957.

extracts of thirty-nine reviews that appeared between 9 July and 26 November 1967 in US-based newspapers.[18] In the Böll Archive in Cologne there are even more. In these reviews Böll is praised for 'capturing the quality of the Irish scene in an unsusual manner, partly because of his alien outlook, but largely because of the imaginative quality of his writing' despite the subject being so familiar.[19] His *Irish Journal* is announced as 'the next best thing to a visit. If you are fortunate enough to be planning a trip to the Emerald Isle, Mr. Böll can tell you what travel agents don't; if you've been to Ireland, the book will tell you what you missed'.[20] Under the telling title of 'German writes a Love Letter to Ireland' a review appeared by a critic, who had obviously travelled in Ireland himself around the same time as Böll, had written about it himself and was therefore especially qualified to judge the other author's work. He humbly and humorously admits:

> Sometimes a man sighs ruefully over the fact that he was behind the door when the talent was passed out. Take my case, for instance, and that of Heinrich Böll. In the early 1950's we virtually toured Ireland together. It is possible that we passed each other on the streets in Dublin or Belfast. But out of this visit Böll, a fine German novelist, extracted this beautiful and evocative 'journal' while I managed only a possibly presentable piece. Yet, I am glad that Böll did for he has written one of the saddest and happiest books about Ireland that we have had in decades'.[21]

Other review titles equally indicate strongly that the book was seen almost exclusively as a book about Ireland and appreciated accordingly: 'Nostalgia for Erin',[22] 'The Mystic and Legendary Irish', [23] 'A Sensitive Diary of Timeless Ireland'[24]. Böll's partiality to his subject is frequently noted: 'Heinrich Böll [...] has written a love letter to Ireland [...] [he] writes with

---

[18] R.L. White, *Heinrich Böll in America 1954-1970*, Hildesheim: Georg Olms 1979, pp. 122-137.
[19] Richard M. Kain, Heinrich Böll on Ireland, *Louisville Courier Journal*, 20 August 1967, in: White, p. 130.
[20] James H. Henson, The Auld Sod, *Tulsa World*, 3 September 1967, in: White, p. 133.
[21] V.P.H., German writes a Love Letter to Ireland, *Omaha World-Herald*, 23 July 1967, in: White, p. 124.
[22] Larry Rumley, Nostalgia for Erin, *Seattle Daily Times*, 6 August 1967.
[23] Alfred Kay, The Mystic and Legendary Irish, *San Francisco Examiner & Chronicle*, 6 August 1967.
[24] C.A.B., A Sensitive Diary of Timeless Ireland, *Buffalo Evening News*, 29 July 1967, in: White, p. 124.

humor, compassion and perspecuity',[25] 'This man knows his Ireland and Irish history. He is obviously familiar with Irish and English literature. And, above all, he is touched, nostalgically, by the simplicity and purity he has found in Irish religious faith'.[26]

However, as early as 1960, John R. Frey of the University of Illinois might have given the most interesting interpretation, as he acknowledges Böll as the filter through which Ireland is seen – but continues to argue strongly that the resulting image remains one of Ireland, with no reference to Germany at all:

> Whether acquainted or unacquainted with the Emerald Island, the reader will find himself immersed in this genuinely Irish atmosphere as conveyed by the totally unbiased Böll, who had previously known only Ireland's gift to the world of literature. What he depicts we see, hear, feel, smell: the Irish landscape, the weather, the city and the country, and above all, the Irish people with all their peculiarities, their plight, their joys and their sorrows. Böll's portrayal, in no way pretentious or overladen with reflections, is not just a composite of sifted observations by an interested and discriminating eye, but of impressions filtered through the fibers of the author's whole perceptive being. It has that blend of realism and fantasy which characterizes Ireland itself [...].[27]

In each context covered in this chapter – within Böll's work, within the tradition of German literature about Ireland, and regarding its international reception – the *Irish Journal* appears to be a book in a league of its own. While the author used his own German background as a frame of reference, there is no question that the book is very much about Ireland and has been received internationally as such, with a notably enthusiastic American response.

---

[25] Larry Rumley, Nostalgia for Erin, *The Seattle Daily Times*, 6 August 1967.
[26] Alvin Beam, A German Writes of Ireland, *The Plain Beaver*, 19 August 1967.
[27] John R. Frey, Heinrich Böll. *Irisches Tagebuch*, in: *Books Abroad* 34, 1960, pp. 58f.

Part IV:

Later Works on Ireland

CHAPTER SIXTEEN

TRANSLATIONS AND REVIEWS

In 1948, long before the first trip to Ireland, Annemarie and Heinrich Böll started translating, hoping to build a new existence that would allow him to concentrate on his own writing and her to give up the often dreaded work as a secondary school teacher. Their first translation, the novel *No name in this street* by Kay Cicellis appeared in 1953 with Böll's publisher Kiepenheuer & Witsch as *Kein Name bei den Leuten*.[1]

Together they translated seven books by Brendan Behan, eight by Eilis Dillon and six by George Bernard Shaw; and in addition books by Flann O'Brien, Tomás O'Crohan, James Plunkett and John Millington Synge.[2]

---

[1] The first translation by Annemarie Böll in 1948, Stephen Spender's essay 'W.H. Auden and the Poets of the Thirties', was accepted by the Munich based *Literary Revue* but not published, cf. *KA 14*, commentary of the *Frankfurter Vorlesungen*, p. 570. See also Irene Hinrichsen, *Der Romancier als Übersetzer, Annemarie und Heinrich Bölls Übertragungen englischsprachiger Erzählprosa*, Bonn: Bouvier 1978.

[2] The long list includes the following:
Translations of **Brendan Behan**: *The Quare Fellow* (1956) – *Der Mann von morgen früh* , Cologne: Gustav Kiepenheuer 1958/9; *The Hostage* (1958) – *Die Geisel*, Cologne: Gustav Kiepenheuer 1958/9; *The Scarperer* (1964) – *Der Spanner*, Cologne/Berlin: Kiepenheuer & Witsch 1966; *Confessions of an Irish Rebel* (1965) – *Bekenntnisse eines irischen Rebellen*, Cologne: Kiepenheuer & Witsch 1978; *The Big House* (1957) – *Ein Gutshaus in Irland*, NDR 13 May 1959, printed in: *Stücke fürs Theater*, Neuwied/ Berlin: Luchterhand 1962; *Moving Out* (1967) – *Der Umzug*, 1968; *The Garden Party* (1967) – *Die Garten-Party*, NDR 7 August 1968, printed in: *Zwei Kurzhörspiele*, Berlin: Henschel 1969
Translations of **Eilís Dillon**: *The Coriander* (1963) – *Die Insel des großen John*, Freiburg: Herder 1966; *The Island of Horses* (1956) – *Die Insel der Pferde*, Freiburg: Herder 1964; *The Seals* (1968) – *Seehunde SOS*, Freiburg: Herder 1970; *A Family of Foxes* (1964) – *Die schwarzen Füchse. Die Abenteuer der vier Inselkinder mit der Fuchsfamilie*, Freiburg: Herder 1967; *The Cruise of the Santa Maria* (1967) *Die Irrfahrt der 'Santa Maria'*, Freiburg: Herder 1968; *The Sea Wall* (1965) – *Die Springflut*, Freiburg: Herder 1969; *A Herd of Deer* (1969) *Peter der*

Most of the primary translation work was actually done by Annemarie as Heinrich Böll freely admitted:

> With regard to the translation work [...]. I really enjoy it: it is a tremendous stylistic exercise and an excellent way to explore another author's world of imagery and thought. It does not interfere with one's work. It is a slog only in quantitative terms; but in fact 90% of the work is actually done by my wife.[3]

In a long interview published in 1975, Böll describes his role as looking through Annemarie's translation, discussing it with her and making suggestions at times, stressing that he really enjoyed the editing of translations by others or his own.[4] Arguably in many cases he provided the same help for Annemarie's translations as she provided for all his writing. However, as his name was established and recognizable it is likely that they kept it on to ensure a stronger appreciation for the often poorly paid translation work. In his lectures at the university in Frankfurt, published as

---

Kundschafter: abenteuerliche Sommerferien an der irischen Küste, Freiburg: Herder 1972; *The Shadow of Vesuvius* (1977) *Im Schatten des Vesuvs: Timon erlebt die letzten Tage von Pompeji,* Freiburg: Herder 1980.

Translation (by Annemarie Böll only) of **Elgy Gillespie**: The Country Life Picture Book of Ireland (1980) – *Irland,* Munich: Delphin 1982

Translation of **Flann O'Brien**: *The Hard Life* (1961) – *Das harte Leben,* Hamburg: Nannen 1966

Translation of **Tomás O'Crohan**: *The Islandman* (1929) – *Die Boote fahren nicht mehr aus,* Freiburg: Herder Freiburg/Olten: Otto Walter 1960

Translation of **James Plunkett**: *Strumpet City* (1969) – *Manche, sagt man, sind verdammt,* Reinbek: Rowohlt 1972

Translations of **George Bernard Shaw**: *Caesar and Cleopatra* (1898) – *Caesar und Cleopatra,* Frankfurt: Suhrkamp 1965; *Man and Superman* (1903) – *Mensch und Übermensch,* Frankfurt: Suhrkamp 1972; *Candida* (1905) – *Candida,* Frankfurt: Suhrkamp 1971; *The Revolutionist's Handbook and Pocket Companion by John Tanner* (1903) – *Handbuch des Revolutionärs,* Frankfurt: Suhrkamp 1972; *The Apple Cart* (1930) – *Kaiser von Amerika,* Frankfurt: Suhrkamp 1973

Translations of **John Millington Synge**: *The Playboy of the Western World* (1907) – *Ein wahrer Held,* Cologne: Kiepenheuer & Witsch 1960; *Riders to the Sea* (1905) – *Unser Schicksal ist die See,* Cologne: Kiepenheuer & Witsch 1969.

[3] Letter from Heinrich Böll to his publisher J.C. Witsch, 30 June 1956, see Stadt Köln & Heinrich-Böll-Stiftung (ed.): *Heinrich Böll Life and Work,* edited by R. Böll, V. Böll, K.H. Busse, M. Schäfer, Göttingen: Steidl 1995, translation by David McLintock, p. 29.

[4] Böll, Linder, *Drei Tage im März,* p. 60.

the *Frankfurter Vorlesungen* in 1964, he gives another reason why he liked translation, even preferred it at times to writing:

> [...] I became aware that the German literature of the postwar period in its entirety is a literature in search of a language, and then I knew why I often prefer to translate than to write myself: to carry something from foreign terrain into the territory of one's own language is a way of finding ground under one's feet.[5]

Russel West-Pavlov argues that Böll's description of 'foreign terrain' and of 'ground under one's feet', is like his notion of a 'habitable language in a habitable land' [the title of his *Frankfurter Vorlesungen*] a metaphor pertaining directly to 'the shattered urban fabric of postwar Germany and to its literary landscape'.[6] He refers to a later comment of Böll's in the *Frankfurter Vorlesungen*, that after the war there was a 'unique situation of equality', when everyone was without possessions and argues that in a situation of 'ubiquitous scarcity, one took whatever one could get one's hands upon; in a parallel situation of literary poverty, translation enacted an analogous relationship of appropriation'.[7] While 'appropriation' sounds overly possessive and not congruent with Böll's vision of open human connections and being bound within a neighbourly context, the comparison of having to start again from zero, both in real life but also in writing, has merit. However, at the same time it needs to be treated with care as Böll's interest in international, especially Irish, writers was nothing new and did not start only after the war. But it added to his own writing and arguably what attracted him most to Irish writers was the closeness of everyday language and poetic imagination.[8] This becomes obvious in his introduction to the new translation of Synge's *Playboy*, where he argues that the poetic richness of everyday language in Ireland Synge notices in

---

[5] Böll, Frankfurter Vorlesungen, *KA 14*, p. 168 [Nach der Lektüre dieser Erzählung wurde mir bewußt, daß die deutsche Nachkriegsliteratur als Ganzes eine Literatur der Sprachfindung gewesen ist, ich wußte auch, warum ich oft lieber übersetzte als selbst schrieb: Etwas aus einer fremden ins Gelände der eigenen Sprache hinüberzubringen, ist eine Möglichkeit, Grund unter den Füßen zu finden.]
[6] Russell West-Pavlov, *Transcultural graffiti: diasporic writing and the teaching of literary studies*, Amsterdam/New York: Rodopi 2005, p. 65.
[7] Ibid. West-Pavlov goes further then to maintain that translation is an act of cultural exchange which 'instantiates the shifting and processural relationships between peripheral and major literary systems', a distinction which is unlikely to have found Böll's favour given its implication of a ranking of different literatures.
[8] See also Hinrichsen, *Der Romancier als Übersetzer*, p. 219.

1907 could still be easily found more than five decades later.[9] While he mentions numerous other Irish writers such as O'Casey, O'Connor, Beckett, Yeats, Joyce and Shaw, the example he gives for this poetry of the everyday language is asking an old woman in Ireland for directions. Böll draws from this the view that poetry comes naturally in this country. He traces the origins for this to the 'passionate word culture' of the Celts, their indomitable, often cruel imagination, the fact that it was forbidden to speak Gaelic in Ireland for centuries and that this Celtic creativity was brought to fruition in the English language and brought a special, Irish blooming.[10]

The translations of Irish literature by the Bölls were particularly numerous in the late 1950s and 1960s, perhaps because their enthusiasm for their newly found second home was then at its highest. In 1958, in parallel with the writing of Heinrich Böll's novel *Billard um halb zehn* (*Billiards at Half-past Nine*), Annemarie and Heinrich Böll translated Tomás O'Crohan's *The Islandman* (*Die Boote fahren nicht mehr aus*) and also Brendan Behan's *The Big House* (*Ein Gutshaus in Irland*). Another of their translations of Brendan Behan's plays, *Die Geisel* (*The Hostage*) caused some consternation and a public exchange of open letters in 1963. Böll answered, 'as Catholic writer and translator', a letter to him by Monsignor Erich Klausener, the press officer of the Catholic Dioceses of Berlin (in which Klausener had questioned among other things whether the play – which according to him only presented 'poor devils, prostitutes, homosexuals and hypocrites'[11] – was worthy of translation) by pointing out twice that he ('the writer of the letter') did not exist as a translator, that he only appears jointly with his wife in this capacity, in fact he develops a further identity in the satirical letter.[12]

---

[9] Böll, Zur neuen Übersetzung von Synge, in: *KA 12*, pp. 47-50.

[10] Ibid, p. 47 [die leidenschaftliche Wortkultur der Kelten, ihre unbezähmbare, oft grausame Phantasie; die Tatsache, daß sich in Irland, wo es jahrhundertelang verboten war, gälisch zu sprechen, die keltische Imaginationskraft dem Englischen mitgeteilt hat, es zu einer besonderen, der irischen Blüte trieb]. For all his love of Irish literature, Böll goes beyond it in his examples, he also mentions Charles Dickens and Welsh writer Dylan Thomas, whom he calls one of the greatest poets and someone who made artistic use of everyday language. See also Böll's article on Thornton Wilder in 1964 under the heading 'Poesie des Alltäglichen' ('Poetry of the Everyday') in *KA 14*, pp. 131f.

[11] Cf. *KA 14*, commentary, Erich Klausener, Anfrage an Heinrich Böll – Bietet uns der katholische Dichter und Übersetzer 'Brot'?, pp. 485-496, 489.

[12] Cf. Böll, Antwort an Msgr. Erich Klausener, in: *Petrusblatt. Katholische Kirchenzeitung für das Bistum Berlin*, 1 December 1963, *KA 14*, pp. 74-84, 75 &

The translation of Robin Flower's English version of Tomás O'Crohan's *The Islandman* (a direct translation from Irish to German was not possible as the Bölls did not have any Irish) is, apart from Eilís Dillon's *The Island of Horses* (which has been a bestseller for children and also been published by popular paperback publisher dtv), their most popular translation of Irish literature. It was republished in 1983 by the Lamuv Publishing House.[13] Since then, the book has gone into its ninth edition. This is also reflected in later German publications on Ireland such as Ralph Giordano's *Mein irisches Tagebuch*, in which he summarizes on several pages the Bölls' translation of *The Islandman* and declares himself as being hooked on the text.[14]

In a study on the translation shifts from Tomás Ó Criomhthain's *An tOileánach* to the Bölls' *Die Boote fahren nicht mehr aus* by Nóilín Nic Bhloscaidh and myself, we found a number of interesting developments. One was that in contrast to the English translation, which retains strong traces of an Irish oral tradition, in German a lot of them are omitted. Interjections such as 'Yerra' and 'Wisha' are often left out. The same goes for interjections which indicate a strong oral tradition like 'you may be sure', 'believe me' or 'I tell you'. On the other hand, the exclamation 'Dar Muire', is translated as 'Holy Mary' or 'In Mary's name'. In the German version it is altered variously, to 'Bei der heiligen Jungfrau' ('Holy Mary'), 'In Gottes Namen' ('In Gods name') and, in one instance, somewhat surprisingly, to 'Zum Teufel noch mal' ('By the devil') probably to avoid repetition. There is also an example of a successful change that required a cultural shift, where Oscar of Irish mythology becomes Hercules from Greek mythology - 'denn niemand hat mich je wieder für so etwas wie einen Herkules erklärt' ('no one declared me to be a Herkules') using the Greek mythology for the translation of the English 'that I was in any way an Oscar', a reference that would not have made sense to most German readers.[15]

However, Hinrichsen indicates that the translations of the Bölls at times lacked precision and that Gaelic terms, for example in Flann O'Brien's

---

78 as well as background, p. 483.
[13] Headed by Heinrich Böll's son René Böll at the time.
[14] Ralph Giordano, *Mein irisches Tagebuch*, p. 43.
[15] G. Holfter, N. Nic Bhloscaidh: 'From Tomás Ó Criomhthain's *An tOileánach* to the Bölls' *Die Boote fahren nicht mehr aus*', in: M. McCusker, C. Shorley (eds) *Reading Across the Lines*, Dublin: Royal Irish Academy 2000, pp. 27-38.

The Hard Life were often not, or inaccurately, translated.[16] A review by Rosenstock of the translation of Behan's *The Scarperer* on the other hand points out that for once all nuances of Irish life are taken care of with unprecedented sensitivity.[17]

Assessing the overall volume of translation of 20th century Irish literature, the Bölls are probably second only to Elisabeth Schnack, the grande dame of translating Irish literature into German. (In the last twenty years Hans-Christian Oeser has contributed much too, especially regarding translations of contemporary literature.) Outside of Irish literature two translations of the Bölls in particular are well known: J.D. Salinger's *The Catcher in the Rye* (*Der Fänger im Roggen*) and Judith Kerr's *When Hitler Stole Pink Rabbit* (*Als Hitler das rosa Kaninchen stahl*). The translation of Irish literature accounted for approximately one third of their translation work.

Böll's reviews of Irish authors and other articles with Irish themes and Ireland as point of reference

Following on from the review about Francis Stuart mentioned earlier, which he wrote before he came to Ireland, Böll continued to write about other Irish writers and Irish topics. Apart from the *Irish Journal* and the film script (that will be analysed in the next chapter), Böll's writing about Ireland and its people, consisting of only a handful of articles, is not particularly voluminous given his impressive overall output. However, the frequency of references to Ireland and its authors in a huge variety of different contexts shows how important Ireland and Irish writers had become as a point of comparison, as a kind of critical framework for his thoughts and arguments or just as a context for examples he uses to make points.[18] In a preface to 'Unfertig ist der Mensch' ('Unfinished is man'), a new journal, written in 1966, Böll argues that art does not give comfort, that art is creating beauty and poetry, but comfort is given by religion and people. By way of an example, he tells the story of George Bernard Shaw, 'the great mocker', who lying on his deathbed was very glad to receive a visit by the wife of his friend, the writer Sean O'Casey, and said a few

---

[16] Cf. Hinrichsen, *Der Romancier als Übersetzer*, pp. 190f.
[17] Georg Rosenstock, Neue Übersetzung von Brendan Behan, in: *Die Zeit*, No. 49, 2 December 1966, p. II.
[18] See last volume of the Cologne edition with an index of places and people mentioned in all of Böll's works: *Registerband,* Kölner Ausgabe, volume 27, edited by Klaus-Peter Bernhard in cooperation with Ulrich Stenzel, Cologne: Kiepenheuer & Witsch 2010 (*KA 27*).

days before his death that is was nice to feel the touch of a soft Irish hand and to hear the sound of a soft Irish voice.[19]

Böll had already written an article on Sean O'Casey's writing, which appeared in early 1957, 'Die Welt Sean O'Caseys' (The world of Sean O'Casey). Böll also mentions other Irish writers such as James Joyce, William Butler Yeats, George Bernard Shaw and Oscar Wilde. As later on in the *Irish Journal* he refers specifically to Swift's *Modest Proposal: For Preventing the Children of Poor People in Ireland from Being a Burden to Their Parents or Country, and for Making Them Beneficial to the Public* (*Bescheidener Vorschlag, zu verhüten, daß die Kinder armer Iren ihren Eltern oder dem Lande zur Last fallen*), written in 1729. Böll takes the opportunity to refer to contemporary poverty and the annual emigration of 40,000 people, and explains that poverty at the time of O'Casey's play, *Red Roses for me (Rote Rosen für mich)*, set in 1913 when the country was still waiting for its freedom, would have been even worse. The 'real' Ireland is described as 'humble, loveable, unwoken'.[20] Böll describes elements of life there as follows: 'Fuchsia flowers, a statue of the holy virgin, piety, dullness, the century old pressure of poverty. Poetry lies on the streets in Ireland'.[21] The creative ability to transform everyday encounters through language was portrayed by Böll in the chapter 'The Dead Redskin of Duke Street', in the person of the poetic policeman. The poetry in everyday life is clearly central to Böll's view of Ireland and Irish literature, and is mentioned several times.[22] But beyond this poetic disposition of a whole country, encapsulating strong humanity as well as literature, there are also evidently individual writers Böll feels particularly close to.

One of the most frequently mentioned authors is Brendan Behan. Böll refers to him continually in reviews and short essays, especially in the context of Catholicism.[23] After Behan's death, Böll wrote an article

---

[19] Böll, Vorwort zu 'Unfertig ist der Mensch', *KA 15*, pp. 269-273, 270.
[20] [das eigentliche Irland: demütig, liebenswürdig, unerwacht], in: 'Die Welt Sean O'Caseys', *KA 10*, pp. 181f.
[21] Ibid. [Fuchsienblüten, eine Marienstatue, Frömmigkeit, Dumpfheit, der jahrhundertealte Druck der Armut. Die Poesie liegt in Irland auf der Straße.]
[22] See for example the aforementioned 'Zur neuen Übersetzung von Synge' (1961), *KA 12*, pp. and also 'Über Synge, *Ein wahrer Held*' (1961), *KA 12*, pp. 174f.
[23] For example 'Das Zeug zu einer Äbtissin' [All necessary requirements for an abbess], a review of Mary McCarthy's *A Catholic Childhood*, *Spiegel*, 2 May 1966, p. 152 and 'Warum so zartfühlend? Über Carl Amery *Fragen an Welt und*

specifically about him, using the opportunity to pick a few bones with German Catholicism and showing his personal affinity with Behan. Böll equates Dublin and Cologne, the latter including, in his opinion, two of the few areas of any German city where Behan would have felt at home. Both areas are closely connected to Böll and his wife – the Eigelstein area in the north of the city is described as part of Annemarie's daily walk to school for eleven years and the area around the Severin's Gate was passed by Böll on his way to school for nine years.[24] The similarity between the specific neighbourhoods in Dublin and Cologne that Böll points out here consists of the vulgarity, the friendliness and the profusion of Catholic-proletarian melancholy which he sees as defining characteristics of these areas in Dublin and Cologne. Further parallels, though this time not expressly stated, seem to be the family background of Behan and Böll, both traditionally Catholic and anti-clerical at the same time. However, Böll is at pains to point out that the German understanding of 'Catholicism' is at odds with the situation in Ireland and by way of example he mentions the different approaches to excommunication which seemingly was no obstacle in Ireland to being married or buried by a priest. Böll uses the opportunity to criticise the German Catholic Youth movement that failed to provide a meaningful resistance to re-armament. Likewise, the understanding of sexual immorality is, according to Böll quite different in Ireland from what it is in Germany, where prostitution is allowed and he believes sexual immorality more often than not results from a desire to be part of the fashionable set. In Ireland, on the other hand, it is a question of passion, and people know that human nature is fallible and neither moralists nor the frequenters of brothels are able to appreciate this. Within this specific argument Böll incongruously introduces a general exasperation with his home country: 'In our country nearly everything is the other way round compared to Ireland'.[25] He also points out the different attitude that existed in the Ireland of Behan's youth towards alcohol, quoting him that it was seen as a victory against the odds to succeed in getting drunk in times of poverty. Böll ends the article with a comparison of Behan and Joyce and praise of Ireland's capital: 'In many ways Behan was the opposite of James Joyce, who was hardly at all a "personality" but almost exclusively a writer, and at the same time both are unthinkable without and inseparable from this unique city, called Dublin.'[26] While Böll sees

---

Kirche', *Spiegel*, 15 May 1967, p. 140.
[24] Cf. Böll, Brendan Behan, *KA 14*, pp. 401-404.
[25] Ibid., p. 131.
[26] Ibid., p. 132. [In manchem war Behan das Gegenteil von James Joyce, der fast gar nicht "Persönlichkeit" war, sondern fast nur Autor, und doch waren sie beide

Behan as contrasting with Joyce in certain respects, the closeness Böll feels towards Behan is obvious.

Ireland, Irish writers and Irish Catholicism continued to be a point of reference for Böll in his writing throughout the 1960s and 1970s. Sometimes it was Ireland itself that was used to make a point, as that was the Catholic exception to the rule.[27] And sometimes an Irish motif appeared completely out of context and unrecognisable in his books as for example the dogs of Dukinella (on Achill) in his 1964 publication *Entfernung von der Truppe* (*Absent without Leave*, 1965), to which Böll refers in 'Thirteen years later' as 'smuggled in there', into a narration that has absolutely nothing to do with Ireland but very much with Germany.[28] Other references to Ireland appear, for example, when he refers to it in one of his 'Briefe aus dem Rheinland' ('Letters from the Rhineland'), as a pious country where nevertheless bus drivers and conductors could go on strike for five weeks without being accused of letting the nation down.[29] Böll wrote several of these 'Letters from the Rhineland', numbers XI to XVIII, in Dugort on Achill, during his stay there between 5 May and 1 September 1963.[30] The 'Letters' were essays for a weekly newspaper, *Die Zeit*, commenting satirically on current affairs and political developments under the pseudonym Lohingrin. The narrator describes in 'Brief aus dem Rheinland XVII' a trip with the family to Italy (while Böll himself was with his family in Ireland) and sketches a scene of his oldest son being in love with the waitress, both communicating only through shy encounters, whereas her mother is described as a great woman with beautiful eyes[31] – reminiscences of the *Irish Journal* chapter 'Mrs D.'s Ninth Child'.

Ireland is mentioned also in another context: terrorism in 1970s Germany and the heated public debate arising from it, which was one of the most difficult times Böll had with his homeland. In one of the most detailed

---

undenkbar ohne und unlösbar von dieser einmaligen Stadt, die Dublin heißt.]

[27] Cf. 'Mauriac zum achtzigsten Geburtstag' published in *Le Figaro Littéraire*, 14 October 1965 (Un parfum de pin et de vignoble), see *KA 14*, p. 339.

[28] Heinrich Böll 'Dreizehn Jahre später', commentary, in: *Werke 1966-68*, Kölner Ausgabe volume 15, edited by Werner Jung, Cologne: Kiepenheuer & Witsch 2005, p. 518 (in the following abbreviated as *KA 15*).

[29] Böll, Brief aus dem Rheinland XIII, in: *Die Zeit*, 28.6.1963, cf. *KA 14*, pp. 33-35. See *KA 14*, p. 427, commentary on Brief aus dem Rheinland XI.

[30] See ibid.

[31] Böll, Brief aus dem Rheinland XVII, in: *Die Zeit*, 23 August 1963, cf. *KA 14*, p. 53.

accounts about his perceptions of the situation, the book *Eine deutsche Erinnerung* (A German Remembering), of 1979, based on a long interview with René Wintzen, Böll tries to come to terms with the terrorist experiences, calls for a careful analysis of the phenomenon and its origin and disregards comparisons with Brittany, Corsica and Ireland as there was no base within the population in Germany and no directly visible political aim. But he also argues that, when talking about terrorists, one of the most distinguished and honourable statesmen and politicians of the 19th century (sic!) was Eamon de Valera, who sixty years previously was regarded as one of the worst terrorists in British history.[32] However, Böll continues that he never thought it possible that the 'concept' of the German Baader-Meinhof group was feasible or realisable.

The most prominent introduction of Irish authors in his writing can be found in Böll's novel *Gruppenbild mit Dame* (*Group Portrait with Lady*) published in 1971 the publication of which was one of the main reasons he was awarded the Nobel Prize. William Butler Yeats appears here as the favourite writer of the heroine's mother Helene, who is also well-informed on Ireland's history and presence and is familiar with the names of Patrick Pearse, James Connolly and James Larkin. This preference for Irish revolutionaries and radical thinkers indicates a special interest in political struggles in Ireland. She is very enthusiastic about 'these Finns' which according to the narrator must most likely have been the Fenians, and her strong preference for Ireland takes on romantic, and even sentimental aspects.[33] Beckett appears as well, with references to his publication in Germany and the indication, that, had he been available already at the specific time, he certainly would also have been among the treasured books of the heroine, Leni, the 'lady' referred to in the title.[34] As McGowan

---

[32] Böll, *Eine deutsche Erinnerung*, p. 79 (in: *KA 25*, p. 366). [Und wenn man über Terroristen spricht, darf man auch nicht vergessen, daß einer der ehrwürdigsten und verehrungswürdigsten Staatsmänner des 19. Jahrhunderts, ein gewisser Eamon de Valera, Präsident der Republik Irland, Ministerpräsident etliche Male, vor sechzig Jahren einer der schlimmsten Terroristen der britischen Geschichte war.]

[33] Heinrich Böll, *Gruppenbild mit Dame*, in *Werke* Kölner Ausgabe vol 17, edited by Ralf Schnell, Cologne: Kiepenheuer & Witsch 2005, pp. 72f. (*KA 17*). See Moray McGowan, 'Pale Mother, Pale Daughter? Some Reflections on Böll's Leni Gruyten and Katharina Blum', in: *German Life and Letters*, 37/ 3, 1984, pp. 218-228 for further references and intertextual links between Leni Gruyten and Katharina Blum with Irish myths and especially Yeats's 'Cathleen ni Houlihan'. Also see Christine Hummel, *Intertextualität im Werk Heinrich Bölls*, Trier: WVT 2002, pp. 230-235.

[34] Böll, *Gruppenbild mit Dame*, p. 22.

points out, the view of Irish history adopted here is largely uncritical, presented mainly as 'a centuries-long struggle against an alien colonial presence'.[35]

Böll's interest in Irish history had already become apparent in his review 'Kennedy, Irland und der große Hunger - Über Cecil Woodham-Smith, *The Great Hunger*', (Kennedy, Ireland and the Great Hunger – On Cecil Woodham-Smith's *The Great Hunger*), written in 1963. He declares that he would have read the book (some 510 pages) even if it had been ten times its length – and even then still with 'engaged empathy'. He traces a certain 'backwardness' (that he is careful to mention only in inverted commas) in Ireland from the time of the Famine to the time of writing, and explains that the Famine is the only reason that such 'backwardness' can still exist among a people of such talents and how misplaced prejudice could begin, following the stream of starving emigrants who, often ill, had to start again with nothing. Böll declares that he himself was occasionally guilty of an arrogant smile, complaining at times about aspects of Irish life that seemed backward and absurd, but stresses that after reading Woodham-Smith's study the lack of comprehension gave way to understanding and realisation of the circumstances.[36]

An article about Northern Ireland of 1970 is among the last publications on Ireland by Böll. In 'Die Ursachen des Troubles mit Nordirland' (The reasons for the troubles in Northern Ireland), Böll convincingly argues that power questions are behind the 'Troubles', and contrasts the Catholic and Protestant sides by comparing the young Catholic woman Bernadette Devlin with Ian Paisley. Surprisingly, he describes Paisley in the clothing of an Anglican minister.[37] Böll could be accused of a lack of differentiation using the simple antipodes of Catholicism and Protestantism without acknowledging different dissenting groups within Protestantism who were at various times also subjected to suppression by the State.

One more publication should not be overlooked here, even though Ireland is not expressly mentioned: Böll's 1963 publication 'Anekdote zur Senkung der Arbeitsmoral' ('Anecdote on lowering work morale'), in which a

---

[35] McGowan, 'Pale Mother, Pale Daughter? Some Reflections on Böll's Leni Gruyten and Katharina Blum', p. 221.

[36] Cf. Böll, Kennedy, Irland und der große Hunger, *Der Tagespiegel*, 11 August 1963.

[37] Heinrich Böll, *Essayistische Schriften und Reden 2*, Cologne: Kiepenheuer & Witsch 1979, p. 461; first published in *Süddeutsche Zeitung* 21/22 February 1970.

relaxed, poorly dressed fisherman at a harbour 'at a western coast of Europe' (which for Böll is very likely to be Ireland) is enjoying sunshine and life without worrying about the future, sharply contrasted with a nervous, excited (German) tourist, taking pictures with his camera, advocating extra work in order to make more and more profit so that in the end he can enjoy the sunshine – and finally realising that it is not the fisherman who is to be pitied but himself. The fisherman embodies an approach to life which is not directed towards profit making and teaches the tourist (who embodies the attitude of the industrial age) a clear lesson about how to live life.[38]

What is gently wrapped up in the story is Böll's criticism of an uncritical belief in growth for its own sake. This was a recurring theme to which he referred much more bluntly in discussions, for example one with his colleagues such as Siegfried Lenz and Günter Grass, in which Böll exclaimed that simple arithmetic was sufficient to see that six percent growth actually meant in sixteen or seventeen years one hundred percent and revealed the madness of believing in the growth agenda.[39] Thanks to the Kölner Ausgabe, a corresponding text has come to life, 'Anekdote vom deutschen Wunder' (Anecdote of the German miracle), written as early as 1955 and not previously published.[40] Again, it contains a conversation in which growth is described, here more blatantly as a paper exercise, not connected to actual work at all but only by transferring money between accounts and accordingly improving creditworthiness, as explained by a father following his son's question on what 'the German miracle' actually is. As in the later 'Anekdote zur Senkung der Arbeitsmoral', the father remains ruminative in the end ('and if he has not become melancholic due to too much thoughtfulness he will be a rich man today').[41]

---

[38] *Das Heinrich Böll Lesebuch*, Munich: dtv 1982, pp. 223-225 and *KA 12*, pp. 441-446. In this context see also Eoin Bourke's paper, 'Heinrich Böll's 'Anekdote zur Senkung der Arbeitsmoral' and the Growth Illusion' at the Galway German Colloquium VII in 1993, in which he contextualises Böll's essay with Richard Douthwaite's critical analysis of Ireland from 1992, *The Growth Illusion*.

[39] Siegfried Lenz, *Über Phantasie – Gespräche mit Heinrich Böll, Günter Grass, Walter Kempowski, Pavel Kohout*, Hamburg: Hoffmann und Campe 1982, p. 179. See also Heinrich Böll, Ich bin kein Repräsentant – Gespräch mit Hanjo Kesting, in: *Die Zeit*, 23 December 1977, p. 36 and *KA 25*, pp. 226-254, especially 235-237. Thanks to Markus Schäfer for help in identifying the references.

[40] Böll, Anekdote vom deutschen Wunder, in: *Werke 1954-1956*, Kölner Ausgabe volume 9, edited by J. H. Reid, Cologne: Kiepenheuer & Witsch 2006, pp. 104f.

[41] Ibid,, p. 105. The commentary on p. 439 further refers to an essay Böll's ('Auferstehung des Gewissens') from 1954 in which he maintains that it is

The divide between money and morals continued to exercise Böll. And while the following text has no direct link to Ireland, it might be an indication why his texts can still provide insights, whether read in Germany or Ireland. Arguably Böll's emotional appeal, shortly before his death, for savings, albeit savings in the right place and not starting with the vulnerable and easy targets first, has special resonance when read in Ireland after the demise of the Celtic Tiger:

> Of course it is understandable that people who are doing ok are afraid of all changes as they think everything is taking a turn for the worse. What the politicians, the responsible politicians, have to make clear to us, is, that we all have to save – not with the unemployed but with the whole bureaucracy, all the unnecessary administration and also in everyday life. The cuts are made in the wrong places, hitting the recipients of social security payments, the unemployed, the old age pensioners. The cuts need to be implemented from the top down and a politician would need to dare to make the cuts first at the top and then to go downwards. Then by implication we will all have less than we have now, all of us, every single one. We cannot go on as we do now, I cannot express it any other way.
> We live in a waste society, an all round society of waste, that pretends that waste is growth. I actually believe that some of the politicians of our present government but which government is immaterial, have understood this. But they don't have the courage to save from the top. Starting with themselves actually, we all have to make sacrifices. It would need to hit the civil servants, employees, every single profession.[42]

---

blasphemy to call an economic flowering a 'miracle'.

[42] Böll, Es stirbt täglich Freiheit weg, in *Die Zeit*, 26 July 1985 [Natürlich muß man verstehen, daß Menschen, denen es gut geht, vor jeder Veränderung Angst haben, weil sie denken, es kommt schlechter. Was die Politiker, die verantwortlichen Politiker, uns klarmachen müssen, ist, daß wir alle sparen müssen, nicht an den Arbeitslosen, an der ganzen Bürokratie, an der ganzen überflüssigen Verwaltung und auch effektiv sparen müssen im Alltag. Gespart wird an der falschen Stelle, bei Sozialhilfeempfängern, bei Arbeitslosen, bei Rentnern. Das Sparen muß von oben nach unten gehen, und ein Politiker müßte den Mut haben, oben zu sparen, mit Sparen anzufangen und dann nach unten gehen. Da werden wir alle notwendigerweise weniger haben als wir jetzt haben, alle, alle. So geht das nicht weiter, ich kann es nicht anders ausdrücken.
Wir leben in einer Verschwendungsgesellschaft, auf jede Weise Verschwendungsgesellschaft, die Verschwendung als Wachstum ausgibt. Ich glaube schon, daß manche Politiker der jetzigen Regierung, aber ganz gleich welcher Regierung, zu dieser Einsicht gekommen sind. Aber sie haben nicht den Mut, oben zu sparen. Auch an sich selber übrigens, wir müßten alle abgeben. Es müßte die Beamten, die Angestellten, alle Berufe betreffen].

Böll's passionate plea for a different accountability by everyone within society, for a careful handling of resources and shared responsibility, as expressed in this text and many others directed at West German society, is surely not only applicable there but is a reminder of unequal values in the modern world. He recognises both individual and political responsibilities. Taken together with his 'Anekdote zur Senkung der Arbeitsmoral' it is clear that this is not to be a small-minded approach but is one that involves humour and enjoyment of life. For Böll the experience of 1950s Ireland was a direct antidote to an irresponsible and blinkered belief in material growth for its own sake. Instead, it was a country, as he happily noted, where bankers could go on strike for months and life simply went on.[43]

---

[43] For example *Im literarischen Kaffeehaus*, WDR/NDR/Freies Berlin, 21 December 1967, conversation between Heinrich Böll, Hans Mayer and Marcel Reich-Ranicki on the occasion of Böll's 50th birthday. Böll was referring here to the bank strike between early May and the end of July 1966 – and emphasised that the strike was not condemned by the church but actually supported by some priests.

Chapter Seventeen

The Emerald Isle in Black and White— The Film *Children of Eire*

> *I wrote a film about Dostoyevsky which I still consider to be a homage to the Russian soul and Russian literature: In the Soviet Union it caused deep mortification officially; I made a film about Ireland, which – as I thought and still think – bordered on adulation. In Ireland it resulted in vicious name-calling and when I was there on one of my visits my neighbour asked: 'Are you not afraid to be stoned?'*
> —Heinrich Böll, Shalom, 1978[1]

Up to 2006, one could wonder whatever happened to the film *Children of Eire*.[2] No one seemed to know about it anymore, Böll specialists as well as German Hibernophiles tended to react with surprise when they heard that Böll had not only written the *Irisches Tagebuch* but also the script for the TV film about Ireland, broadcast in Germany in 1961 and in Ireland in 1965. Similarly forgotten in both Germany and Ireland were the strong reactions the film caused when it was broadcast in each country – great

---

[1] [Ich habe einen Film über Dostojewskij geschrieben, den ich – immer noch – für eine große Hommage an den russischen Geist und die russische Literatur halte: In der Sowjetunion hat er offiziell tiefe Gekränktheit bewirkt; ich habe einen Film über Irland gemacht, der – wie mir schien und immer noch scheint – ziemlich nah an Schmeichelei grenzte. In Irland gab es wüste Beschimpfungen, und als ich wieder einmal dort war, sagte mir eine Nachbarin: „Haben Sie nicht Angst gesteinigt zu werden?"] Heinrich Böll, Shalom, quoted in *Rom auf den ersten Blick*, Munich: dtv 1991, pp. 213-224, 220.

[2] See Holfter, From bestseller to failure? Heinrich Böll's *Irisches Tagebuch* (*Irish Journal*) to *Irland und seine Kinder* (*Children of Eire*), in: C. Schönfeld (ed.): *Processes of Transposition: German Literature and Film*, Amsterdamer Beiträge zur neueren Germanistik, Amsterdam/Atlanta: Rodopi 2007, pp. 207-222, 208. The following chapter contains an update and more information regarding the reception of the film in Ireland.

enthusiasm in Germany and, when shown four years later in Ireland, outrage from many Irish viewers, leading to a significant controversy.

Since then, though, it has been broadcast a number of times on TV (even on such coveted primetime slots as Christmas Day on RTE 2 in December 2006), at Böll weekends and conferences as well as during film festivals. In 2010 Fintan O'Toole called it '[a] prescient vision of Ireland, through a 1960 lens' and argues that the film would have been viewed nostalgically only a couple of years earlier (ie. before Ireland's economic crash) but made for uncomfortable viewing in 2010, especially with regard to its focus on emigration: 'Physically and literally, Böll's vision may be very distant. Psychologically and imaginatively, it feels all too close'.[3]

So what was Böll's vision, why did it cause such strong reactions – and how did Böll respond to them? The image Böll conveyed of Ireland in the film is in many ways similar to what he portrayed in the *Irish Journal*. Themes such as emigration, religion and time feature prominently. It is not the expressly personal, subjective and partial description of the book, though.

Böll used many quotations, attributed to Irish saints such as Columba or Brigid, or taken from writers such as Monk Gibbon, Fiona MacLeod, and W.B. Yeats, though often not expressly mentioning their Irish provenance. As in the *Irish Journal* his own descriptions are lyrical rather than factual accounts of Ireland and its special features, for example in the attributes he gives time: 'Still, time doesn't show its rational face, where clock hands and numbers determine its physiognomy. It is only there, goes to and fro like the tide coming in and out, returns all the time. It pushes forward, pushes towards game and bet.'[4]

The structure of the film broadly follows the life cycle, starting with children going to school, then mentioning universities and Irish literature, entertainment for younger and older generations like the cinema, dancing,

---

[3] Fintan O'Toole, A prescient vision of Ireland, through a 1960s lens, in: *Irish Times*, 17 April 2010, Weekend Review p. 9.
[4] [Noch zeigt die Zeit nicht ihr vernünftiges Gesicht, ihre Oberfläche, wo Zeiger und Zahlen ihre Physiognomie bestimmen. Sie ist nur da, geht hin und zurück wie Ebbe und Flut, kehrt immer wieder. Sie drängt, drängt aber auch zum Spiel, zur Wette.] Heinrich Böll: *Irland und seine Kinder*, first printed in *Westdeutscher Rundfunk. Jahrbuch 1960/1961*. Cologne 1961. In: *KA 12*, pp. 179-193, commentary pp. 565-575.

travelling shows, dog races. Religion and church festivals are featured prominently as are – to German eyes – exotic work activities such as shark fishing. Following a still shot of graveyards, school children are filmed again as the last scene. This cycle is reinforced through the narrative; the starting and finishing paragraph, each describing Irish children, are nearly identical: 'all of royal ancestry, free as kings, as long as they are children' (first paragraph) and 'almost all of royal ancestry, living in a royal landscape, free as kings, as long as they are children' (last paragraph).[5] The emphasis on children that is also expressed in the choice of title has some special resonance for Böll. In a letter to his fiancée in November 1940 he had already written: 'God left us with three possibilities to find the last glimmer of paradise, to be happy. The artists, the lovers and the children (...) they suffer infinitely and often they are infinitely happy'.[6] A similar theme is still expressed in the *Frankfurter Vorlesungen* where he refers to his abhorrence of cowered and tamed children and emphasises the need for free children.[7] A rather special and unsual freedom was in Böll's opinion given to the children of Ireland - 'the great freedom' to be allowed to be poor.[8] The tricky theme of poverty had in earlier draft scripts been introduced from the beginning: Böll had started his text (which was originally entitled 'Insel der Abschiede' – 'Island of Farewells') with the demand that one would need different eyes to understand the island:

> Anyone who wants to understand Ireland and her children should be required to exchange the eyes currently used to make sense of the surroundings, and instead to use new ones: not everything that appears to be poor is poor, what looks meagre is not humble but proud.[9]

---

[5] [Sie alle stammen von Königen ab, sind frei wie Könige, solange sie Kinder sind.] Böll: *Irland und seine Kinder*, in *KA 12*, p. 179; [fast alle stammen sie von Königen ab, leben in einer königlichen Landschaft und sind frei wie Könige, solange sie Kinder sind], ibid., p. 193.
[6] [Gott hat uns drei Möglichkeiten gelassen, die letzten Schimmer des Paradieses zu finden, glücklich zu sein: den Künstler, den Liebenden und die Kinder [...] sie leiden unendlich und sind oft unendlich glücklich]. Böll, *Briefe aus dem Krieg 1939-1945*, vol 1, 9. November 1940, p. 131.
[7] [Ein Königreich für ein Kind, das eins sein, das frei sein durfte.] Böll, *Frankfurter Vorlesungen* (1964), *KA 14*, p. 187.
[8] "Sie dürfen - eine große Freiheit - arm sein", Böll: *Irland und seine Kinder*, p. 180.
[9] [Wer Irland und seine Kinder und die hier gezeigte Bildfolge verstehen möchte, müsste eigentlich aufgefordert werden, anstelle der Augen, die ihm gegenwärtig dazu dienen, seine Umwelt zu betrachten, andere einzusetzen: was hier arm wirkt, ist nicht immer arm, was ärmlich wirkt, nicht immer bescheiden, sondern stolz.]

Though there is an approximation of a utopian idea, Ireland is no paradise as Böll makes clear. Only children enjoy all freedom, as adults they have to face the 'reasonable' time, have to emigrate—not only because of economic necessity but also because of the 'strictness' (likely to be a euphemism for 1950s cultural narrowmindedness) that led to writers such as Joyce and Beckett having to leave the country. [10]

In the film, time is often personified, as a figure offering hours in vain,[11] existing only, moving like tide movements,[12] depending on the fastest horse or dog,[13] appearing unreasonable[14] and mad[15]. But not only time seems to have different qualities and characteristics in this description of Ireland – Böll sees the country as a place that is full of paradoxes, where exaggeration is law and heartfelt children's prayer, pious men and utter desperation exist side by side.[16] The travellers (or 'Irish gypsies', as Böll calls them)

> find neverending space and time on the small island of Ireland, time for them is only in the form of seasons, weather, birth, death, growing up of children and horses. Death, birth and hunger are their only punctuality, 'because the stars that wake up the winds waft through their blood'.[17]

Heinrich Böll: manuscript for *Irland und seine Kinder*, no title, no date. Historisches Archiv Stadt Köln. 'Eyes' had a special meaning for Böll as is obvious here – they incorporate both perspective and approach. Especially in his essay 'Bekenntnis zur Trümmerliteratur' this concept has been developed by Böll to a kind of poetological system (see Päplow, pp. 83-94). He also used the concept as a title for an introduction to a collection of essays, literature and photos about and of the Soviet Union, see Böll, Wer Augen hat zu sehen, sehe!, in: *UdSSR – Der Sowjetstaat und seine Menschen*, Stuttgart: Belser 1970, pp. V-IX.

[10] 'Das Land, das seine Kinder liebt, ist eifersüchtig auf sie und streng zu ihnen, wenn sie erwachsen sind. [...] Geboren sind viele Dichter in dieser Stadt [...] Gelebt haben die meisten von ihnen anderswo; anderswo sind sie begraben.' Böll, *Irland und seine Kinder, KA 12*, pp. 179f.
[11] '[...] auch die Zeit wartet, sie scheint ihre Stunden vergebens anzubieten, vergebens ihre Zeiger zu bewegen, vergebens pünktlich zu sein'. Ibid., p. 181.
[12] Ibid., p. 183.
[13] Ibid.
[14] Ibid., pp. 183 and 189.
[15] Ibid., p. 183.
[16] [Wo Übertreibung Lebensgesetz ist, wohnen inniges Kindergebet, fromme Männer und tiefe Verzweiflung nahe nebeneinander]. Ibid., p. 186.
[17] [finden sie die Unendlichkeit des Raumes und der Zeit. Zeit ist für sie nur Jahreszeit, Wetter, Geburt, Tod, Heranwachsen der Kinder, der Pferde. Tod, Geburt und Hunger sind ihre einzigen Pünktlichkeiten, 'denn die Sterne, die Winde

Ireland is portrayed as a place where statues of Mary rather than clocks are to be found in airports,[18] where religion has almost become nature[19] and time has 'no reasonable face, only a heart, a rhythm and a melody'.[20]

Viewers in Germany liked Böll's black and white portrayal of Ireland. When it was shown on German television on 8 March 1961, 47% of the potential audience watched the film, according to infratest,[21] and comments by viewers and reviewers alike were very positive.[22] The *Mangfallbote* praised the 'lyrical description, which concerned itself not only with reality but managed to conjure the atmosphere beyond the realities, as is only possible with the poetic word'.[23] The *Rheinische Post* declared that it 'seemed to be composed according to musical rules', and that it was artistic and balanced.[24] Letters to the editor of the *TV Fernsehwoche* from viewers in Berlin and Siegen congratulated the TV programmers on the excellent feature, 'a symphony of word and image', noting that it not only informed the audience about Ireland but 'gave [the viewer] an artistic experience.'[25] Böll's hope of creating a suggestive image through a strongly imposed form seems to have been successful and was expressly appreciated. The film was awarded a prize as 'best documentary' in 1961

---

erwecken, wehen durch ihr Blut'.] Ibid., p. 187.
[18] Ibid., p. 184.
[19] Ibid., p. 185.
[20] [Wo die Zeit kein vernünftiges Gesicht hat, nur ein Herz, einen Rhythmus und eine Melodie]. Ibid., p. 189.
[21] Renowned German market research group, founded in 1947, since 1948 specialised in radio and later television market research.
[22] Information according to infratest material in the Böll files in the Historisches Archiv Köln.
[23] [sondern eine poetische Schilderung, die deshalb nicht weniger den Realitäten nachging, aber hinter den Realitäten die Atmosphäre spürbar werden ließ, wie es eben nur dem dichterischen Wort gegeben ist], N.A., Die poetische Reportage, *Mangfallbote* (Bad Aiblingen), 4 March 1961.
[24] [Das wirkte nach musikalischen Gesetzen komponiert, war kunstvoll und—im Blick auf das gesamte Fernsehpublikum—wohl nur gelegentlich zu anspruchsvoll formuliert.] N.A., Dichterische Dokumentation, *Rheinische Post*, 10 March 1961.
[25] '[…] eine Sinfonie von Wort und Bild', R.A., Neunkirchen/Siegen; 'Der Bericht über die 'grüne Insel' war nach meinem Dafürhalten eine in Bild und Wort gelungene Komposition. Sie ließ die Fernseher nicht nur etwas über Irland sehen und hören, sondern vermittelte den Zuschauern ein künstlerisches Erlebnis.' F. Sch. (Berlin-Wilmersdorf), Dank für die 'grüne Insel', *TV Fernsehwoche,* 2 April 1961.

and chosen as the German contribution for the international film competition 'Prix Italia'.[26]

The film was received very differently in Ireland. Böll's film was shown in Ireland as part of the series 'As others see us'. It created great controversy, resulting in one critic demanding an apology from the German government. It can be assumed that it had a fairly large viewing audience given the letters to the editor in different newspapers and the fact that there had been a long article beforehand in the *RTV Guide* by Patrick Gallagher introducing the Irish audience to Heinrich Böll and the film. Gallagher mentions meeting him in Cologne a few years before when Böll 'had just made a name for himself as a satirist whose novels nonetheless had a spare human passion' and declares that *'Children of Eire* is a film of considerable beauty, and to me a perfectly fair and valid camera and poet's eye view of aspects of the West of Ireland.' He also gives a warning:

> Essentially, the film is the view of a poet, and some of us believe that poetic truth beats literal truth hands down. That, however, is a subjective judgement of 'Children of Eire'. Viewers should watch for themselves. The odd ear may burn, but not many an eye will tire of the photo-imagination that pervades the film.

That this warning was necessary became obvious in the studio discussion that followed the programme. Three Irishmen, agricultural editor Patrick O'Keefe, trade unionist Donal Nevin, and author and playwright John O'Donovan, had, it seems, an interesting discussion. As Gabriel Fallon wrote in the *Evening Press* – the 'pleasing, if somewhat limited German film of Irish life' was well worth showing 'if only for the lively discussion it provoked'. John O'Donovan in particular, was quite simply disgusted. In an article in the *Sunday Press* he stated: 'I say this disgraceful production must be withdrawn [...] little was left out of 'Children of Eire' that could help to exhibit us as the most hapless and hopeless race in the northern hemisphere.' Not all commentators agreed with him, one writing that 'How one could see it as a picture of the whole country beats me', comparing it to images of Ireland by Joyce, Kavanagh and Shaw, and concluding:

> To me, 'Children of Eire' was what Mr. Nevin and Mr. O'Keeffe claimed it was: a poet's-eye view of a very real place. What if the poet happens to have a touch of the satirist? We have produced so many poet-satirists

---

[26] Cf. *KA 12*, background *Irland und seine Kinder*, p. 565.

ourselves that we cannot reasonably complain. 'Children of Eire' was in many ways reminiscent of 'Man of Aran'. The essential difference was that in shooting the German film the camera was more sharply focussed. (*Irish Press*, 6.2.1965)[27]

Though Böll probably had no satire in mind when writing *Children of Eire* he would surely have been pleased with the comparison with Joyce, Kavanagh and Shaw.

Many viewers though were disgusted and a heated discussion in the 'Letters to the editor' sections of the major Irish newspapers lasted for weeks. In order to give a representative flavour, selected letters from just one newspaper on two days are presented. The following four letters appeared on 5 February 1965 in the *Evening Press* under the heading 'This view of Ireland'. They give an indication that the annoyance and anger expressed by John O'Donovan was not his alone:

> Let us hope that the German film-makers who made 'The Children of Eire' film shown on T.E. are not allowed near Ireland again. It would indeed be very hard to produce a more unbalanced film than that shown. A film which states that the Irish economy is always near catastrophe, and a reference to 'penny-in-the-slot religion' as well as many other grossly misleading statements cannot be allowed to pass without some form of protest.
> If Ireland's economy is so near catastrophe why then do so many German firms set up factories here? If this is a general indication of German views on Ireland we would be better off without them.
> —Annoyed, Griffith Avenue, Drumcondra
>
> Having watched the German-made film 'Children of Eire' on Telefis Eireann and waited in vain for some acknowledgement of modern Ireland's comparative prosperity, my grandfather rubbed his glasses thoughtfully, saying: 'Maybe we should have sided with Churchill, after all!'
> This remark amused me as much as the film exasperated me. I well remember how my grandfather, in common with many other Irishmen,

---

[27] In the discussion about Böll's portrayal of poverty, the letters of Francis John Byrne, University College Dublin (10 February 1965) and J.W. Millar are of interest, the former claiming that Böll was remarkable insofar as he "however perversely, delights in this state of affairs" referring to the poverty and dirt of Irish life, and, as a reaction to the "soulless new Germany of the Wirtschaftswunder". Millar replies that it was very far from the truth that Böll saw poverty as a virtue, explaining that he had the benefit of knowing Böll personally and having discussed the issue with him numerous times.

refused to believe the facts about Nazi Germany. In 1945, when Pope Pius XII confirmed what the Allies had been telling us for the previous five years he grudgingly conceded that there must have been some truth in all the stories!

The unspeakable sufferings of the Jews, the terrifying fanaticism of the Hitler regime had left him unmoved twenty odd years ago – it was all not business of ours. But one German commentator, because he presented an unfair and one-sided picture of Ireland, changed his mind about the whole German nation! In one half-hour he achieved what Churchill's oratory and Hitler's devilry had failed to do in five long years!
—C.H., Blackrock

I watched the programme 'As Others See Us' on T.E. I was disgusted at the comments made by Donal Nevin and Patrick O'Keeffe in the discussion on the programme. Where are our full blooded Irishmen? My blood boiled at the summing up of the film by these two 'doormats'.

The film was an exaggerated, untrue account of any part of Ireland. In future please, let us have people on TV who will not be afraid to speak their minds.

Like John O'Donovan, I would like to go to Germany to make a film 'Children of Germany'.
—Angry, Rialto

I saw the Telefis Eireann programme – 'Ireland, as others see us', shown on Tuesday night and the discussion which followed. I was indeed very surprised at the views of both Mr. Nevin and Mr. O'Keeffe on the film and I would like to congratulate Mr. O'Donovan on his outspoken criticism with which I entirely agree.

Personally, there wasn't a sentence in the commentary that I could agree with. The shots of rural Ireland to me were a disgrace – all one could see were boarded-up houses with the roofs blown off, very very old people, country roads just like overgrown laneways, etc. Indeed if the film is for distribution in Germany, it would not, in my opinion show a true picture of rural Ireland today. As Mr. O'Donovan said, I too, would like to get an opportunity of presenting rural Germany on film.

I think it was a very distorted picture of rural Ireland.
—Disgusted, Donnybrook

Four days later, on 9 February 1965, equally robust arguments, this time criticising the critics and defending the film, could be found in the same newspaper:

Dublin Doesn't Want To Know Once ... Jack(een) is alright
Surely the maker of the German film 'Children of Eire' wished to present to an intelligent section of the German people, a pictoral story of a part of Ireland which they would find interesting.

Anyone who knows Achill would agree that it was a most sensitive, perceptive picture. A moving and charming hundred per cent honest film, it showed the west as it is, steeped in tears. But Dublin doesn't want to know because Jack(een) is alright.
—Westerner, Kimmage

A TRUE PICTURE

Having read the one-sided comments on the film 'Children of Eire' I feel compelled to reply.

To 'J.M.' I wish to say that although I heard the remark "penny-in the slot religion" I did not hear the slightest tone of sarcasm or humour. Nor was there any quip made about religion.

'Annoyed' states that it would be hard to produce a more unbalanced picture. It would be true to say that it would be quite impossible to produce a more unbalanced view than the one forwarded by 'Annoyed'.

'C.H.' tells us little about Naziism, a subject about which I am sure he knows very little. Try as I do I still can not find the link between Naziism and 'Children of Eire'.

'Angry' calls two prominent Irishmen 'doormats'. This is not only untrue but also indiscreet and ignorant. Only two persons on the panel discussed the film in a fair, sensible and intelligent manner.

To my mind the film projected a remarkably true image of Ireland. Everything the camera filmed is true, as for the narration this with a few exceptions is also true.

In conclusion I wish to ask those people who commented on this film not to be prejudiced and above all don't be afraid to admit especially to yourselves that this film IS a true picture of Ireland.
—E.Tuthill, 291 Ballyfermot Rd. Dublin 10

ALL DUBLIN ADDRESSES

When I read the letters in your columns which criticised the German film 'Children of Eire' the first thing I noticed was they all had Dublin addresses.

Now it cannot be denied by anybody that Ireland is one of the most impoverished countries in Western Europe; and with this in mind the German film makers evidently came to Ireland.

Naturally they decided to operate outside the capital city which, in almost every country gives an artificial picture of how most people live, and this they did fairly and squarely.

A million people – mostly working age – left this country in recent years to find employment elsewhere – empty houses – old people – young children.

As for the religious aspects of the film, I myself was surprised at how deeply religious the people are, outside our capital. As for the 'penny-in-the-slot offerings', it was apparently new to the Germans – let's hope they catch on! I think it's a good idea and by no means wrong.

As for the Irishman's attitude to time, again I think the film was correct.

Some time ago I was out for a spin on a motor bike. About 10 miles outside Dublin I came across an itinerant encampment. One of them stopped me and asked me what day it was!

So all you Dublin critics with your nice jobs and comfortable homes, think of your less fortunate countrymen. Let's hope this film will encourage continental industrialists to come here to help make it a better land to live in. Time has proved we cannot do it ourselves.

—Facts First, Ferguson Road, Drumcondra.

WHAT WAS OBJECT?

It is quite obvious that most of the comments were made by individualists who are biased in their attitudes, in particular C.H. from Blackrock. This bias renders all criticism next to useless, for unless we view these things with open minds we cannot fairly assess the qualities or failures of such a production.

Next, we should, if we wish to judge the film fairly, ask ourselves 'What did it set out to do?' It did not purport to constitute either a fair, balanced or comprehensive picture of Ireland, of life in Ireland, so why criticise it if it does not? The great majority of the scenes in the film are still to be seen and are not even rare in Ireland. Moreover, I wonder if the critics really think that this film, when shown will lead people to believe what they saw is a comprehensive picture of Ireland? – of course not, they must think that continentals are absolutely ignorant.

There is nothing interesting to a continental about skyscrapers, traffic jams, cement silos, and airports. The picture which was depicted was a very interesting and poetic one, which, I imagine, will do more for the Irish tourism than any brochures. The sooner Irish people get rid of their inferiority complex the better.

I also would like to make a film 'Children of Germany' but I doubt if it would lead people to believe that Germany was anything but a prosperous, industrious, and modern nation of people no matter what kind of unbalanced picture I would show. It seems to me that these critics cannot see beyond their noses, and do not give anybody any credit with having a little intelligence.

—Satisfied, Donore Avenue, Dublin 8.

Similar arguments and sentiments on both sides can be found in the many letters that were sent to the other newspapers. In the *Irish Times* numerous letters were printed between 6 February and 6 March 1965.[28] Taken

---

[28] Also notable is the less intense but longer lasting parallel discussion that took place mainly in the *Irish Times*. It also had to do with Irish-German relations and started on 5 February 1965 under the heading 'Verboten'; the last letter on this was printed on 24 March. This debate took issue with foreigners, especially Germans,

together with equally or even more passionate statements in the *Evening Press*, the *Irish Press*, the *Sunday Press*, and the *Irish Independent* we find a very emotional debate for over a month with several dozen letters to the editor, in basically all larger daily or weekly papers.

It is clear that the debate raised larger issues than the film itself. It was also very much an Irish debate about where Ireland stood and where it should go, how to react to a portrayal that conflicted with the self-image at least some people had, how to engage with the outside world generally and, possibly most of all, about which values to follow. There is obvious pride in the economic development that had taken place and was not reflected in the film. Clearly one reason for the negative reception of the film was the delay of its broadcast in Ireland. It needs to be remembered here that the Irish economic situation was changing considerably in the early 1960s (the film was written and shot in 1960 but not shown in Ireland until 1965). Sean Lemass, the new Irish Taoiseach, had created a fairly successful economy, lowering unemployment and improving the balance of trade (which according to Böll's film was heading for a catastrophe which only thanks to support from the emigrants to the US etc was avoided). The 'age of innocence' of Ireland had ended.[29] Modernising changes had certainly already started in the late 1950s but were confined mainly to urban areas, foremost Dublin. Changes in Achill, where a substantial part of the film was shot were far slower. And while it was picked up by 'Facts First' in one letter quoted above, the discussion mainly took place in Dublin, making the debate an example of the city-country divide. Nevertheless, there are indications that people in the west were not always overjoyed either – according to a long article in the *Evening Press* on 17 February 1965, 'German T.E. film slammed', the Castlebar Urban Council decided to protest to Bord Failte 'against the slur cast on this country by the West German company who made the film *Children of Eire*'. While there seems to have been no unanimous condemnation (one person on the Council

---

who had acquired properties and land in Ireland and then erected barbed wire fences. This exchange of opinions though, while using emotive terms such as 'Herrenvolk' and 'Lebensraum' moved on from only Irish-German relations to include also the multi-faceted connection with Britain. Taken together it seems fair to say that unlike the reported friendliness towards Germans in the 1950s, in the mid-1960s there were at least in sections of the Irish population also strong feelings against German visitors and neighbours.

[29] See Brian Fallon, *An Age of Innocence – Irish Culture 1930-1960*. Dublin: Gill & Macmillan 1998.

defended the film), according to the chairman, Mr J. Chambers, people on Achill Island were 'ripping mad over the film'.

Heinrich Böll quickly became aware of negative reaction to the film. Only a few weeks after the Irish broadcast he wrote an attempt to answer his critics which was subsequently published in the March edition of *Hibernia*.[30]

Above his article, a picture of Böll with a cigarette between his fingers and seemingly about to make a point is printed as well as excerpts of different statements under the heading 'A controversial film', ranging from John O'Donovan's 'I say this disgraceful production must be withdrawn' and Patrick Gallagher's opinion that it presents the view of a poet to Gabriel Fallon's viewpoint that it is a 'pleasing if somewhat limited' film that provoked a lively discussion.

In his reply, Böll makes five points in order to clear away misunderstandings, arguing that he does not really have anything to say in defence of the film because he feels he had not really commited any offence but that he was rather misunderstood by some people.

First, he states that he has published 'some 17 books, mostly novels and short stories, all dealing with Germany' (some of them having caused a lot of grief there) and that a comparison is needed between his writings about Germany and Ireland: 'I think it would then be quite clear that *Children of Eire* and *Irisches Tagebuch* are thoroughly friendly in tone, indeed sweet, and this is absolutely genuine, arising out of the author's complete sympathy with and for his subject.' Second, he argues that there was neither any attempt nor chance to give a complete picture of Ireland, only 'to show a small part of what I consider beautiful and poetic in Ireland, and what I feel to be the most painful problem confronting your country; the emigration of young people'. His third point is that both book and film are admittedly historical ('I feel there is room for correction, but not apologies') and a lot has changed, but economic progress and development of tourism also leads to Ireland losing parts of its poetry and warming hospitality, naturalness and peace. He sees these changes with mixed feelings: 'I am delighted at this development, because it will possibly help

---

[30] Heinrich Böll, A reply to critics of *Children of Eire*, in: *Hibernia*, No. 29, March 1965, p. 15. Further attention was drawn to it by large advertising of *Hibernia* for their March edition in the *Irish Times,* which included the short titles of the main articles - 'Critics of *Children of Eire*' in Böll's case - five lines of the text and his name, see *Irish Times*, 6 March 1965, p. 8.

to stem the flow of emigration. At the same time, however, it saddens me, for it will alter the character of your country'. He notes that writers such as 'Frank O'Connor and Sean O'Faolain are living in Ireland again, and others like Brendan Behan, are dying there'. His fourth point is the often misunderstood subject of poverty and his view that he considers even the poorest inhabitant of a village in the West of Ireland richer than someone in a city flat in Germany or England. His final point is that it is not the job of a writer to show the economic progress of a country but rather for a statistician or economist.

The strong reactions to the film in Ireland clearly had an impact on Böll. To avoid similar criticism about the book he added in 1967 the essay 'Thirteen years later' (referring to the elapsed time since his first visit to Ireland in 1954 and the many changes in the economy) to the English translation of *Irisches Tagebuch*, trying to explain why he had not referred to the economic improvement that Ireland had experienced since the late 1950s, and stating his love for Ireland. He also added a brief foreword: 'The Ireland described in this book is that of the mid-1950s. My comments on the great changes that have taken place in that country since then are contained in the Epilogue', perhaps to make sure that no-one would be upset and stop reading before having reached the end.

The film, or better said, the hostile reactions to it, did not end Böll's enjoyment of Ireland. Only two months after the film was aired he spent a month in Achill and in each of the following two years he returned for several months again. But it had left a mark and even years later Böll referred to the negative reception of his film in Ireland. He also used it as an example of unwittingly hurting people and admitted that he realised he had not taken into account natural sentiments.[31]

---

[31] See quote at beginning and for example *Im literarischen Kaffeehaus*, WDR/NDR/Freies Berlin, 21 December 1967, conversation between Heinrich Böll, Hans Mayer and Marcel Reich-Ranicki on the occasion of Böll's 50th birthday.

PART V:
LEGACY

CHAPTER EIGHTEEN

REVERBERATION

Quite apart from the ongoing interest in the *Irish Journal* and to a lesser extent in the film *Children of Eire*, Böll's relationship with Ireland has continued to fascinate and has been the focus of numerous articles, radio programmes and films in Germany.[1] For example, in 2009 a 48-page brochure by Bernd Erhard Fischer and Angelika Fischer, *Das Irland des Heinrich Böll* [Heinrich Böll's Ireland] was published. With many photos and quotes, especially from Böll's letters home, this publication provides an introduction to Heinrich Böll's time in Ireland and is clearly aimed at German tourists. It is referred to on the Achill Island tourism webpage.[2] Clearly a lot is to be said for Eda Sagarra's description: 'Heinrich Böll, Father of German tourism in Ireland'.[3] Even nowadays tourists, and not only German ones, still seem to successfully take up Böll's challenge in his foreword to the *Irish Journal* to find the Ireland he described: 'This Ireland exists: but whoever goes there and fails to find it has no claim on the author.'

What about the legacy of Heinrich Böll overall? A lot has happened since his death that seemed unimaginable during his lifetime, first and foremost the reunification of Germany in the eventful years of 1989/1990. Böll's

---

[1] One of the better ones, a 30-minute film from 1996 by Wibke Kämpfer and produced by Gunter Hanfgarn, that was later also translated into English and shown under the title *A second home – Heinrich Böll in Ireland*, was a production of the radio and television station Deutsche Welle: *Zwischen den Heimaten* ('Between homes'), 'a documentary on Heinrich Böll's second home in the west of Ireland'. It contains interviews with a number of local people and also with René Böll, Erich Kock, who worked as Böll's secretary for a time, and with Hugo Hamilton, who was at the time writer-in-residence at the cottage. Beate Kuhn and Marc Delestre's film *Die Achill-Island – Ein irisches Insel-Tagebuch* (Bayrischer Rundfunk 2005) also used interviews with Achill people as well as short excerpts from *Irland und seine Kinder*.
[2] http://www.achilltourism.com/store/irlanddasboll.php (accessed 20 April 2011).
[3] Eda Sagarra, Heinrich Böll, Father of German Tourism in Ireland, in: G. Holfter (ed.), *Irish-German Literary and Cultural Connections*, pp. 13-18.

name was often invoked when it came to assessing the changes, the specific characteristics of life in West Germany and their portrayal. From 1992, when an international conference in Cologne and a voluminous edited book[4] about him commemorated the 75th anniversary of his birth, there have been regular events and reflection on his place as a writer and a political and social commentator. Quite often there was a split between appreciating him as one or the other – either as a literary figure or as an important voice offering intellectual leadership and shaping political consciousness in Germany from the 1950s to his death.[5] While there are some voices claiming that public interest in Böll's life and work is long gone,[6] there are many indications to the contrary. In 2007, in time for the anniversary of Böll's 90th birthday, a number of activities took place in order to commemorate the writer. It was also an occasion to take stock and ask 'What stays?', as in the *Zeit Magazin* devoted to Böll and offering different view points.[7] Helge Malchow, head of Kiepenheuer & Witsch, Böll's publisher, took the opportunity to point out the important influence Böll had on a number of the new German writers, naming especially Ralf Rothmann, Ingo Schulze and Katja Lange-Müller – he could have added many others. He admitted that even the publishing house was surprised how well a new edition of Böll's short stories sold when published in 2005 – over 20,000 copies within weeks.[8]

---

[4] Bernd Balzer (ed.), *Heinrich Böll 1917-1985. Zum 75. Geburtstag*, Bern, Berlin et al: Peter Lang 1992.
[5] See for example Reinhard K. Zachau, *Heinrich Böll: Forty Years of Criticism*, Drawer, Columbia: Camden 1994.
[6] See Christian Linder, *Das Schwirren eines heranfliegenden Pfeils. Heinrich Böll – Eine Biographie*, Berlin: Matthes & Seitz 2009, p. 10. Linder seems not particularly impressed by Böll's writing though more than half of the text consists of Böll quotes. He also claims that Böll lacked analytical intelligence (p. 286). Interestingly, in over 600 pages of biography Linder covers Ireland and the *Irish Journal* in less than two pages and mentions Behan, Synge, Swift and Yeats not once. He concentrates mainly on his thesis that Böll's writing motivation was mostly connected with his mother and a 'defence of childhood' – a claim Linder had already made in an earlier 1978 biography. Neither his own book nor the numerous (rather mixed) reviews of it sit easily with his stated belief that there is no longer any interest in Böll.
[7] Cf. *Zeit Magazin*, no 32, 2 August 2007, see especially pp 12-21.
[8] Cf. Thomas Linden, Einfach wesentlich – Gespräch mit Verleger Helge Malchow zum 90. Geburtstag von Heinrich Böll, *Bergische Landeszeitung*, 20 December 2007, p. 12.

Of considerable importance also is the 27 volume 'Kölner Ausgabe', the Cologne edition of Böll's works published between 2002 and 2010, that brought into the public domain many previously unpublished early stories as well as much background information. The edition has overall enjoyed critical acclaim and there have been page-long articles about Böll and his ongoing relevance in leading newspapers and journals.[9]

Furthermore, there is a strong legacy beyond the literary and artistic fields. Heinrich Böll's name was chosen as the name of a foundation, that later became associated with the Green Party.[10] Annemarie Böll pointed towards the aims the foundation was to have:

> A foundation carrying my husband's name should be a collection point and support area, a place of remembrance for groups and individuals who try to create a more human, peaceful and fair world – who attempt to continue what he tried to do on his own, as well as with other writers, with his limited possibilities, but with all his energy.[11]

---

[9] See for example Volker Weidermann, Unser Hemingway – Heinrich Böll, ein Moralist? Stimmt nicht. In seiner Werkausgabe trifft man auf einen selbstironischen Modernisierer der deutschen Literatur, in: *Frankfurter Allgemeine Sonntagszeitung*, 9 January 2011, p. 19 and Ulrich Greiner, Der Schriftsteller des Mitleids – Wir sollten ihn wieder lesen: Heinrich Böll, in: *Die Zeit*, 27 January 2011, pp. 49f. A dissenting voice is Werner Bellmann, who was originally involved in the project, and who is very critical of editorial mistakes and appreciative of the wealth of new material available, cf. Werner Bellmann, Heinrich Bölls *Irisches Tagebuch*. Kritische Anmerkungen zur Neuedition in der Kölner Ausgabe, in: *Wirkendes Wort* 60 (2010) vol 1, pp. 157-165.

[10] It was chosen with two other foundations to be jointly associated with the party under the heading of 'Rainbow Foundation' (Regenbogenstiftung). Some time later again, it was decided to have just one foundation in order to avoid duplicate cost and structures. After a long discussion the name of Heinrich Böll was chosen in 1997, with the runner-up of Petra Kelly, who had been among the founders of the Green Party in Germany and incidentally was a politician also well-known in Ireland. The foundation is particularly concerned with political, educational and ecological developments and argues that Böll's promotion of citizens' participation in politics is the model for the foundation's work. The foundation is active not only within Germany but has 28 offices around the globe (unfortunately not in Ireland).

[11] [Eine Stiftung, die den Namen meines Mannes trägt, sollte ein Sammelpunkt, ein Stützpunkt, ein Ort der Erinnerung und Unterstützung für Gruppen und Einzelpersonen sein, die versuchen, eine menschlichere, friedlichere und gerechtere Welt zu bauen – die versuchen, fortzusetzen, was er als Einzelner oder zusammen mit Schriftstellerkollegen mit seinen begrenzten Möglichkeiten, aber mit Einsatz aller Kraft zu leisten versucht hat.] Initiative zur Gründung der

Also in literary terms, Böll's name and work still have currency outside Germany. Australian author Richard Flanagan uses the basic outlines of Böll's novel *The Lost Honour of Katharina Blum* for his acclaimed novel *The Unknown Terrorist* (2007) transporting Böll's story from the terrorist scare in Germany in the early 1970s into the globalist world of post 9/11. In an interview in autumn 2007 Ian McEwan named Böll, Kafka and Thomas Mann as his role models, adding that he loved Böll's style, the slow, nearly frozen unfolding.[12] New editions in the US of his works in 2010 as well as new contracts with Russia in 2009, and Spain and Italy in 2010[13] indicate that Böll is not only still an international bestseller but a 'longseller'.

Legacy in Ireland

The question remains to what extent Böll has entered the Irish consciousness beyond being a German Nobel Prize winner for literature who had some link to Achill Island.[14] A former member of the German Embassy recalled that during a state visit to Ireland of the former German President Richard von Weizsäcker in 1992, the then Irish President Mary Robinson declared in jest that if Ireland did not already have a national saint, Heinrich Böll would be a suitable candidate.[15]

While this indicates a strong admiration of Böll by Mary Robinson, it is not always clear whether this appreciation is shared more widely, although there seem to be signs that it might have become more widespread now in the last few years. An indication here could be how much he has become part of contemporary discourse in Ireland. There is clearly an increased awareness of and interest in the film, as was seen in the previous chapter, quite apart from the active and diverse engagement with the *Irish Journal* described in an earlier chapter. Irish writers and artists, foremost amongst

---

Heinrich-Böll-Stiftung (ed.), *Stiften gehen*, Bornheim-Merten: Lamuv 1987, p. 10.
[12] 'Ich liebe den Stil von Böll, dieses langsame, wie erfrorene Entfalten'. Ian McEwan, Wir müssen zweihundert Jahre vorausdenken, *Frankfurter Allgemeine Sonntagszeitung*, 21 October 2007, p. 25.
[13] Information of Markus Schäfer, Böll Archive Cologne and Iris Brandt, Kiepenheuer & Witsch, 20 January 2011.
[14] See for example the obituaries in Irish newspapers upon his death: Death of Heinrich Böll, *Irish Times* 17 July 1985, p. 1; Heinrich Böll dies, aged 67, *Irish Times* 17 July 1985, p. 6; Böll got last rites, *Irish Times* 19 July 1985, p. 5; W. German literary giant Böll dies, *Irish Independent*, 17 July 1985.
[15] Letter from Dr. Klapper, German Embassy Dublin, 25 November 1992.

them Hugo Hamilton, show a great interest in Böll's work and his relationship with Ireland. Recent examples also include artist Declan Clarke's acclaimed video *Cologne Overnight*, interweaving the collapse of the Cologne History Archive in 2009 and the loss of many of Böll's papers with footage of the destruction of Cologne in 1942 and the the deserted village on Achill.[16] Also, a physical reminder of Böll has a key role in maintaining and expanding Böll's legacy in Ireland – his former cottage.[17]

The Heinrich Böll Cottage on Achill Island

> For me to spend some time in Böll's cottage now, in that room with the window looking down over Nangle's valley to the sea at Dugort, brings back at the same time one of the most moving fiction writers and the enthusiasm and the integrity of my father. It is a room to conjure ghosts in, to urge one on to labour, while great fuchsia bushes hang their flowers drenched with mist before the window. Deora Dé; the Tears of God. Time stands cautious, and the act of writing becomes a greater labour of love.[18]

Without a doubt the most important place of remembrance and ongoing legacy is the Heinrich Böll cottage in Dugort, Achill Island with its writers/artists-in-residence scheme. The idea was born during a writers' workshop on Achill conducted as part of Scoil Acla, in a discussion between Clodagh King and John F. Deane. Clodagh King then contacted Annemarie Böll, Heinrich's widow, and René Böll, his son. The Böll family very much supported the idea and with some financial backing from the Heinrich Böll Foundation, then in Cologne, the cottage was

---

[16] It was praised as the hightlight of the Kilkenny Arts Festival 2010, see http://www.theflyonthearchitecturalwall.org/ (accessed 28 April 2011). See also Declan Clarke, The Weather over Germany, Heinrich Böll's literature of ruins, in: *Cabinet*, 39/2010, pp. 28-32.

[17] Another institution in Ireland, the Centre for Irish-German Studies at the University of Limerick is also doing its share to acknowledge Böll's central position in the context of its work. The 1st Conference in Irish-German Studies and founding event of the Centre for Irish-German Studies at the University of Limerick in September 1997 had a strong emphasis on Heinrich Böll, with an exhibition of Böll's life and work, opened by the late Viktor Böll, nephew of Heinrich and long term director of the Heinrich Böll Archive. There were also a number of papers on Böll, in the overall context of German-Irish connections in arts, music and literature, politics, history and business. The 9th Conference in 2007 on the *Irisches Tagebuch* has already been mentioned.

[18] John F. Deane, in: John McHugh (ed.), *The Heinrich Böll Cottage on Achill Island*, Dooagh: The Heinrich Böll Committee 1998, p. 60.

officially opened as an artists' residence on 21 March 1992. A Heinrich Böll Committee had been formed just two months before in late January 1992, with Clodagh King, John F. Deane and Tom McNamara among others. René Böll came over for the opening, and the German Ambassador at the time, Mr. Martin Elsässer, was there as well as the first residents of the cottage, Tom LeBlanc, a Sioux Indian writer, and the Irish poet Macdara Woods. Later the same year, on 4 August, President Mary Robinson came to visit. The list of Irish and international artists who have been in the Böll cottage since then is long – among others, writers Deirdre Madden, Anne Enright, Paul Durcan and Hugo Hamilton, also sculptor John Behan and composer Michael Holohan. Other guests with links to the Böll family have included the German politician Petra Kelly and German writer Günter Wallraff.

In 1998, in order to contribute to the celebrations of the 80th anniversary of Böll's birth, a small book was published by the Committee, dedicated to the memory of Clodagh King, who had died in 1995. It gives some background and examples of the work of a number of the artists-in-residence and is a tribute to the amazing inspiration of the cottage: 'I spent a fortnight in the cottage in 1992 and I found it an unusually productive period. It is a perfect place to work in, remote, quiet but also with access to other villages. It is a great privilege to be able to make use of it' (Leland Bardwell); 'The Böll house is a place of peace which personally I found to be a paradise for a writer' (Eamonn Sweeney); 'The three weeks in May '92, which I spent at the Böll House are among the happiest of my artistic life' (John Behan).

In June 2001 the Böll family agreed to sell the cottage for £100,000 to the Heinrich Böll Committee which became transformed into the Heinrich Böll Association and was registered as a limited company and charity in order to obtain funding through the Department of Arts, Heritage and Gaeltacht, the Arts Council and Mayo County Council. Donncha Ó Gallchobhair, former Minister for the Gaeltacht, pointed out at the time that it was 'a great honour for Achill to have Heinrich Böll locate here'.[19]
The effort to buy the cottage was well supported by the community and writers with links to Achill such as Paul Durcan (who wrote much of his poetry collection *Greetings To Our Friends in Brazil* during a month long stay there). He stated in a letter that was attached to the proposal for the purchase and refurbishment of the cottage: 'The whole project of the

---

[19] Ibid.

Heinrich Böll Cottage is constantly validated by a sense of the presence of the original Writer Resident himself as the master author who understood the necessity of privacy and the rightness of solitude.'[20]

This privacy and solitude can, however, be challenged at times. One occupant of the Böll cottage, the writer Eamonn Sweeney, wrote in an article printed in the *Irish Times* in 1997, that each day he received a dozen or so of Böll's compatriots who were visiting the house. This obviously had some result on his lifestyle, preventing him from having lie-ins: 'as the thought of an unshaven novelist in his boxer shorts being accidentally camcordered by literary tourists from Frankfurt is not a pleasant one.'[21]

In order to avoid too many disruptive visits, particularly from German tourists, a sign was placed outside the cottage, asking for respect of the privacy of the occupants – written in German and English. The sign itself also has 'Heinrich-Böll-Cottage' written in large letters and the background of the cottage is a good photo opportunity and also a compromise for visitors who have sometimes come a long way to see Böll's cottage.

Unfortunately, for some visitors this seems insufficient. Celebrated writer Claire Keegan, another beneficiary of the writer-in-residence scheme devoted one of her short stories to such an unwanted visitor.[22]

---

[20] Sheila Sullivan, The writer's residence, *Irish Times*, 29 August 2001, p. 10. Thanks to Hermann Rasche for pointing out the article to me.
[21] Eamonn Sweeney, Böll's Notion, *Irish Times*, 18 July 1997, p. 10. My own experiences nine years later around the same time of the year would indicate a downturn in (German) tourist numbers, though occasionally buses or individuals stopped briefly to take pictures.
[22] Claire Keegan, The long and painful death, in: *Walk the Blue Fields*, London: Faber & Faber 2008, pp 1-20. In the story the narrative voice is that of a female writer who has come to the Böll cottage for two weeks, '[...] hungry to read, and to work' (p. 4). Keegan describes in detail the position and surroundings of the house on Achill, and its layout including Böll's study, 'a small room with a disused fireplace, and a window facing the sea' (p. 6). The story evolves around the conflict of the narrator's wish for privacy and her need to write and the disturbing intrusion of a German professor of literature, who calls and insists on visiting the cottage. When he comes later, he does little more than insult her rather than providing any information about Böll as had been hoped by the narrator beforehand (as '[s]he felt at a loss and slightly ashamed, knowing so little about the man in whose house she was staying'). In the story the narrator revenges

Sign at the entrance of the Böll cottage in Dugort

However, overall the whole scheme has been very successful, and continues to be supported by the Arts Council, Mayo County Council and the Goethe-Institut. The aims followed are very simple, very straightforward, as John McHugh, the secretary of the group, explains:

> People are invited who are creative – writers, visual artists, translators or composers. They just come to Achill and they have time, it is of direct benefit to the artists. The scheme fulfils this aim very well and that's why it gets the funding. But there are three other aspects to it – firstly, how it relates to the community, allowing for some contact between the artist and the community, without prescribing it, but welcoming and facilitating it if wished. So sometimes there have been visits and readings in schools or art workshops for the elderly. Another aspect is to recognise the tradition of Achill Island to be a place to which writers and artists have come for the last hundred years and to build and foster a continuation of this tradition. Through the Böll cottage new people are brought in and in a number of cases Achill permeates through their work which obviously is very good for Achill in order to maintain a profile as a place, as an island, from a

---

herself by writing about the episode and then extending it fictionally by letting the professor die of cancer, 'a long and painful death' (title and last sentence, p. 20).

national and international base. And last but not least it is felt that it is the best memorial that can be made for Heinrich Böll on Achill Island – a place where people come to work and where there is a feeling that 'the man himself' would have approved and welcomed it.[23]

Well over one hundred artists and writers have benefited from the scheme so far.

The Committee is involved not only in the selection of the writers and artists who are invited to come, the upkeep of the house as a place with a good atmosphere, a home for the artists (a major facelift was given to the cottage in 2005 which added flowerbeds outside, underfloor heating and a number of other mod cons) but they also put a lot of work and effort into the organisation of readings, exhibitions, involvement in Scoil Acla and the organisation of Heinrich Böll weekends. Further activities include essay competitions with Böll-connected topics in local secondary schools.[24] The varied programmes of the Böll weekends, combining lectures and exhibitions on Böll as well as local history, national art and often readings by internationally acclaimed writers (for example in 2010 the reading and discussion with Booker Prize winner John Banville and Kathrin Schmidt, winner of the German Buchpreis, chaired by Hugo Hamilton) with guided walking tours to points of interest, seem a winning formula to ensure ongoing interest.

The Böll family has strongly supported the project from the beginning, when Clodagh King approached Annemarie Böll, half a dozen years after Heinrich's death. Annemarie, who was over eighty years old at the time of the opening, was not able to attend, but René Böll, who had become the main point of contact, did come. He has returned often, attending and contributing to the activities, which is much appreciated in Achill. For him, many childhood memories are connected to Keel and Dugort; for the locals, some of whom have known him since he was a boy, he is very much part of the place. From a German perspective, one could have hoped that the Heinrich-Böll-Cottage would have continued to receive funding not only from the Irish side but also from the Heinrich Böll Foundation and possibly the German Government, as one would be hard pushed to

---

[23] Conversation John McHugh, 21 August 2006.
[24] See also Edward King, John McHugh, The work of the Achill Heinrich Böll Association and the Heinrich Böll Residency Programme, in: G. Holfter (ed.), *Heinrich Böll's 'Irisches Tagebuch' in Context*, Irish-German Studies 5, Trier: WVT 2010, pp. 23-25.

imagine a better enterprise to foster intercultural understanding and support of cultural links and joint heritage. However, the way it is run now, with an Irish and mainly Achill-based Heinrich Böll Committee, has provided a close connection to the local community, achieving a great record of activities and enjoying a lot of support and interest on Achill and nationwide. And the impact of Böll on Achill is resonant not only with its Irish inhabitants, as the memoirs of American former *Irish Times* journalist Sheila Sullivan, *Follow the Moon*,[25] or Belgian visual artist Francis van Maele's inclusion of Böll family photos in his 2007 book of Achill photographs show.[26]

Conclusion

'She smiled at me, and I smiled back' (p. 8), a sentence in the second chapter, is repeated at the very end of the *Irish Journal*, thereby enclosing the text between the chapters 'Arrival II' and the last chapter 'Farewell'. Böll captures here his whole relationship with Ireland. It was a happy, smiling and generally sympathetic relationship, allowing for idiosyncrasies and misunderstandings. It was built on literature, due to his early reading of and a lifelong preference for Irish literature and writers, most explicitly Behan, Swift and Synge but with great reverence also for Joyce, Yeats, O'Casey and others. It was the most important relationship Heinrich Böll had throughout his life with any foreign country. It was at once an intellectual affinity and an actual experience of living at the western edge of Europe and a retreat. The specific way of life attracted him and his family: an easily misunderstood appreciation of a simple way of life and his encounters with Irish people, especially on Achill Island; the poetical everyday communication as well as a perspective strongly anchored in religious beliefs which at least partly fulfilled his dream of a society permeated by other, Christian values.

What this book set out to do was to show the multifacetedness of Heinrich Böll's relationship with Ireland, which, having started with fairy tales, became a reality. It had a strong personal dimension for him and his wife. Not only the *Irish Journal* but a good number of Böll's other writings were inspired by Ireland. All this is not to minimise the many other

---

[25] Sheila Sullivan, *Follow the Moon – A Memoir*, Dublin: Currach 2006, especially chapter 9 'In search of Heinrich Böll', pp. 149-164.
[26] Francis Van Maele, *Dugort – Achill – Photographs 2005-2007*, Dugort: Redfoxpress 2007.

interests and effects Böll had in literary, cultural and political matters of his time, both in Germany and internationally. Böll's literary work overall, before and after the *Irish Journal*, was firmly anchored within contemporary Germany. But there is no doubting the enormous impact the *Irish Journal* had on Irish-German relations and the German view of Ireland.

Not only the *Irish Journal* but also Böll's film and his and Annemarie's translations continue to provide cultural and historical insights, or are rediscovered as doing so. His film is not only a historical document of a bygone era but also a case study of how (Irish-German) discourses can boil hotly, be forgotten and resurface in other forms. While among the German reading public the *Irish Journal* has been an ongoing catalyst to ponder German life and values (and dream of Ireland), the film led to a controversional argument about Irish realities and ambitions and the question to what extent the outsider can or should make statements on Ireland – a discussion repeated some forty years later on account of remarks by the then German Ambassador Christian Pauls.

We will never know what Heinrich Böll's opinion would be of the Celtic Tiger and its demise. Böll clearly viewed Irish modernisation in the 1960s with mixed feelings. He had strong and sometimes contradictory views, but what is beyond dispute is his passionate engagement with his surroundings and his often questioning and critical involvement in the political, cultural, social and literary sphere. But concentrating only on Böll's public persona often leads to overlooking his strong commitment to his writing as art. The *Irish Journal* is a fine example of his literary achievement.

In time, a new translation of the *Irish Journal* might make it more accessible to younger Irish readers, and a broader general interest in Böll's works, not only his novels but also his essays, will with any luck re-establish itself.

Böll was an author of his time – but he still has a lot to tell us today.

SELECTED BIBLIOGRAPHY

I. Primary Literature by Heinrich Böll

Böll, Heinrich: *Acquainted with the Night* translated by Richard Graves, New York: Holt 1954.
—. Als Gott die Zeit machte, *FAZ,* 19 July 1956, No. 166, p. 8.
—. Am Rande Europas, in: *Magnum,* 2 /1955, issue 10, p. 48.
—. An Approach to the Rationality of Poetry, translated by Leila Vennewitz, in: *Heinrich Böll – On his Death – Selected obituaries and the last interview*, Bonn: Inter Nationes 1985, pp. 32-46.
—. *And Never Said a Word,* translated by Leila Vennewitz, New York: McGraw-Hill 1978.
—. Anekdote zur Senkung der Arbeitsmoral, in: *Das Heinrich Böll Lesebuch*, Munich: dtv 1982, pp. 223-225.
—. A reply to critics of *Children of Eire*, in: *Hibernia* 1965, p. 15.
—. Auf einer kleinen Insel, *FAZ,* 14 May 1955, No. 112, p. 42.
—. Bete für die Seele des Michael O'Neill, *FAZ,* 26 February 1955, No. 48, p. 32.
—. Betrachtungen über den irischen Regen, *Neue Zürcher Zeitung,* 4 February 1956, No. 332 (8), p. 4.
—. Bilder aus Irland, in: *Westermanns Monatshefte* 97 (1956), No. 8, pp. 14-21.
—. *Briefe aus dem Krieg 1939-1945*, edited by Jochen Schubert, Cologne: Kiepenheuer & Witsch 2001.
—. Das Zeug zu einer Äbtissin, *Spiegel,* 2 May 1966, p. 152.
—. Das neunte Kind der Mrs. D., *Aufwärts* 9, No. 8, 15 August 1956.
—. Der Abschied von Irland fiel schwer, *FAZ,* 9 March 1957, No. 58, p. 38.
—. Der erste Tag, *FAZ,* 24 December 1954, No. 299, p. 39.
—. *Der Mann mit den Messern*, Stuttgart: Philipp Reclam jun. 1959.
—. Der tote Indianer in der Duke Street, in: *Jahresringe 55/56*, ed. Kulturkreis im Bundesverband der deutschen Industrie, Stuttgart 1955, pp. 206-209 / *FAZ,* 31 March 1956, No. 77, p. 46.
—. Die Ursachen des Troubles mit Nordirland, *Süddeutsche Zeitung* 21/22 February 1970.

—. Ein paar Worte über ein paar Wörter, die uns da dauernd um die Ohren fliegen, in: Petra K. Kelly, *Um Hoffnung kämpfen - Gewaltfrei in eine grüne Zukunft*, Bornheim-Merten: Lamuv 1983, pp. 7-11.
—. *Eine deutsche Erinnerung - Interview mit René Wintzen*, Cologne: Kiwi 1979.
—. Es könnte schlimmer sein, *FAZ*, 8 January 1957, No. 6, p. 8.
—. *Essayistische Schriften und Reden I, 1952 - 1963*, edited by Bernd Balzer, Cologne: Kiwi 1979.
—. *Essayistische Schriften und Reden II, 1964 - 1972*, edited by Bernd Balzer, Cologne: Kiwi 1979.
—. Gedanken eines reisenden Zahnarztes, *FAZ*, 6 March 1956, No. 56, p. 8.
—. *Gruppenbild mit Dame*, Cologne: Kiwi 1971.
—. *Haus ohne Hüter*, Cologne: Kiwi 1954.
—. Ich bin kein Repräsentant – Gespräch mit Hanjo Kesting, in: *Die Zeit*, 23 December 1977, p. 36.
—. *Irisches Tagebuch*, with material and a comment [Nachwort] by Karl Heiner Busse, Cologne: Kiwi 1988.
—. *Irisches Tagebuch*, with materials and photos, edited by René Böll and a comment [Nachwort] by Jochen Schubert, Cologne: Kiepenheuer & Witsch 2007.
—. *Irish Journal*, New York/Toronto/London/Sydney: McGraw-Hill 1967 (translated by Leila Vennewitz).
—. Mayo - God help us, *FAZ*, 7 July 1956, No. 156, p. 41.
—. Porträt einer irischen Stadt, *NDR*, 25 March 1955 / *FAZ*, 26 March 1955, No. 72.
—. *Rom auf den ersten Blick - Landschaften, Städte, Reisen*, Munich: dtv 1987.
—. Skelett einer Siedlung, *FAZ*, 16 July 1955, No. 162, p. 40.
—. Torfklumpen im Kaminfeuer, *FAZ*, 26 August 1955, No. 197, p. 6.
—. Über Religion und Kirche – Interview von Robert Stauffer, broadcast on *Deutschlandfunk*, 12 January 1982, later published in *Konkret*, No. 6, 28 May 1982, pp. 115-117 under the title 'Die Kirche fault'.
—. Warum so zartfühlend? Über Carl Amery *Fragen an Welt und Kirche*, *Spiegel*, 15 May 1967, p. 140.
—. *Was soll aus dem Jungen bloß werden*, Munich: dtv 1983.
—. Wenn Seamus einen trinken will, *FAZ*, 3 August 1956, No. 179, p. 10.
—. *Werke 1936-1945*, Kölner Ausgabe volume 1, edited by J. H. Reid, Cologne: Kiepenheuer & Witsch 2004.
—. *Werke 1946-1947*, Kölner Ausgabe volume 2, edited by J. H. Reid, Cologne: Kiepenheuer & Witsch 2002.

—. *Werke 1947-1948*, Kölner Ausgabe volume 3, edited by Frank Finlay and Jochen Schubert, Cologne: Kiepenheuer & Witsch 2003.

—. *Werke 1949-1950*, Kölner Ausgabe volume 4, edited by Hans Joachim Bernhard, Cologne: Kiepenheuer & Witsch 2003.

—. *Werke 1951*, Kölner Ausgabe volume 5, edited by Robert C. Conrad, Cologne: Kiepenheuer & Witsch 2004.

—. *Werke 1952-1953*, Kölner Ausgabe volume 6, edited by Árpád Bernáth in cooperation with Annamária Gyurácz, Cologne: Kiepenheuer & Witsch 2007.

—. *Werke 1953-1954*, Kölner Ausgabe volume 7, edited by Ralf Schnell in cooperation with Klaus-Peter Bernhard, Cologne: Kiepenheuer & Witsch 2006.

—. *Werke Haus ohne Hüter 1954*, Kölner Ausgabe volume 8, edited by Jochen Schubert, Cologne: Kiepenheuer & Witsch 2009.

—. *Werke 1954-1956*, Kölner Ausgabe volume 9, edited by J. H. Reid, Cologne: Kiepenheuer & Witsch 2006.

—. *Werke 1956-1959*, Kölner Ausgabe volume 10, edited by Viktor Böll, Cologne: Kiepenheuer & Witsch 2005.

—. *Werke Billard um halb zehn (1959)*, Kölner Ausgabe volume 11, edited by Frank Finlay and Markus Schäfer, Cologne: Kiepenheuer & Witsch 2002.

—. *Werke 1959-1963*, Kölner Ausgabe volume 12, edited by Robert C. Conrad, Cologne: Kiepenheuer & Witsch 2008.

—. *Werke Ansichten eines Clowns (1963)*, Kölner Ausgabe volume 13, edited by Árpád Bernáth, Cologne: Kiepenheuer & Witsch 2004.

—. *Werke 1963-1965*, Kölner Ausgabe volume 14, edited by Jochen Schubert, Cologne: Kiepenheuer & Witsch 2002.

—. *Werke 1966-1968*, Kölner Ausgabe volume 15, edited by Werner Jung in cooperation with Sarah Troost, Cologne: Kiepenheuer & Witsch 2005.

—. *Werke 1969-1971*, Kölner Ausgabe volume 16, edited by J. H. Reid, Cologne: Kiepenheuer & Witsch 2008.

—. *Werke Gruppenbild mit Dame (1971)*, Kölner Ausgabe volume 17, edited by Ralf Schnell and Jochen Schubert, Cologne: Kiepenheuer & Witsch 2005.

—. *Werke 1971-1974*. Kölner Ausgabe volume 18, edited by Viktor Böll and Ralf Schnell in cooperation with Klaus-Peter Bernhard, Cologne: Kiepenheuer & Witsch 2003.

—. *Werke 1974-1976*, Kölner Ausgabe volume 19, edited by Werner Jung, Cologne: Kiepenheuer & Witsch 2008.

—. *Werke 1974-1976*, Kölner Ausgabe volume 20, edited by Ralf Schnell and Jochen Schubert in cooperation with Klaus-Peter Bernard, Cologne: Kiepenheuer & Witsch 2009.

—. *Werke 1979-1981*, Kölner Ausgabe volume 21, edited by Jochen Schubert, Cologne: Kiepenheuer & Witsch 2006.

—. *Werke 1981-1984*, Kölner Ausgabe volume 22, edited by Jochen Schubert, Cologne: Kiepenheuer & Witsch 2007.

—. *Werke 1985-1985*, Kölner Ausgabe volume 23, edited by Hans Joachim Bernhard and Klaus-Peter Bernhard, Cologne: Kiepenheuer & Witsch 2007.

—. *Werke Interviews I 1953-1975*, Kölner Ausgabe volume 24, edited by J. H. Reid and Ralf Schnell, Cologne: Kiepenheuer & Witsch 2009.

—. *Werke Interviews II 1976-1979*, Kölner Ausgabe volume 25, edited by Robert C. Conrad and Werner Jung, Cologne: Kiepenheuer & Witsch 2010.

—. *Werke Interviews III 1980-1985*, Kölner Ausgabe volume 26, edited by Jochen Schubert, Cologne: Kiepenheuer & Witsch 2010.

—. *Werke Registerband*, Kölner Ausgabe volume 27, edited by Klaus-Peter Bernhard in cooperation with Ulrich Stenzel, Cologne: Kiepenheuer & Witsch 2010.

—. Zur Verteidigung der Waschküchen, in: Ferdinand Melius (ed.): *Der Schriftsteller Heinrich Böll*, Cologne/Berlin: Kiepenheuer & Witsch 1959, pp. 33-36.

Böll, Heinrich and Linder, Christian: *Drei Tage im März*, Cologne: Kiepenheuer und Witsch 1975.

Böll, Heinrich and Limberg, Margarete: 'Freedom is Fading Every Day' – The last major interview, 11 June 1985, in: *Heinrich Böll – On his Death – Selected obituaries and the last interview*, Bonn: Inter Nationes 1985, pp. 22-31.

Böll, Viktor (ed.): *Das Heinrich Böll Lesebuch*, Munich: dtv 1982.

Böll, Viktor and Matthaei, Renate (eds): *Querschnitte - aus Interviews, Aufsätzen und Reden von Heinrich Böll*, Cologne: Kiwi 1977.

II. Secondary Literature

Alten, Philipp: Heinrich Böll: Der lesende Soldat – eine Teilrekonstruktion auf Grundlage der veröffentlichten Feldpostbriefe, in: Werner Jung, Jochen Schubert (eds): *'Ich sammle Augenblicke' - Heinrich Böll 1917-1985*, Bielefeld: Aisthesis 2008, pp. 49-80.

Balzer, Bernd: *Das literarische Werk Heinrich Bölls – Einführung und Kommentare*, Munich: Deutscher Taschenbuch Verlag (dtv) 1997.

Balzer, Bernd (ed.), *Heinrich Böll 1917-1985. Zum 75 Geburtstag*, Bern, Berlin et al: Peter Lang 1992.
Balzer, Bernd: *Heinrich Bölls Werke,* Cologne: Kiwi 1977.
Barrington, Brendan (ed.): *The wartime broadcasts of Francis Stuart 1942-44*, Dublin: Lilliput 2000.
Bellmann, Werner: Heinrich Bölls *Irisches Tagebuch.* Kritische Anmerkungen zur Neuedition in der Kölner Ausgabe, in: *Wirkendes Wort* 60 (2010) vol 1, pp. 157-165.
Bermann, Richard: *Irland*, Berlin: Hyperionverlag 1914.
Bernhard, Hans Joachim: Es gibt sie nicht, und es gibt sie, in: Renate Matthaei (ed.): *Die subversive Madonna: Ein Schlüssel zum Werk Heinrich Bölls.* Cologne: Kiepenheuer & Witsch 1975, pp. 58–81.
Böll, Alfred: *Die Bölls. Bilder einer deutschen Familie*, Bergisch Gladbach: Lübbe 1981.
Böll, René: Shapes Taking Form, in: Heinrich Böll Stiftung (ed.): *Ansichten - Die Romanskizzen Heinrich Bölls – In View: Heinrich Böll's Novel Sketches*, Berlin: Heinrich Böll Stiftung 2010, pp. 8-10.
Born, Nicolas and Jürgen Manthey (eds): *Literaturmagazin 7 – Nachkriegsliteratur*, Reinbek: Rowohlt 1977.
Bourke, Eoin: *Das Irlandbild der Deutschen*, Schriftenreihe des Deutsch-Irischen Freundeskreises in Baden-Württemberg e.V., No. 4, Tübingen: Deutsch-Irischer Freundeskreis Baden-Württemberg 1991.
—. Romantisierende Irlandbücher = versteckte Deutschlandbücher? Das Irlandbild in den neueren deutschen Reiseliteratur, in: W. Segebrecht, C. Conter, O. Jahraus, U. Simon (eds): *Europa in den europäischen Literaturen der Gegenwart*, Frankfurt: Peter Lang 2003, pp. 187-199.
Brown, Terence: Saxon and Celt: The Stereotypes, in: Wolfgang Zach and Heinz Kosok (eds), *Literary Interrelations*, vol. 3, National Images and Stereotypes, Tübingen: Narr 1987, pp. 1-10.
Budhlaeir, Caítriona: Critical and experimental approached to translations of Heinrich Böll's prose into Irish, MA thesis University of Limerick 1996.
Butler, Michael (ed.): *The Narrative Fiction of Heinrich Böll – Social conscience and literary achievement*, Cambridge: CUP 1994.
Carthy, Una: Heinrich Böll – Redensarten, in: Jeff Morrison and Florian Krobb (eds), *Prose Pieces*, Konstanz: Hartung-Gorre 2008, pp. 159-168.
Cash, William: *The Third Woman*, London: Little, Brown & Company 2000.
Clarke, Declan: The Weather over Germany, Heinrich Böll's literature of ruins, in: *Cabinet*, 39/2010, pp. 28-32.

Conard, Robert C.: *Heinrich Böll*, Boston: Twayne 1981.
Cosgrave, Mary, Paul Henry and Achill Island, in: Ullrich Kockel (ed.), *Landscape, Heritage and Identity*, Liverpool: Liverpool University Press 1995, pp. 93-116.
Dohmen, Doris: *Das deutsche Irlandbild – Imagologische Untersuchungen zur Darstellung Irlands und der Iren in der deutschsprachigen Literatur*, Amsterdam/Atlanta: Rodopi 1994.
Donoghue, David: Heinrich Böll and a Changing Ireland, in: G. Holfter (ed.), *Irish-German Literary and Cultural Connections. 50 Years Heinrich Böll's 'Irisches Tagebuch'*, Irish-German Studies V, Trier: WVT 2009, pp. 33-36.
Elborn, Geoffrey: *Francis Stuart: A Life*, Dublin: Raven Arts 1990.
Eliot, T.S.: *Four Quartets*, London: Faber and Faber 1979.
Fallon, Brian: *An Age of Innocence—Irish Culture 1930-1960*. Dublin: Gill & Macmillan 1998.
Finlay, Frank: *On the Rationality of Poetry: Heinrich Böll's Aesthetic Thinking*, Amsterdam/ Atlanta: Rodopi 1996.
Fischer, Bernd Erhard and Fischer, Angelika: *Das Irland des Heinrich Böll*, Berlin: Edition A B Fischer 2009.
Fischer, Joachim: *Das Irlandbild der Deutschen 1890-1939*, Heidelberg: Winter 2000.
Gerstenberg, Joachim: *eire - Ein Irlandbuch*, Hamburg: Broschek 1940.
Gibbon, Monk: *Western Germany*, London: B.T. Batsford 1955.
Giordano, Ralph: *Mein irisches Tagebuch*, Munich: dtv 1999.
Giraldus Cambrensis: *The history and topography of Ireland*, edited by John Joseph O'Meara, Harmondsworth: Penguin1982.
Görtz, Franz Josef: Heinrich Böll – More than a Writer – On the death of the winner of the Nobel Prize for Literature, in: *Heinrich Böll – On his Death – Selected obituaries and the last interview*, Bonn: Inter Nationes 1985, pp. 7-9.
Grub, Frank Thomas: ‚Bei mir regnet's schon': Irland aus DDR-Sicht, in: Monika Unzeitig (ed.), *Grenzen überschreiten – transitorische Identitäten*, Bremen: edition lumière 2011, pp. 67-80.
Grubbe, Peter: Die immergrüne Insel, in: *Valhagen & Klasings Monatshefte*, Berlin/Bielefeld, 60/1952, issue 6, pp. 605 - 609.
—. *Wo die Zeit auf Urlaub geht - Irland, die Insel der Elfen, Esel und Rebellen*, Wiesbaden: Brockhaus 1954.
Gurjewitsch, Anton: *Das Weltbild des mittelalterlichen Menschen*, Munich: C.H. Beck 1980.
Haefs, Gabriele: *Das Irenbild der Deutschen - dargestellt anhand einiger Untersuchungen über die Geschichte der irischen Volksmusik und*

ihrer Verbreitung in der Bundesrepublik Deutschland, Frankfurt a.M./Bern/New York: Peter Lang 1983.

Hamilton, Hugo: *Die redselige Insel,* Munich: Sammlung Luchterhand 2007.

—. Introduction, in: Heinrich Böll, *Irish Journal,* Brooklyn, NY: Melville 2011, pp. vii-xiv.

Happe, Hans A.: *Irland und die Emigration - Die Bedeutung des Auswanderungsphänomens,* Aachen: Rader 1987.

Hayton, David W.: From Barbarian to Burlesque: English Images of the Irish c. 1660-1750, in: *Irish Economic and Social History* XV/1988, pp. 5-31.

Heinen, Richard: Geh nach Irland – Das Irlandbild in *Haus ohne Hüter,* in: Gisela Holfter and Joachim Lerchenmueller (eds): *Yearbook of the Centre for Irish-German Studies 1998/99,* Trier: WVT 1999, pp. 66-76.

Helm, Melanie: *Spes contra spem – Ansätze zu einem Kirchenbild der Zukunft bei Heinrich Böll,* Münster et a: Lit 2005.

Hennig, John: Goethes Irlandkunde, in: *Deutsche Vierteljahrsschrift für Literaturwissenschaft und Geistesgeschichte* (= *DVjs*) 21, 1957, pp. 70-83.

—. Irish-German Literary Relations, in: *German Life and Letters,* No. 3, 1950, pp 102-110.

—. Mile-stones of German-Irish Literary Relations, in: G. Holfter, H. Rasche (eds), *Exil in Irland – John Hennigs Schriften zu deutsch-irischen Beziehungen,* Trier: WVT 2002, pp. 174-177.

—. Studien zur deutschsprachigen Irlandkunde im 19. Jahrhundert, in: *DVjs* 47, 1973, pp. 167-179.

—. Studien zur Geschichte der deutschsprachigen Irlandkunde bis zum Ende des achtzehnten Jahrhunderts, in: *DVjs* 35, 1961, pp. 617-629.

Hinrichsen, Irene: *Der Romancier als Übersetzer - Annemarie und Heinrich Bölls Übertragungen englischsprachiger Erzählprosa,* Bonn: Bouvier 1978.

Hoffmann, Gabriele: *Heinrich Böll,* Bornheim-Merten: Lamuv 1986.

Hohn, Hans Willy: Zyklizität und Heilsgeschichte – Religiöse Zeiterfahrung des europäischen Mittelalters, in: Rainer Zoll (ed.), *Zerstörung und Wiederaneignung von Zeit,* Frankfurt: Suhrkamp 1988, pp. 120-142.

Holfter, Gisela: Deutsche Literatur weltweit? Die Rezeption Heinrich Bölls und seiner Werke, in: S. Kirkbright (ed.): *Cosmopolitans in the Modern World.* Munich: Iudicium 2000, pp. 179-192.

—. *Erlebnis Irland - Deutsche Reiseberichte über Irland im 20. Jahrhundert*, Grenzüberschreitungen series, No. 5, Trier: WVT 1996.

—. Fasziniert von Irland - eine Untersuchung über die Begeisterung für Irland bei deutschen Schriftstellern in den 50er bis 70er Jahren von Heinrich Böll bis Arno Schmidt, in: Hasso Spode (ed.): *Goldstrand und Teutonengrill - Kultur- und Sozialgeschichte des Tourismus in Deutschland 1945 bis 1989*, Berlin: Verlag für universitäre Kommunikation, Berichte und Materialien No.15, 1996, pp. 137-145.

—. From bestseller to failure? Heinrich Böll's *Irisches Tagebuch (Irish Journal)* to *Irland und seine Kinder (Children of Eire)*, in: Christiane Schönfeld (ed.): *Processes of Transposition: German Literature and Film*, Amsterdamer Beiträge zur neueren Germanistik, Amsterdam/ Atlanta: Rodopi 2007, pp. 207-222.

—. »... und es ist nicht gut für einen Autor, über einen Gegenstand zu schreiben, den er zu sehr mag« – Heinrich Böll und Irland, in: Werner Jung, Jochen Schubert (eds): *'Ich sammle Augenblicke' - Heinrich Böll 1917-1985*, Bielefeld: Aisthesis 2008, pp. 153-164.

Holfter, Gisela and Nóilín Nic Bhloscaidh: From Tomás Ó Criomhthain's *An tOileánach* to Böll's *Die Boote fahren nicht mehr aus*, in: M. McCusker, C. Shorley (eds): *Reading Across the Lines*, Dublin: Royal Irish Academy 2000, pp. 27-38.

Holfter, Gisela and Hermann Rasche (eds): *Exil in Irland – John Hennigs Schriften*, Trier: WVT 2002.

—. 'German travel literature about Ireland – the saga continues', in J. Conroy (ed.): *Cross-Cultural Travel*, New York et al: Peter Lang 2003, pp. 459-468.

Holl, Karl: *Die irische Frage in der Ära Daniel O'Connells und ihre Beurteilung in der politischen Publizistik des deutschen Vormärz*, Universität Mainz 1958 (PhD Thesis).

Hoven, Herbert (ed.): *Die Hoffnung ist ein wildes Tier - Der Briefwechsel zwischen Heinrich Böll und Ernst-Adolf Kunz 1945-1953*, Cologne: Kiwi 1994.

Huber, Lothar and Robert C. Conard (eds): *Heinrich Böll on Page and Screen*, Publications of the Institute of Germanic Studies, vol. 71, 1997 and *University of Dayton Review*, vol. 24/3, summer 1997.

Huber, Victor Aimé: *Skizzen aus Irland - oder Bilder aus Irlands Vergangenheit und Gegenwart von einem Wanderer*, Stuttgart/ Tübingen: Cotta 1838.

Hummel, Christine: *Intertextualität im Werk Heinrich Bölls*, Trier: WVT 2002.

Initiative zur Gründung der Heinrich-Böll-Stiftung (ed.), *Stiften gehen*, Bornheim-Merten: Lamuv 1987.

Jähn, Alexandra Lisbeth: Tabakgenuß als Kommunikation – Vom Rauchen, Reden und Schweigen bei Heinrich Böll, MA thesis, Universität Bayreuth 1995.

Jaspert, Willem: *Irland*, Berlin: Karl Siegismund 1938.

Johann, A. E. (Alfred E. J. Wollschläger): *Heimat der Regenbogen - Irland, Insel am Rande der Welt*, Gütersloh: Bertelsmann 1953.

—. In Irland ist niemand einsam, in: *Westermanns Monatshefte,* 106, issue 8, 1965, pp. 67-78.

—. *Irland - Heimat der Regenbogen*, Munich: Heyne 1979.

—. *Sohn der Sterne und Ströme*, Gütersloh: Bertelsmann 1955.

Jong, Cornelius de: *Reisen nach dem Vorgebirge der guten Hoffnung und nach Irland und Norwegen in den Jahren 1791 bis 1797*, Hamburg: Hoffmann 1803.

Joyce, James: Irland - Insel der Heiligen und Weisen, in: James Joyce, *Kleine Schriften*, edited by Klaus Reichert, Frankfurt: Suhrkamp 1987, pp. 165-191.

Jurgensen, Manfred: *Das fiktionale Ich - Untersuchungen zum Tagebuch*, Bern: Francke 1979.

Kaiser, Joachim: The Suffering and Greatness of Heinrich Böll – on the death of a distinguished writer, in: *Heinrich Böll – On his Death – Selected obituaries and the last interview*, Bonn: Inter Nationes 1985, pp. 17-21 (German version in *Süddeutsche Zeitung*, 17 July 1985).

Keegan, Claire: The long and painful death, in: *Walk the Blue Fields*, London: Faber & Faber 2008, pp. 1-20.

Kennedy, S.B.: *Paul Henry*, New Haven/London: Yale University 2000.

Klieneberger, H. R.: Ireland Through German Eyes 1844 - 1957 – The Travel-Diaries of Jakob Venedey and Heinrich Böll, in: *Studies*, (Dublin) 1960, pp. 373-388.

Kluge, Hans-Dieter: *Irland in der deutschen Geisteswissenschaft, Politik und Propaganda vor 1914*, Frankfurt a.M./Bern/New York: Peter Lang 1985.

Kohl, Johann Georg: *Reisen in Irland* (2 vols), Dresden/Leipzig: Arnold 1843.

Krobb, Florian and Sabine Strümper-Krobb: Übersetzung und Rückübersetzung: Bölls *Irisches Tagebuch*, in: Gisela Holfter, Hans-Walter Schmidt-Hannisa (eds): *German-Irish Encounters – Deutsch-irische Begegnungen* Irish-German Studies 2, Trier: WVT 2007, pp. 185-195.

Krusche, Dietrich and Alois Wierlacher (eds): *Hermeneutik der Fremde*, Munich: Iudicium 1990.

Kühn, Dieter: *Auf dem Weg zu Annemarie Böll*, Berlin: Heinrich-Böll-Stiftung 2000.

Kurz, Paul Konrad: *Apokalyptische Zeit – Zur Literatur der mittleren 80er Jahre*, Frankfurt a.M.: Josef Knecht 1987.

Küttner, Karl Gottlob: *Briefe über Irland an seinen Freund, den Herausgeber*, Leipzig: Johann Philipp Haug 1785.

Ladenthin, Volker: Misanthrop und Philanthrop - Ein Essay über die Beziehung zwischen Arno Schmidt und Heinrich Böll, in: *Wirkendes Wort*, 38/3, 1988, pp. 359-370.

Lee, J. J.: *Ireland 1912 - 1985 – Politics and Society*, Cambridge: Cambridge University Press 1989.

Leerssen, Joep: *Mere Irish & Fíor Ghael - Studies in the idea of Irish nationality, its development and literary expression prior to the nineteenth century*, Amsterdam/Philadelphia: John Benjamins 1986.

Lenz, Siegfried: *Über Phantasie – Gespräche mit Heinrich Böll, Günter Grass, Walter Kempowski, Pavel Kohout*, Hamburg: Hoffmann und Campe 1982.

Linder, Christian: *Das Schwirren eines heranfliegenden Pfeils. Heinrich Böll – Eine Biographie*, Berlin: Matthes & Seitz 2009.

Loest, Erich: Schon kichert die nächste Wolke - Eine Irland-Reise - dreißig Jahre nach Heinrich Böll', *Süddeutsche Zeitung*, No. 242, p. III, 19./20. October 1985 (also in: Erich Loest, *Wälder, weit wie das Meer*, Munich: dtv 1992, pp. 131-139).

MacBride, Seán: *That Day's Struggle – A Memoir 1904-1951*, edited by Caitriona Lawlor, Dublin: Currach 2005.

Mansergh, Martin: Heinrich Böll and Ireland. 50 Years *Irisches Tagebuch*: Political Connections and Developments in Comparison, in: G. Holfter (ed.), *Irish-German Literary and Cultural Connections. 50 Years Heinrich Böll's 'Irisches Tagebuch'*, Irish-German Studies V, Trier: WVT 2009, pp. 9-11.

MacBride, Seán: *That Day's Struggle – A Memoir 1904-1951*, edited by Caitriona Lawlor, Dublin: Currach 2005.

McConnell, Winder: The Image of Ireland and the Irish in Medieval German Vernacular Literatur, in: Albrecht Classen (ed.): *Medieval German Literature*, Göppingen: Kümmerle 1989, pp. 105-116.

McDonagh, Theresa: *Achill Island – Archaelogy – History – Folklore*, Tullamore: I.A.S. Publications 1997.

McGowan, Moray: Pale Mother, Pale Daughter? Some Reflections on Böll's Leni Gruyten and Katharina Blum, in: *German Life and Letters*, 37/3, 1984, pp. 218-228.
McHugh, John (ed.), *The Heinrich Böll Cottage on Achill Island*, Dooagh: The Heinrich Böll Committee 1998.
McIlroy, Brian: *Irish Cinema: an Illustrated History*, Dublin: Anna Livia Press 1988.
McNally, Kenneth: *Achill*, Newton Abbot: David & Charles 1973.
McNicholl, Rachel: Heinrich Böll's Other Ireland, in: J.L. Flood (ed.): *Common Currency - Aspects of Anglo-German Literary Relations since 1945*, Stuttgart: Hans-Dieter Heinz 1991, pp. 71-86.
Morton, H.V. [Henry Canova Vollam]: *The Magic of Ireland*, London: Eyre Methuen 1978.
Nägele, Rainer: *Heinrich Böll – Einführung in das Werk und die Forschung*, Frankfurt: Athenäum Fischer Taschenbuch 1976.
Ó'hUiginn, Seán: Heinrich Böll's *Irisches Tagebuch* Fifty Years Later, in: Gisela Holfter (ed.), *Irish-German Literary and Cultural Connections. 50 Years Heinrich Böll's 'Irisches Tagebuch'*, Irish-German Studies V, Trier: WVT 2009, pp. 37-42.
O'Keeffe, William: Western Approaches: Heinrich Böll in Normandy and Ireland, in: Gisela Holfter (ed.): *Heinrich Böll's 'Irisches Tagebuch' in Context*, Trier: WVT 2010, pp. 89-98.
O'Loughlin, Michael: *Another Nation*, Dublin: New Island Books 1996.
O'Neill, Patrick: *Ireland and Germany - A Study in Literary Relations*, New York: Peter Lang 1985.
Oehlke, Andreas: *Die Iren und Irland in deutschen Reisebeschreibungen des 18. und 19. Jahrhunderts*, Frankfurt a.M. et al.: Peter Lang 1992.
Pater, Siegfried: *Achill Island – Bilder und Geschichten einer irischen Insel*, Bonn: Retap 2000.
Päplow, Thorsten: *"Faltenwürfe" in Heinrich Böll's 'Irisches Tagebuch'*, Munich: Iudicium 2008.
—. Identität und Heimat. Heinrich Bölls *Irisches Tagebuch*, in: Ulrich Breuer, Beatrice Sandberg (eds): Grenzen der Identität und der Fiktionalität, Munich : Iudicium 2006.
Preuß, Helmut: Von der Kunst der Reiseschilderung in Heinrich Bölls ‚Irisches Tagebuch' - eine Sprach- und Strukturanalyse in exemplarischer Darstellung, in: Eberhard Ockel (ed.): *Sprechwissenschaft und Deutschdidaktik*, Kastellaun: Henn 1977, pp. 244 - 255.
Pribil, Dorothee: Heinrich Bölls 'Irisches Tagebuch', Gießen 1989 (unpublished academic essay).

Prodaniuk, Ihor: *The Imagery in Heinrich Böll's Novels*, Bonn: Bouvier 1979.

Pückler-Muskau, Hermann Fürst von: *Briefe eines Verstorbenen - Ein fragmentarisches Tagebuch aus Deutschland, Holland, England, Wales, Irland und Frankreich, geschrieben in den Jahren 1826 bis 1829*, 2 volumes, first and second part edited by Günter J. Vaupel, Frankfurt a.M./Leipzig: Insel Verlag 1991 [Stuttgart: Hallberger 1831].

Pückler-Muskau, Hermann: *Tour in England, Ireland and France in the years 1828 and 1829 by a German Prince*, 4 vols, translation by Sarah Austin, London: Wilson 1832 [published as *Touring England, Ireland, and France: in the years 1826, 1827, 1828, and 1829. With remarks on the manners and customs of the inhabitants, and anecdotes of distinguished public characters. In a series of letters by a German Prince*, Philadelphia: Carey, Lea & Blanchard, 1833].

Raddatz, Fritz: *Lieber Fritz. Briefe an Fritz J. Raddatz 1959-1990*, Reinbek: Rowohlt 1991.

Rasch, Wolfdietrich: Zum Stil des *Irischen Tagebuchs*, in: Marcel Reich-Ranicki (ed.): *In Sachen Böll*, Cologne: Kiepenheuer & Witsch 1968.

Reich-Ranicki, Marcel (ed.): *In Sachen Böll*, Cologne: Kiepenheuer & Witsch 1968.

Reich-Ranicki, Marcel: Writer, Jester, Preacher, in: *Heinrich Böll – On his Death – Selected obituaries and the last interview*, Bonn: Inter Nationes 1985, pp. 10-13 (German version in *Frankfurter Allgemeine Zeitung*, 18 July 1985).

—. *Deutsche Literatur in West und Ost. Prosa seit 1945*, Munich: Piper 1963.

Reid, James H.: *Heinrich Böll: a German for his time*, Oxford: Berg 1988.

—. Nur 'Gesellenstücke' – Zum Frühwerk Heinrich Bölls, in: Werner Jung, Jochen Schubert (eds), *'Ich sammle Augenblicke' – Heinrich Böll 1917-1985*, Bielefeld: Aisthesis 2008, pp. 9-29

—. Time in the Works of Heinrich Böll, in: *Modern Language Review*, 62/1967, pp. 476-485.

Reinhardt, Regine: Der Blick auf Böll hat Bestand – und verrät so viel über uns Deutsche, in: *irland journal* XVIII, 1.07, pp. 138-143.

Rice, Harry: *Thanks for the Memory*, Athlone: Athlone Printing Works 1952.

Richter, Hans Werner: 'Liebst du das Geld auch so wie ich?' in: H. W. Richter: *Im Etablissement der Schmetterlinge*. Munich: Hanser 1986, pp. 63-79.

Rix, Walter T.: Ireland as a Source of German Interest in the Early Nineteenth Century - From Politics to Literature, in: Wolfgang Zach and Heinz Kosok (eds): *Literary Interrelations*, vol. 1, Reception and Translation, Tübingen: Narr 1987, pp. 21-32.

Rodenberg, Julius: *Die Insel der Heiligen - Eire. Pilgerfahrt durch Irlands Städte, Dörfer und Ruinen*, Berlin: Janke 1860.

Roney, Sir Cusack P.: *How to Spend a Month in Ireland*, John Camden Hotten: London 1872.

Rost, Hans: *Deutschlands Sieg – Irlands Hoffnung*, Stuttgart: Deutsche Verlagsanstalt 1915.

Rousseau-Fischer, Pascale: *Irlande: L'île de Heinrich Böll et Michel Déon*, Université de Lille 1992 (Dissertation).

—. Irlande: le refuge de Heinrich Böll et Michel Déon = Ireland: the refuge of Heinrich Böll and Michel Déon, in: *Etudes irlandaises* 1/1996, vol 21, pp. 65-79.

Sagarra, Eda: Die 'grüne Insel' in der deutschen Reiseliteratur - Deutsche Irlandreisende von Karl Gottlob Küttner bis Heinrich Böll, in: Hans-Wolf Jäger (ed.): *Europäisches Reisen im Zeitalter der Aufklärung*, Heidelberg: Winter 1992, pp. 183-195.

—. Heinrich Böll, Father of German tourism in Ireland, in: G. Holfter (ed.), *Irish-German Literary and Cultural Connections. 50 Years Heinrich Böll's 'Irisches Tagebuch'*, Irish-German Studies V, Trier: WVT 2009, pp. 13-17.

Sauder, Gerhard: Heinrich Bölls Léon-Bloy-Lektüre – Ursprünge eines radikalen Katholizismus, in: Werner Jung, Jochen Schubert (eds): *'Ich sammle Augenblicke' - Heinrich Böll 1917-1985*, Bielefeld: Aisthesis 2008, pp. 31-48.

Schneider, Jürgen and Ralf Sotscheck (eds): *Irland. Eine Bibliographie selbständiger deutschsprachiger Publikationen 16. Jahrhundert bis 1989*, Darmstadt: Verlag der Georg Büchner Buchhandlung 1988.

Schubert, Jochen: Nachwort, in: Heinrich Böll, *Irisches Tagebuch*, edited by René Böll, Cologne: Kiepenheuer & Witsch 2007, pp. 149-195.

Senger, *Max: Irland die seltsame Insel,* Zürich: Büchergilde Gutenberg 1956.

Smyth, Jim: A load of old Boellix, in: *Contemporary Art from Ireland*, edited by European Central Bank, Frankfurt 2005.

Sowinski, Bernhard: *Heinrich Böll*, Stuttgart/Weimar: Metzler 1993.

Sperber, Manès (ed.): *Wir und Dostojewskij. Eine Debatte mit Heinrich Böll, Siegfried Lenz, André Malraux, Hans Erich Nossack*, Hamburg: Hoffmann und Campe 1972.

Stadt Köln and Heinrich-Böll-Stiftung (eds): *Heinrich Böll Life and Work*, edited by R. Böll, V. Böll, K.H. Busse, M. Schäfer, Göttingen: Steidl 1995.

Stephan, Enno: Eins Dritter Dublin, in: *Der Fortschritt* No. 33, p. 3 (part 1), 21. August 1953, in: *Der Fortschritt*, No. 34, p. 5 (part 2); 28. August 1953, in: *Der Fortschritt*, No. 35, p. 5 (part 3); 4. September 1953, in: *Der Fortschritt*, No. 36, p. 5 (part 4); 10. September 1953, in: *Der Fortschritt*, No. 37, p. 5 (part 5) and 18. September 1953, in: *Der Fortschritt*, No. 38, p. 5 (part 6).

Streiff, Eric: *Inseln am Saume Europas - Tagebuchblätter aus Irland*, Zürich: Sanssouci 1982.

Sullivan, Sheila: *Follow the Moon – A Memoir*, Dublin: Currach 2006.

Surenhöfener, Karl: Keine Bomben in Irland, in: *Neues Europa*, No. 24, 3/1948, pp. 15-18.

Titley, Alan: Turning Inside and Out: Translating and Irish 1950-2000, in: *The Yearbook of English Studies*, vol 35, 2005, pp. 312-322.

Ulbrich, Reinhard: *Irland - Inseltraum und Erwachen*, Leipzig: Brockhaus 1988.

Van Maele, Francis: *Dugort – Achill – Photographs 2005-2007*, Dugort: Redfoxpress 2007.

Venedey, Jacob: *Irland*, part I and II, Leipzig: Brockhaus 1844.

Vogelsang, Klaus: Das Tagebuch, in: Klaus Weissenberger (ed.): *Prosakunst ohne Erzählen*, Tübingen: Niemeyer 1985.

Vogt, Heinrich: *Heinrich Böll*, Munich: Beck 1987.

—. *Kulturen der Einsamkeit - Der keltische Rand Europas*, Darmstadt: Wissenschaftliche Buchgesellschaft 1994.

Volkmann, Johann Jacob: *Neueste Reisen durch Schottland und Ireland vorzüglich in der Absicht auf die Naturgeschichte, Oekonomie, Manufakturer und Landsitze der Grossen*, Leipzig: Fritsch 1784 (5 vols).

Vormweg, Heinrich: *Der andere Deutsche – Heinrich Böll*, Cologne: Kiepenheuer & Witsch 2000.

—. 'Heinrich Böll is Dead – An Obituary', in: *Heinrich Böll – On his Death – Selected obituaries and the last interview*, Bonn: Inter Nationes 1985, pp. 14-16 (German version in *metall* No. 15, 26 July 1985)

Walter, Hans A.: *Irland und wir, Deutschlands Kampf – Irlands Hoffnung*, Munich: A. Hertz 1915.

Warner, Patrick: *Irland* (foreword by Alfred Andersch), Frankfurt a.M./Berlin/Wien: Ullstein 1973.

White, R.L.: *Heinrich Böll in America 1954 - 1970*, Hildesheim: Olms 1979.

Woodland, T.W.: *Irisches Tagebuch* by Heinrich Böll, in: *German Life and Letters* 12 (1959/60), No. 1.

Young, Arthur: *Reise durch Ireland nebst allgemeinen Beobachtungen über den gegenwärtigen Zustand dieses Reiches in den Jahren 1776, 1777 und 1778 bis zum Ende des Jahres 1779*, Leipzig: Junius 1780.
Zachau, Reinhard K.: *Heinrich Böll: Forty Years of Criticism*, Drawer, Columbia: Camden 1994.
Zorach, Cecile Cazort: Two Faces of Erin - The Dual Journey in Heinrich Böll's *Irisches Tagebuch*, in: *The Germanic Review* 53, No. 3, 1978, pp. 124-131.
Zuckmayer, Carl: Gerechtigkeit durch Liebe, in: Marcel Reich-Ranicki (ed.): *In Sachen Böll*, Cologne: Kiepenheuer & Witsch 1968, pp. 67-71.
Zylinski, Leszek: *Heinrich Bölls Poetik der Zeitgenossenschaft*, Torun: Uniwersytet Mikolaja 1997.

III. Newspaper articles

Alioth, Gabrielle, Neues altes Irland? *NZZ*, 30 August 2010.
Anonymous: Böll got last rites, in: *Irish Times*, 19 July 1985.
Anonymous: Bölls 'Reise nach Irland', *Kölnische Rundschau*, 5 April 1957.
Anonymous: Death of Heinrich Böll, *Irish Times*, 17 July 1985.
Anonymous: Heinrich Böll dies, aged 67, *Irish Times*, 17 July 1985.
Anonymous: Heinrich Bölls 'Irisches Tagebuch', in: *Die Kiepe*, No. 1, 5 Spring 1957.
Anonymous: Heinrich Bölls 'Irisches Tagebuch', *Freie Presse*, Buenos Aires 24 August 1957.
Anonymous: W. German literary giant Böll dies, *Irish Independent*, 17 July 1985.
Beam, Alvin: A German Writes of Ireland, *The Plain Beaver*, 19 August 1967.
Becker, Rolf: Weil nichts geschah, *Sonntagsblatt* (Hamburg) 5 May 1957 and *Kölner Stadtanzeiger*, 18 May 1957.
Betz, Klaus: Gehversuche, die Träume zu Füßen - Über die eher beiläufige Entdeckung der irischen Seele, *Frankfurter Rundschau*, 14 August 1993.
Blöcker, Günter: Heinrich Böll und Irland, *Der Tagesspiegel*, 21 July 1957.
F[ennell], D[esmond]: Ireland in the Rain, *Irish Times*, 19 April 1958.
Fennell, Desmond: Report from Cologne – Heinrich Böll in Ireland, *Irish Times*, 23 June 1956.

Frey, John R.: Heinrich Böll. *Irisches Tagebuch*, in: *Books Abroad* 34, 1960.
Gerlach, Walter: Im Bild des Auslands das Heimatland getroffen: Auf den Spuren des *Irischen Tagebuchs* – 30 Jahre nach seinem ersten Erscheinen, in: *Börsenblatt* 36, 5 May 1987.
Greiner, Ulrich: Der Schriftsteller des Mitleids – Wir sollten ihn wieder lesen: Heinrich Böll, *Die Zeit*, 27 January 2011.
Haerdter, Robert: Meerumglänzt, in: *Gegenwart* 12, No. 7, 1957.
Hamilton, Hugo: The loneliness of being German, *The Guardian*, 7 September 2004.
Henson, James H.: The Auld Sod, *Tulsa World*, 3 September 1967.
Hohoff, Curt: Bölls *Irisches Tagebuch*. Ein Autor hat sich freigeschwommen, *Rheinischer Merkur*, 12 July 1957.
Hüsgen, Hans Dieter: Liebe zu einem kleinen Land, *Trierische Landeszeitung*, 28 July 1957.
Jelen, Tobias: Die grüne Insel, die Heinrich Böll so mochte – Der Nordwesten Irlands zur Jahreswende: Moor, Heide, Klippen, Sandstrände, Pubs und Guinness, *Landshuter Zeitung*, 16 January 1993.
Kain, Richard M.: Heinrich Böll on Ireland, *Louisville Courier Journal*, 20 August 1967.
Kay, Alfred: The Mystic and Legendary Irish, *San Francisco Examiner & Chronicle*, 6 August 1967.
Linde, Malte: Großer Bahnhof im kleinen Cottage - Das Böll-Haus in Irland wird Begegnungsstätte, *Frankfurter Rundschau*, 9 May 1992.
Maurer, Ramona: Wo die felsigen Berge sanft in den Atlantik fallen – Impressionen aus einem Traumland, *Mitteldeutsche Zeitung*, 24 July 1993.
Morgan, Don: An Irishman's Diary, *Irish Times*, 21 July 2010.
—. In The Rare Old Times, *Irish Examiner*, 21 May 2010.
McEwan, Ian: Wir müssen zweihundert Jahre vorausdenken, *Frankfurter Allgemeine Sonntagszeitung*, 21 October 2007.
Netzhammer, Michael: Tagebuch einer anderen Zeit – Auf den Spuren des Schriftstellers Heinrich Böll: Eine Reise an die irische Westküste, *Badische Zeitung*, 31 May 1998.
Ni Anluain, Éilis: Ceacht Heinrich Böll dúinn, *Irish Times*, 20 June 2007.
Ó Cathaoir, Brendan: An Irishman's Diary, *Irish Times*, 17 June 2002.
O'Faolain, Sean: A land that bewitches, *New York Book Review*, 13 August 1967.
O'Toole, Fintan: A prescient vision of Ireland, through a 1960s lens, *Irish Times*, 17 April 2010.

Pollety, Elfriede: '... wenn er auch nur 765 Meter hoch ist'- Wallfahrt auf den Croagh Patrick - Erinnerungen an Heinrich Bölls 'Irisches Tagebuch', *Straubinger Tagblatt*, 31 July 1993.

Pyle, Fergus: Ireland Through German Eyes, *Irish Times*, 16 April 1983.

Rosenstock, Georg: Manche Länder muß man dreimal sehen, *Die Welt* (Berlin), 8 June 1957.

—. Neue Übersetzung von Brendan Behan, in: *Die Zeit*, No 49, 2 December 1966.

Rumley, Larry: Nostalgia for Erin, *Seattle Daily Times*, 6 August 1967.

Scally, Derek: Berlin as the new Achill – despite Böll, *Irish Times*, 1 March 2008.

—. Berlin Diary, *Irish Times*, 12 February 2011.

—. From Germany to Ireland with love – still, *Irish Times*, 2 December 2010.

Schauer, Rainer: Als Mister Boll Achill Island verließ - Irlands Westen bietet trotz aller Veränderungen noch Ruhe und Abgeschiedenheit, *Bergische Landeszeitung*, 27 July 1986.

Stephan, Enno: Heinrich Böll: Irisches Tagebuch, *dpa-Buchbrief*, 9 September 1957.

Stuart, Francis: Shadow of the Nazis, *Sunday Tribune* (Dublin), 3 March 1985.

Sullivan, Sheila: An Irishwoman's Diary, *Irish Times*, 1 March 2005.

—. The writer's residence, *Irish Times*, 29 August 2001.

Sweeney, Eamonn: Böll's Notion, *Irish Times*, 18 July 1997.

Taucher, Franz: Geliebte grüne Insel, *Deutsche Zeitung und Wirtschaftszeitung* (Stuttgart) 5 June 1957.

Uhlig, Inna: Almost like being there, *Baltimore Sunday Sun*, 20 August 1967.

Weidermann, Volker: Unser Hemingway – Heinrich Böll, ein Moralist? Stimmt nicht. In seiner Werkausgabe trifft man auf einen selbstironischen Modernisierer der deutschen Literatur, *Frankfurter Allgemeine Sonntagszeitung*, 9 January 2011.

Wittstock, Uwe: Wiedersehen mit Bölls grüner Insel, *Die Welt*, 15 March 2007.

Zwick, Christiane: Böll in Irland - Ansichten einer Insel, *Frankfurter Allgemeine Sonntagszeitung*, 22 April 2007.

IV. Film, Internet Material, Radio, Presentations

Clarke, Declan: *Cologne Overnight*, Dublin 2010 (film).
de Valera, Eamon: Address 17 March 1943. *RTE* radio http://www.rte.ie/laweb/ll/ll_t09b.html.
Ferriter, Diarmuid: Eamon de Valera and broadcasting, *RTE 1*, 12 October 2007 http://www.rte.ie/laweb/ll/ll_t09_main_a.html.
Hanfgarn, Gunter and Kämpfer, Wibke: *Zwischen den Heimaten / A Second Home: Heinrich Böll in Ireland*, Deutsche Welle 1996 (film).
Hauptverband des Österreichischen Buchhandels, Mit dtv nach Irland, 9 June 2011,
http://www.buecher.at/show_content.php?sid=94&detail_id=4296.
http://oconnollys.wordpress.com/.
http://www.achilltourism.com/store/irlanddasboll.php.
http://www.amazon.de/gp/cdp/member-reviews/A1DVHWQJR86JZ8.
http://www.amazon.de/gp/cdp/member-reviews-/A1LSD44Q1YZ1HY?ie=UTF8&display=public&sort_by=MostRecentReview&page=2.
http://www.askaboutireland.ie/reading-room/environment-geography/physical-landscape/lakelands-of-westmeath/lough-ree/islands-of-lough-ree/hare-island-the-annals/hare-lodge-and-lord-cast.
http://www.theflyonthearchitecturalwall.org/.
Kuhn, Beate and Delestre, Marc: *Die Achill-Island – Ein irisches Insel-Tagebuch*, Bilder einer Landschaft series, Bayrischer Rundfunk 2005 (film) .
McAleese, Mary: Remarks at an Irish community reception, Berlin, 26 February 2008,
http://www.president.ie/index.php?section=5&speech=474&lang=ire.
Niedecken, Wolfgang: Logbuch 2 October 2010,
http://www.bap.de/start/aktuell/logbuch/berlin-brandenburger-tor.
Reiner, Jule: *Grüß die Lieben in Mayo – Auf Heinrich Bölls Wegen durch Irlands Westen*, Tourism Ireland 2007 (CD).
Schehl, Michael: *Heinrich Böll in Ireland*, Deutsche Welle 2007 (film).